Regeneration

Writing as . . .

Remembering

Reflecting

Re-Sorting

Re-Visioning

Resolving

Restoring

Resonating

Regenerating

re·gen·er·a·tion (*noun*)
1. The act or process of regenerating or the state of being regenerated.
2. Spiritual or moral revival or rebirth.
3. Biology Regrowth of lost or destroyed parts or organs.

The American Heritage® Dictionary of the English Language, Fourth Edition copyright ©2000 by Houghton Mifflin Company. Updated in 2009.

Inspired by classmate Andrew Legare's poetic essay written while he was on Georgia's death row, artist Yvonne Gabriel sought to recreate on canvas the miracle of the seed that managed to germinate in the harsh and hostile environment of a small crack in the cement prison yard. The David-and-Goliath image of a tender plant breaking through almost impenetrably hard cement is repeated in Margaret Eskew's "Sonnet on Foucault," signaling regeneration at incredible odds—the very theme that emanates from many of the selections in this book, giving rise to its title, Regeneration.

Regeneration!

A Journal of Creative Writing

Mercer University
College of Continuing and Professional Studies
Regeneration Writers with
Students, Faculty, Alumni, and Staff

"When we tell our stories authentically, it is not only important to us: our stories become an inseparable part of those who hear them and how they view the world."

The Regeneration Writers Press 2009
Macon, Georgia

Published in 2009 by
Regeneration Writers Press
844 College Street
Macon, GA 31201

regenerationwriters@gmail.com

ISBN 978-0-9843747-0-0

Founded in 1833, Mercer University is a dynamic and comprehensive center
of undergraduate, graduate, and professional education. The University has
approximately 7,300 students and eleven schools and colleges–liberal arts,
law, pharmacy, medicine, business, engineering, education, theology, music,
nursing and continuing and professional studies. Mercer has major campuses
in Macon, Atlanta and Savannah and four regional academic centers across
the state. In addition, it has two teaching hospitals: Memorial Health University Medical Center and the Medical Center of Central Georgia, a university
press, educational partnerships with Warner Robins Air Logistics Center in
Warner Robins and Piedmont Healthcare in Atlanta, an engineering research
center in Warner Robins, a performing arts center in Macon, and a NCAA Division I athletic program. For more information, visit http://www.mercer.edu.

Library of Congress Cataloging in Publication Data

Regeneration! A Journal of Creative Writing

Acknowledgments

Without the leadership and passion for writing and learning of the Regeneration Writers, this collection of short stories, poems, interviews, and essays would never have been written. Without their discipline, skills, and tenacity this collection of creative writing would not have been published. No teacher could have wanted a more insightful, dedicated, engaged, endearing, and enduring group of students.

Once the mandate to write became clear, numerous individuals contributed in various ways toward the clarification and realization of the collective vision of the writing classes. Dean Tom Kail and Liberal Studies Chair Colin Harris offered their blessings on the formation of the classes. Professors Karen Lacey and Thompson Biggers generously agreed to serve as mentors. Incoming Dean Priscilla Danheiser continued unbroken the tremendous chain of support. The Tarver Library staff was incredibly supportive. Dean of Libraries Beth Hammond provided a faculty carrel to house the editing and publishing phases. Ginger Harper of Harper Art in Macon designed the postcard sent out to faculty, staff, students, and alumni inviting them to submit their writings for consideration. Col. Raleigh Mann shared pertinent contact information. Ellen Banas made the drawing of the fetus in the bulb as an illustration. Photographers include Janet Crocker, Barbara Sellers, and Yvonne Gabriel, who also painted the flower emerging through cement.

Four Regeneration Writers attended the Summit on Torture held on the Atlanta campus with scholarship assistance from the conference sponsors. Mrs. Joan Godsey related to the writers her experiences with the Head Start program in Alabama. CCPS secretary Brenda Jackson arranged for rooms and equipment. Tech Services set up websites and resolved program issues.

This project was supported by the Mercer Commons. Thanks to everyone who had a hand in bringing this work to fruition.

Contents

Conversation on Race   65

This Is My Story   91

Essays 209

Biographical Sketches 259

Joan Stockstill Godsey

Sr. Helen Préjean

DEDICATION

to

Joan Stockstill Godsey

&

Sr. Helen Préjean:

Two women of God, who have looked intensely into the faces of God's children and have recognized there the image of God. They are nurturers in the best sense of the word and role models for us all in the struggle for beauty, justice, opportunity, and mercy.

The Regeneration Writers

Cliff Brown

Janet Horne Crocker, Design & Photography Editor

Terri DeFoor, Editor in Chief

Harry Eskew

Margaret Eskew, Production Editor

Elnora Fluellen

Yvonne Gabriel, Art Editor

Gloria Jordan, Associate Editor

Diane Lang

Rosemary McKelvey

Kevin Reid

Barbara Sellers, Research Editor

Zach Wells

_____

Thompson Biggers, Faculty Mentor

Karen Lacey, Faculty Mentor

Duane Davis, Faculty Copy Editor

Jerome Gratigny, Technical Editor

Introduction

We don't all have the same gifts, but we all have gifts. We don't all have the same vision, but we all have vision. We don't all have the same voice, but we all have a voice. Mercer Chancellor Kirby Godsey eloquently proclaimed that it is our job to identify and live out our gifts. That requires sharpening and expanding our vision, and finding and using our own voices. No matter how melodious or beautiful the voice of another is, it is not ours. An authentic voice is always compelling. When it rings true, others sit up and listen; they know we have something to say.

Our stories are crucial to the formation of others and to our recognition of who we are and the directions we have unconsciously chosen in our journey through life. When we tell our stories authentically, it is not only important to us: our stories become an inseparable part of those who hear them and how they view the world. Telling our stories is one important way that we can effect change. These are the authentic stories in narrative, poetic, interview, and essay form of students, faculty, staff, and alumni of the College of Continuing and Professional Studies at Mercer University. We love to tell our stories.

Passion for Lifelong Learning

In the fall of 2009, on the Macon campus of Mercer University, twelve students and one professor came together to imagine, to innovate, to create. Brought together by common purposes to share their love of writing with one another and, through their writing, to reveal some of the meaning of their lives with others, these individuals committed to a year-long study designed to result in the compilation of their work. The

1

magnificent collection that resulted, *Regeneration!*, is symbolic
of the passion for life-long learning demonstrated by these
exceptional students and their beloved professor that is the most
highly valued outcome of educational experience. It is a gift
to us and tribute to these remarkable people who, bonding and
working late in the evenings and early on weekend mornings
over the course of a year, produced a work that connects all of us
who read it to the extraordinary lives of women and men who return to higher education to engage, question, discover, and learn
deeply.

Priscilla Ruth Danheiser, Dean
College of Continuing and Professional Studies

A Gift of Many

One of the significant benefits of living and working in a
community of learners like Mercer is the enrichment that comes
from the many colleagues, both teachers and students, who bring
their gifts to the table for us to partake. Everyone has something
to teach, and everyone has something to learn; and it happens,
often inconspicuously, in ways that mold and shape us toward
who we are continually becoming.

Once in a while, these experiences of teaching and learning become focused in a way that pulls a part of the community
together and produces a landmark expression of insights and discoveries that are the products of a unique educational endeavor.

The collection of written reflections you are about to
read is one of those landmark expressions. It is the product of a
gifted teacher's inspiration and encouragement, several students'
careful, honest, and courageous reflections on their personal
journeys, the creativity of many who are discovering the power
of writing to convey deeper levels of truth, the persistence and
hard work of an editorial group to organize and present this
diverse collection, and the support of an administration that rec-
ognizes and values what these experiences and efforts represent.

Without any of these elements, such a product would not be in our hands; and its presence is a model of the kind of transformation that true educational engagement brings.

The offerings that follow invite reflection, conversation, engagement, and participation in the experiences they set forth. They underscore the truth that education is not a spectator activity but one that involves profound levels of participation. As you read, let their stories become your story; let their passion for justice bring your passion to expression; let their hopes and dreams help you sketch your vision for the future. Nothing says thanks to them more than your willingness to join the journey.

This first edition of *Regeneration!* is a gift of many for which we are grateful.

--Colin Harris, Chair of Liberal Studies, CCPS

Education Changes Us

Sixteen-hour teaching days are not uncommon for professors in the College of Continuing & Professional Studies at Mercer. It was near the end of one of those long days after a class on the Macon campus on Literature of the South that five or six students cornered me, requesting or demanding that the CCPS offer some courses in writing—and that I teach them. Fortunate to still have my cognitive powers about me, although admittedly somewhat reduced by the late hour, I promised the students to address the matter. By the time the Chair of Liberal Studies, Dr. Colin Harris, signed on to the idea, the early nucleus had gathered more students. We started the class with an even dozen students.

Not wanting to disappoint the students and desirous of tailoring the class to their needs and aspirations while remaining true to the Mercer mission, I solicited help from the students in the design of the class. They took an active role in developing the form the class assumed. Students researched the elements of effective writing and led *The Regeneration Writers* in practicing

3

selected writing strategies. One student with prior experience in writing classes introduced the group to an effective process for reviewing each other's works—a sort of round table approach that became a staple of each class meeting. Keeping in mind the results of two disparate writing groups in Michigan--one which disbanded after several years and a second which produced many fine writers including several who are nationally acclaimed--, we made a conscious decision to focus on the positive aspects of each writer's work and to each offer two or three specific suggestions for making each work more effective.

From the outset, all of us wrote and shared our writings in the class setting. We *all* did the assignments. At first, students were wary of critiquing the teacher's work. I tried hard to model how to accept suggestions gracefully and incorporated the ones that made my writing more effective. I also sought to model how to critique a work in such a way as to motivate the writer to continue writing. We worked on disagreeing in an affirming manner. The result was that every student continues to write and share his or her efforts with other *Regeneration Writers*.

Naturally, we made some mistakes as we proceeded, but we did not try to sweep the mistakes under a rug. We clearly identified the mistakes and worked together to reclaim our direction. Amazingly, even when tremendous calamities befell the class—heart surgery on a spouse, the first anniversary of a mother's death, heart catheterization, etc.–, there was a tremendous outpouring of support for the affected student.

The writers decided at the beginning to create a literary journal, which we would call *Regeneration!*, mainly because that is an apt description of what happens to many students in all majors in the CCPS. We elected to open the journal to students outside the class, alumni, faculty, and staff of the CCPS. We received over one hundred entries, more than we could adequately evaluate in the quick timeframe of our sessions. However, they were an indication of the tremendous interest of our college in writing. I include here an email from one of the Regeneration writers, who eloquently speaks for the class:

4

The journal we put together is for me a monument for the start of my second life. What happened in that class was an awakening of a part of me that had been suppressed, neglected and covered in dust. I reconnected with people and stepped back into life. You took me by the hand and opened the door to this wonderful world. To see this immortalized in the form of the journal brings me to tears. All the memories and the good vibes come rushing back as I read our stories. It will be for me one of the most meaningful possessions I have.

The teaching mantra that I share excessively with my students is that if education doesn't change you, you haven't received an education. The secret I haven't been as open to share is that students change me. Their honesty, their openness, and their support help me grow in ways that I never imagined. Through this work, I, along with the students, have truly experienced "regeneration." We hope that these writings will engender new life in you, our reader.

--Margaret Eskew

Uncharted Waters

Among this collection of poetry, narrative, and essay are some truly remarkable works. There are beautiful renditions of individual growth and exploration by emerging student writers, allowing this creative journal to stand as a compelling invitation to current and future students to join the dialog. Faculty, staff, and alumni contributions showcase an amazing diversity of disciplines, interests, orientation, and background, a foundational strength of the CCPS.

With perhaps an unparalleled quest to help students find their own voices, Dr. Margaret Eskew led us tirelessly, sensitively, and superbly toward the realization of our initial vision as we reshaped and refined it through the processes of writing, critiquing, revising, editing, arranging, illustrating, and publishing. All of us involved learned more than the grades we received in our publishing courses reflect. We will all remain forever grateful to her for the willingness to lead us past our initial idea all the way to concrete completion.

We have sailed uncharted waters. When researching other nontraditional programs across the country, we found none that had published a literary journal. In addition, unlike most journals produced by literature departments in traditional undergraduate programs, we have included essays on a variety of subject matter along with creative prose and poetry.

Please enjoy our gift to you, our treasured readers. We invite students, faculty and staff members, and alumni of Mercer's College of Continuing and Professional Studies to join the conversation by submitting their thoughtful works to *Regeneration* for the next publication.

--Terri DeFoor

Dr. Priscilla Danheiser, Dean, CCPS

I Too Have a Dream . . .

. . . that one day the world will be clean and the forests restored; that children will roam free and fear will be no more; pollution will be gone, replaced by perfumes from flowers surrounded by bees; no more artificial colors or additives; a cow, a few tomatoes in my backyard; no more stock market; no more corruption in people's hearts; children who are healthy and educated; no more unfairness to those who are ill-fated. (Yvonne Gabriel)

. . . that there will be true justice for all men: black, white, and men of color; that my son will be released from the chains of the corrupt justice system. (Gloria Jordan)

. . . that America will find the heart of honesty; that all people will treat others like kin; that honest values will be restored within business and government. (Cliff Brown)

. . . that Americans will think a little deeper and move beyond being satisfied with clichés and catch phrases; that they will begin asking questions and pondering conclusions; that they will know a little better why they believe what they believe and be able to share those convictions with others. (Terri DeFoor)

. . . that one day there will be peace in my house. (Diane Lang)

. . . that our nation will find new priorities and that taking care of babies and people in need will become more important and receive more funding than prisons and political campaigns. (Janet Allen Crocker)

. . . that one day the world will live in peace. I realize it is probably hopeless to wish for such a thing, but if every person on

9

earth would stop and consider the welfare and feelings of each other, it could be a reality. Imagine everyone in a world where each person cared about the others. There would be no more hunger, no more wars, less or no crime, and genuine friendship would flourish. Each person would embrace her neighbors regardless of religion, race, ethnic background, or political party. It may only be a dream, but it is my dream. (Barbara Sellers)

. . . that world peace will become a desire and a possibility; that harmony will exist among all citizens of the United States; that we will all be one color, so there will be no racism; that we will all speak one language, so there will be no confusion; that we will all desire peace, so there will be no more war; that we will all have jobs, so there will be no poverty; that we will all be educated, so there will be no illiteracy. (Elnora Fluellen)

. . . that all Americans will have access to basic health care; that the U.S. will abolish the death penalty; that Americans will have access to a college education or the training they need to have a good job; that we will make peace a priority. (Harry Eskew)

. . . that every child will have a quality education. (Zach Wells)

. . . that all people will have an equal chance to pursue life to the fullest; that we might live in a world free from poverty. (Kevin Reid)

. . . that we will learn to listen to the revelations of truth from others and share our revelations of truth with them, so that in this sharing we might arrive at the fullness of truth; that from science we will learn that each action, no matter how small, affects the rest of the world; that our freedom and our well-being are inextricably tied to the freedom and well-being of others throughout the world; that we will all gain the courage to live out the gift we are to the world. (Margaret Eskew)

The Road To Mercer

Regeneration in the Centers

"Regeneration" is a common experience for students in the Regional Academic Centers as they make their way through college after a few years or a few decades out of high school. Some come with fine academic records and a good deal of confidence in themselves; many others have fears about their abilities and may have a rocky academic past.

I will never forget watching "Janice" adjust her graduation cap, using a window in the Sheffield Building on the Mercer Atlanta Campus as a mirror, at the 2001 commencement. It was the end of my first year of teaching in the Regional Academic Centers, and Janice had been in one of my classes. A superior student, she graduated with honors. "You must be excited about graduating," I said. "This is my first graduation ceremony," she beamed. She had dropped out of high school because of a pregnancy and later received her GED. Here she was graduating with honors from Mercer University, while raising a family and working full time.

Janice certainly is not the only Mercerian with a dramatic story. "Tom," a law enforcement officer, developed excellent insights that he believed increased his depth as a person. It was amusing and gratifying to visit him at his internship site in a county sheriff's department--the staff asked him for advice, rather than the other way around. He is now a county sheriff himself.

"Tonya" juggled her full-time course load with raising a family and working at a very demanding job. Extremely organized and motivated, she always submitted her work on time and at a superior level. She excelled in every class she took.

"Betty" worked in a bank and got tired of training the young recent college grads who were quickly moving up the ladder. Hampered by the lack of a degree, she considered herself, in her mid forties, too old to go to college. When she realized she could CLEP a number of courses, she decided to give college a try. She earned a degree in business, which opened up other doors for her.

"Katherine's" mother became gravely ill in another state. Too close to graduating to stop, Katherine drove many hours each week to care for her mother and finish her last course. She came back to work at an internship in Georgia at a very high level—the last requirement for graduation. When she had to go back to her mother's side, she was able to find an agency in that state that would take her for the brief time that remained in her internship. She graduated against great odds.

"Caroline" had wanted to be a teacher ever since she had entered kindergarten herself, but lack of funds prevented her from going to college right after high school. She settled into work and began a family. Needing to keep her job, she assumed it would be impossible for her to live out her dream of becoming a teacher. Then she discovered evening classes at the Centers and jumped at the chance to get her teacher education degree. Now she is shaping the minds of fourth graders.

"Kelvin's" father died when he was 15, forcing him to work every day after school and on weekends pumping gas at a service station—long before self-serve was even dreamed of. The oldest child, his earnings were essential to his family's survival. He barely graduated from high school. He thought many of his high school teachers passed him because they felt sorry for the family. Kelvin got a job in a large corporation and began to move up the ladder bit by bit. After he had worked about 20 years, his supervisor encouraged him to try college.

"Candace," in her early 20s, is often the youngest person in her Center classes. Not interested in the student activities that so many of her friends enjoy at residential colleges, she opted to work during the day. She fits right in with her Center classmates, some as much as three decades older.

Fears about attending Mercer are common with many students. "Darryl" described pulling up to a Center for orientation. He parked at the far end of the lot and sat there for a long time, seriously debating whether to enter the building. He was one of those who had begun college right out of high school and had just had too much fun being a college student to be a good classroom student. In the Culture of Mercer class, Darryl learned how to study, manage his time, and deal with stress and mastered other skills crucial to college success. He was a sincere and ethical person with real leadership abilities.

In a recent email, "Vanessa," a major in human services, related that she had seriously considered dropping out because of her fear of mathematics. Through much soul-searching, Vanessa decided to work at changing her attitude about math and finally took the "dreaded" beginning course. "I love it," she exclaimed in the email. "I think I've discovered the hidden mathematician in me."

The Centers are a place for students to experience regeneration, no matter what their age or background is. Not all are willing or able to make the sacrifices required to succeed in college, adding it to already busy lives. Those who do find themselves richer people and inspire the faculty to do their best for them.

Many CCPS faculty members, including our adjuncts, come to teaching in college as a second career with a wealth of experience behind them. Besides providing students with practical examples, our faculty has a hunger to teach, a hunger that perhaps was not satisfied by their previous work. For me, sharing what I have learned with our adult learners is very meaningful, exciting, and regenerative.

--Laurie Lankin, Ph.D., Associate Professor (Counseling & Human Science)

Just Do It!

What am I doing at Mercer University in the evenings? I am taking classes in the College of Continuing and Professional Studies (CCPS). I am working towards a degree in English. I was born in the Netherlands and I completed my RN degree there. However, professional education in the Netherlands does not include history, math, English or any of those core subjects. When you're in college for nursing, that's what you do: nursing. I spent four years alternating between the classroom and the hospital where we rotated through all the different specialties. My education has served me greatly. It allowed me to access the theater of life where people are born, recover, and sometimes die. The nuns, who ran the hospital like an army, pruned and tweaked us vigorously; they did not hesitate to tell us to go find another profession if we did not measure up.

When I applied for my next job as a flight attendant, my training as a nurse was definitely an asset. I traveled far and wide and lived in the Middle East for a year. Shortly after I arrived in the United States, I passed the RN exam and worked in Grady Memorial Hospital in Atlanta, observing the differences in culture and healthcare. After I got married, it was easy for me to take care of my babies when they came along. Those two babies have turned into beautiful, busy teenagers.

So far I have led an amazing and adventurous life, which is about to take another turn. My children will be going to college soon. I am only forty-five--practically a baby! If I don't get run over by a car, I still have a lot of life left in me. I could go back into nursing, which would make sense, but I want to reinvent myself one more time. Watching my children grow up, I have seen firsthand what a profound difference a teacher makes in a child's life. Of the time that they were awake, my children have spent more hours with their teachers than with me. I don't know if their teachers realize what an integral part they have played in my family's life. I've seen some really bad ones who managed to reduce my children to tears and I've seen the best who made them feel like they could conquer the world. And I've seen everything in between.

Would it be possible for me to be a good teacher? Would I be able to inspire--to bring alive the treasures stored in the books? Would I be able to control a class, or would I be intimidated? I am going to find out. Dr. Eskew, one of the outstanding professors in the CCPS, is my act to follow. What she does in front of a class is pure magic. She has a way of messing with your mind that is entertaining and inspiring. She creates new and improved visions of yourself and shows you the map to stardom in your own Hollywood. I'll never be her, but I have some of my own tricks up my sleeve. I've got nothing to lose. I'm going for it! And I am enjoying the journey.

Since I started going back to school I feel like my brain has taken a membership in the gym: heavy books, stretches of the imagination, cerebral-vascular brainstorming. As we get older we lose muscle mass if we don't exercise and I'm convinced that is what happens to the brain. I could almost feel it rattling around in my skull, screaming for food: "Give me something to do! Something to ponder! Something to memorize."

CCPS meets the challenge. The excellent teachers, outstanding curricula, and personal attention to your unique qualifications and circumstances in life will help you soar to heights you thought you could never reach. Your classmates are strong people who have made the choice to improve themselves, often with full-time jobs. Their strength and determination are incredibly motivating. And you won't meet them anywhere else, because they are at the place where it all happens--at Mercer CCPS. Just do it!

--Yvonne Gabriel

The Call of Books

It was a hot September day. The classroom at my elementary school was full of six-year-olds eager to begin the adventure of learning. At the front of the classroom stood a young woman with pretty red hair and an inviting smile. Over the next few months, I learned many things from her. I soon learned that her name was Mrs. Lawson. She was a caring individual, with the patience of a saint. I will never know how she stood those long, hot days in a room with approximately 30 children.

There was no air conditioning in any of the rooms, only small fans that circulated the heavy, humid air. She persisted in teaching us, and did a magnificent job. I remember reciting the alphabet, learning the sounds of the letters, and finally reading my first "Dick and Jane" book—a significant accomplishment I relished. I also remember learning to write the letters of the alphabet, and struggling with the letters 'S' and 'B'. But most of all, I remember the dedication of Mrs. Lawson. As I grew and passed into higher grades, I decided that I wanted to be a teacher like Mrs. Lawson--one who loved and encouraged the children. She could be stern when she had to be. I remember a boy talking back to her one day and being taken out into the hall. A few minutes later we heard the sound of the paddle as it came into contact with his bottom, followed immediately by the sound of yelling. I swore that would never happen to me, and I hoped that when I became a teacher I wouldn't have to spank anybody.

I made straight A's and loved attending school. Most of my teachers were great and I did well in their classes, but about the time I was in seventh grade I realized that my main focus was on reading and writing. The more difficult task of solving math problems was a chore I did not enjoy, and I struggled through each class. Although not a straight "A" student in high school, I did well in most of the classes. My senior year was a whirlwind of activity. My main priorities were to attend football games, dances, the prom, and graduation. The year passed quickly. When I graduated I was so happy. No more school! I had met the person I thought I would spend the rest of my life with, and we decided to get married. At that time, I had no desire to return to school. Less than a year later my first son was born. I did not work until after he began school at the age of five. Once I began working, there was no time for even the thought of going back to school.

For several years I worked in a weekly newspaper office. The first few years I was the office manager, but then one of the reporters took another job. When I was asked to write weekly features, I was terrified. I knew nothing about reporting or writing, but I accepted the challenge and found myself writing about everything from recipes to a local murder trial. I became intrigued by writing. I was surprised when the local librarian called to tell me about a position that was about to become open at the public library and to encourage me to apply. Excited at the prospect of working at the library, I applied immediately. What could be better than working with books every day? Since my first day of work there in 1989, I have firmly believed that a library is where I was meant to be.

I left my hometown library in 2000 when I moved to Warner Robins. I worked at the Centerville Public Library before coming to Mercer's Tarver Library in 2003. When I came to Mercer to work, I never thought about becoming a student. Once I became aware of the benefits and spoke with a representative of the College of Continuing and Professional Studies, I became determined to work towards a degree. It didn't matter that it might take me several years, or that I would be considered a "nontraditional" student. Attending college was something that I wanted to do.

Although I have worked indirectly in education for nearly 15 years, I do not possess a college diploma. That will soon change. I will graduate in May 2009 with a degree in Liberal Studies with concentrations in writing and literary studies. I am not sure of what the future holds, but I am a lifelong learner. Although I have decided not to teach, I plan to remain under the umbrella of education by continuing to work in a library. One day I will be at work in a library with my framed degrees hanging on my office wall. I will assist a patron with choosing reading material, and pull a book off the shelf with these words on the spine: "By Barbara Sellers."

--Barbara Sellers

My Late Education

In 1976 right out of high school, full of energy and eager for new experiences, I dove into college life. Ready to grow, I wanted to be a writer. I had a lot to say and important ideas to share with the world. Unfortunately, my early English professors did not share my enthusiasm. Steeped in outdated traditions, they were bitter, colorless women who seemed to be extensions of the creaky wood floors. Their duty was to lecture and ours was to replicate on demand the information they delivered. They rigidly adhered to the methods of education described by Paolo Freire as "The Banking Concept of Education." Stern looks and angry red scribbles thwarted any attempts to break away from their rigid curriculum. Fighting a losing battle, I limited my English and literature classes to the minimum required courses. I hadn't come to college merely to memorize someone else's ideas.

The professors in the psych department were slightly more open-minded, albeit a little out of kilter. I changed my major. To satisfy my desire to write, I joined the college newspaper as photo editor with the responsibility for writing cut-lines for the photos. I gained support and recognition for expanding my material into small stories.

Weak in math, I had put off taking statistics until my senior year. An uphill battle from the outset, the class proved to be even more difficult than I had feared. To make matters worse, my professor scheduled me for an internship at Central State Hospital simultaneously with the statistics course. I don't know if the psychology advisor didn't know or if he didn't care that I was not prepared for what I was going into.

It was February, and the cold wind cut through me as I walked up to the looming old building at Central State. Overwhelmed by my assignment, I'd never even been in an institution. A foul odor greeted me as I made my way down the hall through an obstacle course of screaming patients to reach the office to check in with the head nurse. I had hardly had time to introduce myself before she motioned for me to follow her as she provided my orientation:

> *You'll be working in the women's wing. There are a few basic things you'll need to remember: Don't get too close to the large lady in the corner because she won't let you go once she grabs you. If someone is bleeding, bang on the glass, and we'll send someone in. We don't have time to babysit you. Do you understand?*

I took the charts from my supervisor and headed into a large rancid-smelling room full of women. The fluorescent lights flickered, making the grey walls more depressing; the uninviting chairs matched the small row of cloudy windows lining the top of the dingy outer wall. Some of the women seemed fairly normal, some resembled the feral children out of television documentaries, and others appeared comatose, sitting and rocking back and forth. A towering 7-foot tall black woman approached me and took my hand. Wearing a shapeless grey smock, she didn't say a word, but led me around the room in her bare feet, pausing in front of each woman as if to introduce us. When we reached the large woman in the corner, she pulled back and shook her head. Her expressive face, dominated by her large and kind eyes, effectively communicated her thoughts without words. She was warning me to keep my distance.

The tall lady's name was Essie. Her chart indicated mild retardation. She had been institutionalized because her IQ was low. Long arms and huge hands and feet—for which the hospital staff had been unable to locate shoes large enough--accentuated Essie's slender build. Deserted by her family, she

21

had lived at Central State for 40 of her 55 years, never receiving any visitors. There was no apparent reason she couldn't talk–she just didn't. Self-appointed caretaker for the other women, she would pull them apart and rub their heads as if they were small children, should a scuffle ensue. She voluntarily distributed the food trays at every meal--one of the few people permitted to approach the large woman in the back without being nabbed. Kind and hospitable in an otherwise hostile environment, Essie had miraculously found a way to blossom.

At each subsequent visit, Essie greeted me warmly with a big grin, her large, well-spaced teeth gleaming white against her dark skin. She followed me faithfully as I talked with each woman, nodding approval at my comments. Fascinated by my hair, she liked to run her fingers through it, sometimes patiently working each strand of my long blond hair into tight little ropes that stuck up on the top of my head and hung down my back. Not psychotic or violent, Essie really didn't belong in a mental hospital—she was a victim of intolerance and fear. People didn't know what to do with her, so they hid her away.

Meanwhile, my statistics class wasn't going well. Several times I tried in vain to meet with the professor for help. I'd never had trouble with other classes, but I was sinking in this one. One day I left the university discouraged, heading out to my shift at Central State. Threading my way through the maze of confusion to my section, I showed my credentials to the new attendant, who snarled a greeting at me. Entering the day room, I could tell immediately that something was terribly wrong. The women were abnormally quiet and muttering to themselves. Essie was cowering in the corner, her face bruised and her lip busted. Her big beautiful eyes filled with tears as she glanced timidly toward the new attendant, who immediately demonstrated his disdain by flicking his toothpick across the room.

I was livid that the ignorant attendant had done this to sweet Essie. Determined that he not get away with such cruel behavior, I reported him to my supervisor. She affirmed that I'd done a great job but explained that I just didn't understand how difficult it was to find people to work in such poor circumstances for so little pay. My psychology advisor voiced basically the identical argument. In a condescending tone, he contended that I couldn't possibly understand how difficult it was to deal with "those people" and instructed me to keep out of hospital politics. Helpless, I sat down on the marble steps of the psychology building and sobbed.

I wrote letters to everyone I thought might be able to help--from the hospital administrator to the Governor of Georgia. The Governor's office sent me a nicely embossed letter thanking me for my concern and applauding my service to the community. I received a letter from my supervisor thanking me for completing my service. My internship was over.

The "D" I received in statistics confirmed the extent of my ineffectiveness. I didn't put up a fight when my parents suggested that I wasn't cut out for college after all. I found a job in a camera store in Milledgeville–I could sell cameras and teach people how to take photographs--no emotional toll required. I would just go to work, do my job, and draw a paycheck.

I got married and within three months I was pregnant. After my daughter was born, my life was consumed with caring for her. I fell into the pattern of taking the path of least resistance. Bored with family life, my husband sought excitement elsewhere. Life's necessities now began to dictate my schedule. A single mother who worked full time, I deferred my dreams.

I eventually went to work at Mercer University in Marketing Communications. Five years passed with no thought of completing my education. Then Kim Meredith in admissions with the College of Continuing and Professional Studies approached me in her calm and confident manner and skillfully guided me in the development of a plan to get back in school.

The closest discipline to psychology, human services proved to be the fastest path to a degree. Although adding on to an already demanding workday was challenging, the classes were more enjoyable than I had expected. The old creaky literature professors of three decades earlier came back to haunt me. I was one course short of the core requirement: I needed a liberal studies class. Finally, I decided to take the plunge.

It's funny how things happen. The professor for that liberal studies class would change the course of my life. Margaret Eskew reached a part of me that I had given up on years ago. She invited open discussion on issues--as eager to learn as she was to teach. Her openness and her patience made the class so much more than could be reflected in any syllabus or the catalog. With her encouragement, I enrolled in a literature class and eventually enrolled in several writing classes.

Thirty-two years after I started college I finally got an education.

--Janet Crocker

Just Enough

My path to Mercer University began in 1985 when I took my first college course. It was an Introduction to English class at San Antonio College. The class met each Saturday morning with about fifteen adults who had full-time jobs and families. The instructor placed us in circles of five. I completed the class with a grade of "B" and felt really good about my accomplishment. Prior to that, I had never given much thought to attending college. I would often see friends and associates headed to class after work and wonder why they would do such a thing when they could have done something enjoyable. Why sit in a classroom when you don't have to? Maybe it was this line of thought that prevented me from taking another college class for another ten years.

After leaving San Antonio, I spent four years in Italy and three years in the United Kingdom. In 1994 I moved to Bellevue, Nebraska, and in 1995 I gave in to the prodding of my unit commander and took a couple of Information Technology classes at Metropolitan Community College. Still it was no fun having to study and do homework when I really didn't see the benefit of it all.

Attending college part-time was never anything I wanted to do. I had never imagined myself working, taking care of a family, being involved in other activities, and also going to school. It just seemed to be too overwhelming to even think about. To satisfy work requirements and take care of a family was a twenty-four-hour, seven-day-a-week commitment in itself. In the fall of 1998 that all changed.

Assigned to Scott Air Force Base in southern Illinois, by 1998 I had already achieved the rank of Master Sergeant in charge of a work center comprised of 15 junior enlisted personnel. Many of my fellow senior enlisted comrades were winning competitive awards, such as Senior "NCO of the Year," and using that achievement to get promoted to the next higher grade. For the first time in my military career, my commander stressed that those directing and supervising any junior members should be recognized for their efforts. He insisted on doing everything within his power to get us promoted for the work we were doing. He wanted to know what it would take to get me promoted to Senior Master Sergeant, the next grade.

Promotion meant meeting many requirements. Education was the one obligation I was missing. If those interested in a promotion did not have a college degree of some sort, they either had to be close to achieving one or in active pursuit of one. Spurred on by my commander, I started taking classes on the weekend and at night. Every semester, I took some required class--public speaking, programming, economics, accounting, or marketing. I took whatever class was being offered--any class that would help me earn a degree. In May 2000, I received an Associate Degree in Management of Information Systems. In 2001, I was promoted to Senior Master Sergeant. I finally saw the connection between an education and work. I continued to take classes until my retirement from the Air Force.

In the summer of 2003, I left Scott AFB in Illinois for McGuire AFB in New Jersey, where I remained until 2006. I drove one and a half hours to Philadelphia for work each day.

By the time I arrived home from work and took care of my family responsibilities, I was too exhausted for anything other than rest and relaxation. For those three years, I made no advancement at all toward my education. In the summer of 2006 I left New Jersey and moved to Georgia.

Upon my arrival in Georgia, I immediately registered at Macon State and Mercer University. The Veterans Administration in New Jersey that was financing my education insisted that I continue seeking a degree in IT. However, the VA in Georgia strongly suggested a degree in teaching. They reasoned that teachers, especially male teachers, were in great demand while IT jobs were hard to find. Considering what Mercer charged per semester hour, I was quite sure the VA would not agree for me to take classes there. Thus Macon State became my number one choice. Because Macon State offered no evening program in education at that time, I started to focus my attention on on-line schools, not realizing that the VA would not approve that route. Once again the VA suggested that I refocus my attention on a degree in IT since I already had a job in that field. I was shocked when the VA suggested Mercer University. But it seemed that Mercer was my only choice. After careful reconsideration, I decided to register at Mercer.

Since my arrival at Mercer in October 2006, the experience has been fantastic. It has been a total learning situation—a change in my level of consciousness. I've learned almost as much about myself as I have about the subjects I have taken. I've met people who have enriched my life and helped me to overcome the obstacles I've encountered in the educational system. I have finally made the journey from hesitant, sometimes unwilling, and reluctant student to lifelong learner. Mercer University has helped me become the person I was created to be.

--Broderick Booker

Glory Hallelujah!

Forty years ago, when I was all of twelve years old, I watched Mercer baseball games from across the street on my aunt's front porch. I did not dare utter my thoughts aloud: "I wish I could go to college." This was only a secret dream. I understood that as a black child I could not attend college. My family was too poor, and I was too stupid. Still I wondered about college life and felt proud every time I saw a black student attending Mercer.

My free time was spent in the Mercer student center, where I made many friends. Chatting with them about their college life, I secretly envied those who could afford a higher education. By the age of twenty-six I already had three children. The thought of higher education would not seriously enter my mind again until I was forty, when once again I awoke from a recurring dream of hurrying to class and lost homework assignments. I sat on the side of my bed wondering why I thought I could succeed in the academic world of college.

But this time things were different. I had moved into my Habitat home (Habitat house number 13) about a year before. I had been told that I didn't qualify, but yet there I was, in a brand new home of my own. I began to believe that I could accomplish anything with effort and determination. The dreams started again: I would be sitting in class, books on my desk, and pencil in hand.

The day after one of my school dreams, I discussed the possibility of going to college with my three children, who were very supportive. The next week I enrolled at Macon Technical Institute. The first few weeks were terrifying. I felt I was too old, not smart enough, and out of place. "What kept me going?" you might wonder. A young woman from one of my classes stopped me in the hall one day, commenting: "Ms. Jordan, I love being in class with you. You are smart and funny and make learning fun for me. I try every week to get better grades than you. If you make an A, then I want one, too. I am glad you're here." Utterly amazed that I could so positively impact the lives of others, I fought back the tears.

I was nominated for the Georgia Occupational Award of Leadership (GOAL) and placed in the top five. After graduating with honors from Macon Technical Institute, now Central Georgia Technical College, I began work as a paraprofessional at Butler Early Childhood Center. In 2004, I registered at Mercer University.

Being at Mercer has been an awesome experience. How has Mercer impacted me? Mercer has facilitated encounters with wonderful and caring professors and staff. I have made friendships that will last forever. I have had the chance to research my father, a man I have never met, and look into the injustice of his life and the events leading to his death by electrocution in Georgia's prison system. I sat on a panel called "Four Faces from Death Row," representing my father and allowing his story to be heard for the first time.

I am also a member of *The Regeneration Writers*, a writing team of students from the College of Continuing and Professional Studies, who compiled this literary journal, the first of its kind published by nontraditional undergraduate students in the nation—probably in the world. In May, I went to Guatemala with Mercer on Mission, expanding my knowledge and experience as I helped children in an orphanage there.

Attending Mercer has allowed me to be a role model for my children and grandchildren. I will graduate in May 2010 knowing that I am the first in my family not only to graduate from high school, but also to receive a degree from one of the best academic institutions in the world. The habits of inquiry and reflection and the values of integrity, diligence, and community will characterize this grateful and jubilant Mercerian. Glory, Glory Hallelujah! Gloria Jordan is marching on.

--Gloria Jordan

A Long Detour

I was born into a family of educators. Both of my parents were teachers in the local school system. With several decades of teaching experience behind them, they stressed two important lessons. The first lesson maintains that education is the great equalizer. Everything can be achieved through education, even some measure of equality. The second lesson centers around the work ethic. My father constantly reminded me that I would have to outperform my white counterparts, because the playing field wasn't level. I had to work harder and study longer in order to achieve the skills expected by the general population.

I was seventeen years old when I first arrived on Mercer's campus. A recent graduate of Central High School, I was ready to tackle the world. Having already gotten acquainted with several of Mercer's professors from my association with their sons in high school, I felt quite comfortable on campus. There was Joe Hendricks, whose dad was known as "Papa Joe"– Papa Joe is now a Mercer icon recognized for his role in integrating Mercer and his work for civil rights. The fathers of Mark Flick and Travis Tremble were also very well-known professors on the Mercer campus. They made the transition from high school to Mercer easy. Originally, I came to Mercer to study political science, with aspirations of becoming a lawyer. I lived in the dormitory that now houses financial aid and the registration office. The first year went by quite uneventfully, while the second year drastically changed the course of my life, leading to a long detour.

During the beginning of my second year, I met a young lady who was a transfer from Tuskegee University. Although the relationship started out as a bet, a serious courtship soon developed. I no longer concentrated on my studies, often skipping classes to be with my girlfriend. In the end, the relationship failed miserably. I experienced my first real failure in this world– and it didn't even involve academics. I spent the next several days in my fraternity house contemplating my next move. I finally emerged from my valley of despair, deciding that I would leave school to join the Army.

Luckily for me, the Army had several training cycles. I didn't have to wait long before receiving orders. Within three days I left for Fort Leonard Wood in Missouri for basic training, followed by advanced training as a combat engineer. I was willing to accept any difficult assignment, and the Army was happy to oblige. Throughout the course of my twenty-two years in the Army, I traveled around the world and was exposed to a different kind of education. I have lived in several different countries. The interaction with other cultures has given me a priceless education.

Some twenty-eight years later, my detour ended. I found my way back to Mercer to complete my formal education. Somewhere along the line, I traded my dream of becoming a lawyer for working in education to help level the playing field for the young and to instill in them the work ethic modeled by my parents. With a degree in liberal studies and a minor in education from Mercer University, this seasoned soldier and global student will combine the lessons of my parents, the discipline and skills learned in the Army, and the enlightened worldview acquired from my sojourn among different cultural groups toward the preparation of the next generation's community and world leaders. I just wish that my grandmother, Miss Bay, could be here to celebrate with me.

--Kevin Reid

My Season

In her essay "In Search of Our Mothers' Gardens," Alice Walker describes the genius of black women whose creativity was stymied, often having to express itself in some alternative, even contrary, form. Walker's mother's creativity resulted in beautiful flower gardens that transformed her world. Like Alice's mother, I get great satisfaction from tending my garden.

Like Alice herself, I come alive when I express myself in writing. An avid gardener, I often see life through the lens of tilling, sowing, tending, and reaping.

Always hardworking and productive, I found myself at dead center in my life, going through the motions but getting little satisfaction. I had settled for the mundane. There were many hues in my garden of life, but none was brilliant; they were dull and lifeless. Like President Obama, I wanted a startling change for the better. I felt like a flower ready to bloom, awaiting the right circumstances, in need of nourishment, sunshine, and rain to blossom—to show the world my magnificent colors.

My elementary school days promised a harvest of beautiful flowers. My teachers lovingly and skillfully cultivated our young and impressionable minds, encouraging ideas here and severely pruning others. Segregated and located in a poor neighborhood, the school proved to be an oasis for the children needing a rich soil into which to send down their roots. The caring manner in which these sainted teachers toiled to prepare the soil and create conditions for growth among their tender charges inspires me even today.

Sadly, my high school days were not as fruitful; my teachers were not careful gardeners, often allowing weeds to sprout up untilled. The promise of a harvest of plenty appeared to wither from the lack of genuine care evinced by the faculty. Fortunately, my elementary school teachers had already strongly established the roots of knowledge, mitigating the lack of cultivation encountered in this period. Though the plant had been weakened, the time for blossoming had been merely delayed.

A year after the birth of my son, Calvin, I joined the Air Force, hoping to find an atmosphere for strong growth. Mired in the muck of bureaucracy, I despaired at being able to break through the hard dry surface. I pulled up my roots, hoping to plant them in a more fertile soil, taking along the surplus of manure for subsequent cultivation.

For my daughter, Alysha, I became like a tree standing by the waters--I would not be moved. I provided the shade and protection for her to grow strong in my embrace. She provided for a while the sunshine of my life, her radiance and beautiful spirit lending me the strength to reach beyond my own courage. I didn't want her to experience a world where her vision and growth would be stifled by others. Nestled safely in my embrace, she could perceive of a world without false boundaries and limits.

In the corporate world, acid rain and polluted waters slowly poisoned my soul, surrounding me with strong vines that choked me and suppressed the vibrant being within. Rules prohibited personal expression, thereby deferring dreams. "Would my dreams dry up like a raisin in the sun?"

Drowning in pessimism, I quit my job and stepped out on faith, determined somehow to penetrate the negativity that was all around. Confident that there was a flower somewhere beneath the surface waiting to emerge, I sought once again to bask in the sun, yearning for my true colors to break through. While I was testing the soil of freedom, Kenny came into my life, providing sorely needed nourishment for my withering plant. Kenny, Jr., his handsome ten-year-old, helped me remember the beauty and innocence of youth. I glimpsed once more the promise of a resplendent future. We became a family.

For almost 30 years, I had toiled—the massive amount of my energy having been spent in vain. I had worked hard, yet the harvest was minute in comparison to my labor. There was sand amidst the rich soil. I once again planted seeds of hope, scattering prayers for a new beginning. I applied for the Veterans Administration Vocational Rehabilitation Program, where the land was very hard to plow. I fought for the right to return to college. I prayed for a miracle.

With the confirming letters of the VA in hand, I was negotiating enrollment at Macon State when the miracle letter arrived: I had gained provisional admission to Mercer University! Determined to prove myself, I enrolled in one of the required core courses, LBST 175, where my sleeping passion for writing awakened. I gained confidence in using my own voice once again. The familiar works of James Baldwin and Alice Walker fused with the writings of Parker Palmer and Richard Rodriguez, creating an awakening within me, resonating with something in my soul. The mandated journal turned out to be a blessing in disguise as I began to learn more about myself through reflections on my thoughts, desires, goals, and accomplishments.

I toiled and sweated in the various courses needed for my academic program, hesitating only momentarily at some new challenge. My vision of teaching writing to inner city children grew clearer and clearer. The time to apply myself to my studies was a gift I did not take lightly. I was proud of the work I had accomplished. I could witness my own transformation from one paper to the next. One day I was invited to become a part of *The Regeneration Writers*, a group of students who had successfully negotiated for creative writing classes and had decided to produce a literary journal. It was for me a rebirth. Learning and working in that incredibly creative and regenerative environment for three sessions went beyond my highest expectations. We became a family, pushing and pulling each other forward toward our potential. Yet, for all of us, life would intervene, sometimes, it seemed, intentionally, to thwart the beauty of our development.

Even as I tended to the needs of my sick mother, my mind worked overtime, churning out ideas for stories or poems I would later process on my computer. Then my husband's illness competed for my time, requiring that I make use of the back burner once again. Although I continually propagated promises for an abundant life, the red clay, the thistles, thorns, and briars seemed often to prevail, delaying the arrival of the harvest. Yet I know, along with King Solomon, that there is a season for everything under the sun: "To everything there is a season, and a time to every purpose under heaven: a time to be born, and a time to die; a time to plant, and a time to pluck up that which is planted" (Ecclesiastes 3:2).

My season has come. The harvest is at hand!

--Elnora Fluellen

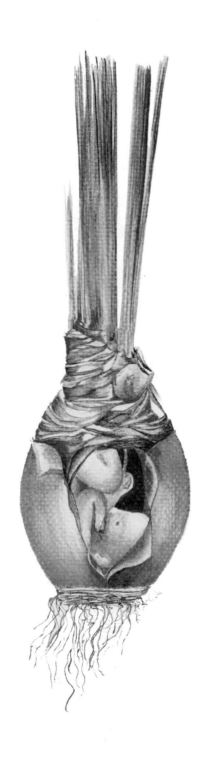

Taking Life

Death Row — April 17, 1987
for H. C. E.

Yesterday I was walking in the prison yard, circling the
100 square feet of brushed and measured concrete enclosed by
12 feet of chain-link fence topped and stranded with barbed
and razored wire. The thought about good fences making good
neighbors crossed my mind, and I laughed. Then I thought about
the Easter weekend beginning today in the journey of the cross,
a long perilous journey through cramped narrow streets, twisted
graveled paths, and the hidden passages of darkness in the human heart. The tortured Bearer would finally hang in the burning
sun and the night would fall upon His sagging shoulders, His
branded and forsaken brow. This journey would culminate in
the bright cool dawn of Resurrection, a gentle man of sorrows
rising from His tomb, freedom and joy emerging victorious from
a cave carved in stone.

I circled the yard and searched within myself for a
celebration of this life, this victory, this white bird of mourning beating its wings against my chest. But I could not find it.
I looked around myself, troubled, the prison on one side, the
bright sun captured in the skylight of the Death House tacked
onto the cellblock like an afterthought. On the other three sides,
more fences. Confused, I searched for the meaning of Easter in
this life, this death, this scene.

I looked across the yard to the grass growing so thick and
carelessly green outside the fences. I breathed deeply, hoping to
partake of the spring freshness and pull it through my veins. A
crack in the concrete caught my eye. I looked again at the grass
outside the fences, then turned back to look down at one small

single-leafed stem rising up from a narrow split in the concrete slab.

My thoughts whirled. My heart jumped. The razor wire glittered in the sun. This small tender sprouting green testified to the simple joy of Easter.

One solitary seed, blown thoughtlessly by the wind or dropped by some passing bird, had fallen helpless into the crack, surrounded by tons of concrete, lacking even the power to crawl free. Yet, with a uniquely frail tenacity and singularity of purpose – inscrutable, indomitable--it had burst forth, singing its brave face into the blazing sun with a bright green duality of song, proclaiming the pain, the joy, the gift of life.

My heart sang out. Even so it sang. Even so sings the human spirit.

--Andrew Legare

A Long Walk Home

The sun was just beginning to touch the tops of the tall Georgia pines as Big Jim walked toward home along the dusty clay horse path that divided Mr. Green's cotton field from the blackberry brush that was mixed with young dogwoods and old cedars. Behind him trailed six-year-old Lucille, who always had a hard time keeping up with her Papa. There were bugs and butterflies to chase. There were wildflowers to pick. There were logs to jump over. There were melodies to hum.

Big Jim looked back at his little girl, one of fourteen little mouths that the Good Lord had charged him with feeding. "C'mon wid yuh, li'l gal. Yo Mama'll be waitin' supper on us." Lucille ended her bunny-hop, and let her bare feet carry her to her papa's side. She grabbed his big, calloused hand and looked up at him.

"Will Mama let me hol' the new baby when it come, Papa? I'll hol' its head right. I knows how."

38

"We'll see 'bout dat, li'l gal. I 'spec you be gittin' 'bout big 'nough."

Big Jim worked for Mr. Bagwell at the lumberyard just out of town. There were always extra orders on Monday. He and his two older boys, Joseph and Isaiah, also took odd jobs on nearby farms. Other than that, he ran a tiny farm on land that he did not own, in return for a share of the meat and crops that he grew. It kept his large and growing family fed and sheltered. It was not an easy living, he thought, but he was a free man. His daddy and mama had been slaves on a large South Georgia plantation; both had died with stooped backs from picking cotton day after day, year after year. Big Jim had been born free in 1872. After Mr. Lincoln declared all slaves free, Big Jim's parents had moved with his three older siblings into the same dwelling where he was now raising his own family. Uncle Willem had stayed behind with his growing family on the old plantation. Other uncles had moved with their wives and families to nearby Macon, hoping for work as free men. Big Jim's daddy had gotten work with Amos Green, a kindly small-time farmer who had managed to eke out a living without the help of slave labor. His son was now in charge of the farm, running it more efficiently than the elder Green, and with only slightly less heart. Sharecropping was not easy, but Jim wore no chains. Though life held many burdens, no one would ever sell his wife or children away from him.

Walking along with Lucille toward home, Big Jim thought about the family he was now raising in that same house where he had been born. It was a relatively sturdy structure that had once been a small barn. It was worn and shabby, with boards nailed haphazardly across places in need of reinforcement. The roof had been patched in several places, and in a strong rainstorm no one could hear the babies cry because the rain hit the tin so hard. Washtubs hung on nails along one side of the house. The younger children played on the large front porch and creaky wooden steps. They ran and giggled on the porch, into the raked dirt yard, and back into the house through the screen door that slammed behind them.

It was a house full of young'uns alright. He smiled at
this rambunctious one next to him, his little Lucille. She would
often go with him on Mondays to the lumberyard, where she
kept the Bagwell's three-year-old son entertained so Mrs. Bagwell could work on the books for the lumber business. Lucille
had her mama's big brown eyes and easy disposition, but she
was built sturdy like her papa. He thought she would make a
fine woman for a husband one day. She would work hard, but
she would find life worth living. In spite of living in a white
man's world, she would be strong, and she would be happy.

"Watcha thinkin' on, Papa?" Lucille squinted her eyes
toward her Papa. "Why you so quiet an' lookin' at me funny?"

"Ha! You is a funny gal. I was thinkin' on yo' tomor-
ras, chil'. I was thinkin' 'bout how things'll be when you has
young'uns yo'self."

"Why you thinkin' 'bout dat, Papa?"

"Well, gal, dat's what grown-up papas think on. We is
good at worryin' 'bout our young'uns."

"Well, don't go a worryin' 'bout me, Papa. I's gonna be
jes' fine!" Lucille skipped on ahead along the path, but stopped
dead as she saw four white men staggering toward them in the
middle of the dusty path.

"C'mere, gal. Stay here wid me." Lucille got behind
her papa, and held tightly to his hand. As she peered at the men
around her papa, she thought she might have seen two of them
earlier at the lumberyard. Mr. Bagwell had yelled something at
them, causing Mrs. Bagwell to stop her work and stare out the
open window toward them. Lucille had noticed her squinched
up face as she turned back to her papers; she looked past Mrs.
Bagwell out the window into the yard as the pair were stomping
toward their wagon, still full of tree trunks, muttering angrily.

Big Jim recognized the same two as regulars at Bagwell's lumber yard. They were brothers from a nearby farm who
hauled in felled trees to have them planed into usable lumber.
They relished in announcing their thoughts on proper racial division loudly; most white folks agreed with them on this point, but

were not quite so publicly belligerent about it. These two were known as general troublemakers. Lately, they had become even more cantankerous, until Mr. Bagwell had had enough. Big Jim had heard him just that morning plainly tell the brothers that he no longer needed their business.

As the brothers and their two companions got closer, Lucille became more anxious. Something was wrong. One of them was holding a brown bottle; another waved a shotgun. One was leading a mule with a pack on its back.

"Hey you, nigger man!" They stopped in the shade of an ancient live oak, blocking the path. "Who said you could be on this land?"

"My name is Jim." Lucille heard her papa say. He held his eyes and head straight and fast, shoulders back.

"Don't you sass me, boy! You ain't nothin' but a nigger, don't matter how that nigger-lovin' Bagwell treats ya! Now, who said you could be here?"

"My name is Jim Johnson." He answered in a plain, strong voice. "I lives on Mr. Green's land. He knows I walks dis path."

"Is that so? Well, you know what I think, Will?" The one in the red shirt addressed the one in the worn blue overalls. Lucille was afraid of their little squinty eyes. "I think what we got us here is a uppity nigger! I'm a thinkin' he don't know his place too good. Whatchu think, Will?" Lucille wanted to go home.

"I think we jes' might hafta teach this uppity nigger a lesson." The one called Will grinned at his brother as Lucille's stomach churned. The other two stood quietly looking at the ground. Big Jim turned to look down at his little daughter. "Honey-chil', now you listen to me. I want fer ya to run home, fas' as yo' li'l legs can run, ya hear me?"

"I want us both to go home, Papa! You come, too!" Lucille tugged desperately at his hand. Why were these men mad at Papa?

"Go now. Mind yur papa. Scat!" The one in the red

41

shirt stomped his foot in the clay toward the little girl, but Lucille held stubbornly to her papa's hand, as tears began to roll down her cheeks.

"No! Papa! You come too!" Big Jim jerked his hand sternly away from his troubled little girl.

"Now you do like I sez, gal! You git home right now!" Her daddy's voice shook with insistence. "You run hard, an' don't look back!"

Lucille began running, while still protesting. "No, Papa! I don't wanna go home wid'out you!" She ran and cried, and hollered, "No, Papa!" over and over.

"Don't look back, Lucille! Jes' keep on uh runnin'!" She could hear his booming instructions behind her as she ran. After what seemed like a long while, she stopped and leaned on a rough-barked tree trunk away from the path where she had left her papa. She was still crying as she tried to catch her breath. Papa had said not to look back. A dark fear crept into her heart. She was afraid to look, and she was afraid not to look. What was happening to her papa? Why were those men mad at him? What were they doing to him? Lucille slid slowly to the ground, falling in a heap and snagging her faded yellow dress. She hid her eyes in the crook of her arm. For a long time, she cried and rocked herself back and forth, exhausted in grief and paralyzed with fear. Eventually, her tears spent, Lucille squinted her eyes closed as tightly as she could, and stood up. She moved away from the tree and turned her whole body toward the spot where she had left her papa. She was far enough away that she couldn't hear anything. After a few seconds, she pried her eyes open slowly, and looked down the path, down into the little valley from where she had run. In the distance she could barely see her papa, her big strong papa, dangling from a fat branch of the old oak tree.

"No, Papa, no!" Lucille screamed and cried as she ran back to her Papa. When she finally got to the big tree, she reached for her papa. She could barely touch his toes, as they trembled and kicked about slightly. His eyes were wide open and his swollen face contorted, but the rope had finally tightened enough to stop his breathing and choking. No one else was there; the men had taught their deadly lesson, and then walked on down the path in the dusk of that ordinary day. Lucille was still crying when she dropped to the ground underneath her papa. Big Jim could do nothing about his little daughter's brutal agony. He placed her destiny into the Good Lord's hands as he slipped from this cold, dark world.

--Terri DeFoor

A Story Retold

John sat quietly with his back to the wall, the silence broken only by the constant ticking of the clock, precious time fading. A father waited to die.

"Hey, Slim, when they come for ya, man?"

"Later today, dawg."

The conversation seemed to stop almost mid-sentence.

Peter sat on a hard stool listening to each footstep as men shuffled past his cell. Like his grandfather before him, today was his day to face judgment. Sitting quietly with his back to the wall, Peter's thoughts turned to his grandfather. How many times had he asked his mother about the final days of his grandfather's life? Each time she had recounted the scene of her father sitting with his back to the wall, waiting until death came to call.

How horrible it must be to know you are innocent and are sentenced to die anyway—thinking that the truth will set you free. But it doesn't. You sit. You wait. The clock ticks. Time slips away, carrying your life with it. His grandfather had only had one visitor, his mother, to whom he spoke minutes before his execution. He was twenty-six when he died in the electric chair at Reidsville Prison in 1957: tried, convicted and sentenced by Jim Crow laws. Fifty years later, that same justice system held Peter's fate as well.

"Peter, Peter Johnson?" The call of his name interrupted his reverie. "To the door!" Soft brown eyes looked upward. Refusing to allow anyone to know how anxious he really was, Peter stood, nodded, and sauntered to the opening in the cell door. With outstretched arms his hands automatically came together; the handcuffs clicked as they fastened about his wrists.

"Your mother is downstairs. She wants to visit. Next time put her on your card or we won't let her in."

The old elevator clickety-clacked to the next floor. He saw her as soon as the doors parted. She was seated behind the crystal glass divider, watching as he walked towards her. A smile greeted a smile. Picking up the phone to communicate, Peter allowed himself for the first time to acknowledge the pain hidden behind her familiar façade. Both pretended that things were normal. What is normal?

A strong hand tapped his shoulder: "It's time to go." Peter rose and looked into his mother's chocolate brown eyes and mouthed the words: "Love you, ma." Then he quickly turned and went out the door. I won't look back. She is watching me and her eyes are fighting back tears. It's okay! She will be okay, if I just don't look back.

The sound of the door echoed what seemed like an eternity--not in her ears but in her heart.

The guard ushered Peter into an office. Glancing around the room, Peter noticed a tall, white man with piercing blue eyes who motioned to him.

"My lawyer is not here, sir."

"Don't matter, son. I have things to do. Here's the deal."

"But, it's not fair. I didn't do it! I am innocent."

"Not my job to prove your innocence, son. My job is to prosecute. Do two years, or I will send you away for twenty. Your choice. I will convince the jury that it was you–innocent or not. Officer, I am finished with Mr. Johnson."

The rest of the day was a haze for Peter. Where is justice? Where is Lady Liberty? Where is my freedom?

Peter's father sat on his bunk, his back touching the wall

of his dark prison cell, a letter crushed in his hand. What have
I done? Why can't I get myself together? They have given my
son two years in jail and I sit here in prison helpless to help him
or myself. Tears fell. A heart ached. Thoughts were interrupted:
"David, David Johnson. Front and center. Your mother's
here for a visit!"

--Gloria Jordan

Reflection on Prisons

My thinking about prisons has shifted over the last de-
cade, mostly attributable to the people I have met, the materials
I have read, and the experiences I have had. The changes I have
experienced were not always dramatic. The small incremen-
tal changes, however, have added up over time, pointing me in
directions I never thought possible.

Like Sr. Helen Préjean, the nun who became the spiritual advisor to two men on death row at Angola State Prison in
Louisiana and wrote a book about it—Dead Man Walking--, I
naively thought that everyone got what he or she deserved. If
you did the crime, you got the time—and the punishment that
went along with it. A student of World War II, I had read and
heard first hand accounts from Nazi prisons and concentration
camps. I became physically ill after reading an entire book of
the death sentences meted out to citizens who opposed the Nazi
line—becoming especially disconcerted when I read the sentence of the father of Solomon Raditzsky, who had spoken to my
class. Loyal American that I am, I knew that my country would
not condone such cruel and unjust practices. My study of World
War II has profoundly influenced the person I have become
and the way I perceive others—especially the least of these our
brothers and sisters.

As I prepared my dissertation on the language of Adolf
Hitler for publication, I was approached in my role as Director of

the Center for Intercultural Studies at Xavier University of Louisiana to host a forum on the death penalty. I was working hard to build students up and didn't consider "prison concerns" within the scope of my duties—there was an entire infrastructure to be built for study abroad and student scholarships to procure. So it was with not a little resentment and a good deal of impatience that I agreed to read one chapter of *Dead Man Walking*. I read through the entire night, finishing the book around 10 a.m. The daughter of a lawyer, Sr. Helen had put together a convincing casebook on the influence of election year, race, class, ethnicity, and geography on the death penalty. I agreed to host the forum on the death penalty with Sr. Helen as the keynote speaker along with the Assistant District Attorney of New Orleans, the chair of the department of sociology at Tulane, and several other notable participants. Over 3,000 participated in the various sections of that unforgettable two-day symposium, another milestone. Prisons moved off dead center in my life.

When I moved to Georgia, I decided to keep a low profile. I put my extracurricular efforts into Habitat for Humanity and later into the Fuller Center for Housing with founder Millard Fuller. Then one day Dot Pinkerton of the Light House Mission came into my office. She was determined that I would help her write a grant for the Mission. She won, and I was gradually pulled more and more into rehabilitation work with her. I began to meet the men who had come out of prison, sometimes after more than forty years behind bars. I listened to their stories, witnessed their struggles, and learned firsthand the almost impossible hurdles that awaited them. Unwittingly, I had put faces to the group designation. I could no longer just think in the abstract. This made life so much more complicated.

Dot prodded me about going into the prisons—the work of rehabilitation, she preached, had to begin in the prisons so that the men would be able to make it on the outside once they were released. I managed to clear my schedule to go to the prison on Fulton Mill Road right off Eisenhower Parkway in Macon, Georgia. Giving up my keys and purse was unnerving, but not nearly as much as the sound of the locks clicking behind me. I found myself in a large room full of lifers and only a few guards. I began deep breathing, realizing that the guards would be hard put to contain any violence that might erupt.

The program Dot had planned for that night was an address by a lifer who had received a life sentence when he was sixteen and had just been released thirty years later. The son and daughter of the woman he had killed on that fateful night would speak. The ex-convict addressed the group, expressing genuine remorse for his actions on that night, vowing that if he could, he would give his own life to bring back the woman he had killed. I saw the brother and sister stand up and move toward the podium, not knowing if this would be the moment of their revenge. A retired policeman, the son knew how to smuggle in a gun undetected. A breathtaking silence reigned in the room as the brother and sister embraced their mother's murderer, vowing to help him adjust to life outside of prison, even promising financial assistance. The brother confessed that he had indeed once intended to smuggle in a gun, shoot his mother's murderer, and then turn the gun on himself. The effect of witnessing first hand such forgiveness was visible on the faces of the lifers. I have never before or since witnessed the tremendous power of forgiveness in any other place, not even in the church, which is founded on forgiveness. From the expressions on their faces, it seemed that each man was yearning for the forgiveness he had watched almost magically unfold that evening.

The life-changing, life-sustaining power of forgiveness ceased that night to be a theoretical construct. It was real. It had happened in a prison and turned my world upside down. Following that sacred moment, Dot spontaneously announced that Dr. Eskew would say a few words. I groped my way to the microphone, having no idea what would proceed from my mouth. With the picture of the brother and sister embracing the murderer of their mother emblazoned on my mind's eye, I recited the words to the *Sacred Harp* hymn I had learned as a child: "I will arise and go to Jesus. He will embrace me in his arms. In the arms of my dear savior, oh, there are ten thousand charms."

I returned to my seat, still trying to piece together what had happened there. I looked up to see a line that seemed about a mile long, snaking around the room. Shocked, I realized that the line was for me. The lifers wanted to talk to me. I couldn't imagine why. Pressing little pieces of paper into my hand, they all wanted to know about the ten thousand charms. Dot had told them earlier in the service that I taught writing. Now they were imploring me, begging me, to return and teach them to write. Already reeling from the lesson in forgiveness, I bore patient witness to a powerful force driving man after man forward to claim a remnant of his voice and to make a connection with the spiritual. I left, never to forget their embrace that evening.

Back at Mercer, I walked into the LBST 175 class I taught. The reading assignment for the evening was John Wideman's "Our Time." Like the men I had met in that prison, Wideman's brother Robby's voice had been silenced by a life sentence. John had attempted to channel Robby's voice through this essay. Awkwardly trying to find a point of connection between the class and the essay, I asked if anyone could identify with anything in the story. After a long silence, Gloria Jordan raised her hand in affirmation, confessing that she could identify with just about everything in the story. Not prepared for the answer Gloria would give, I pressed for details: "My father was executed in 1957 in Georgia's electric chair."

All of us in that class felt a cold shiver travel down our spines. Finally finding my voice, I thanked Gloria for her trust and confidence in us—for her bravery and honesty. Several other students encouraged by Gloria's lead described how their lives had become entangled in the criminal justice system. That evening was pivotal in the direction I took in studying prison literature and teaching writing. I stood in awe of Gloria and others who had managed to achieve so much at such great odds, who were standing before me with tremendous skills and insight, trust, positive expectations, and excitement about life. Philosopher and educator Paolo Freire would have smiled: that evening the students taught the teacher.

At the Prison and Jail Project in Americus, I learned that one African American woman had been jailed because of debt. When she could not pay the fine assessed, she was forced to stay at the detention center, which she left each day to go to work. Her detention center "rent," bus fare for work, and a very small amount for food left her less than $5 each month for the remainder of her expenses—including paying off the ever increasing fine. The state that was settled by people from the debtors' prisons in England had returned some of the least of these its citizens to a debtors' prison.

Prisoners on work release in Macon have to procure a job. Governor Perdue makes it easy for these men to provide the labor for his chicken factory in Perry. A bus transports the men to and from Perry for $10 each way. The men work ten-hour shifts, preparing chickens for the market. The first man on the assembly line reaches down into a basket of live chickens, selects one, and hangs it by the feet from the overhead conveyor belt. The chicken is not too happy about the whole process, squawking and letting fly its excrement in all directions. The man at the second station gets to slit the throat of the struggling bird—a fine way to ease an ex-convict back into society. That is about all the description I was able to tolerate. I wondered how this would affect the soon-to-be-released offender. Spending ten hours a day six days a week for maybe minimum wage in a chicken factory is hardly anyone's dream of freedom. Then try reestablishing yourself on that amount of money. The prison cell begins to be inviting. Without support, it is difficult at best for anyone imprisoned for a long period of time to make it on the outside. I tasted the hopelessness and despair of those who finally find release from their prisons.

Then I met one young man who had been in the prison system for nine years for a crime he didn't commit. He was told to plead guilty or the judge would put him under for twenty years. When he protested his innocence, the judge averred that innocence or guilt was not the question. The truth didn't make the young man free, but intervention finally pried him loose. He was required to report to the jail on a regular basis. If all the beds at the jail were filled, he was commanded to report back the next week. If the beds weren't filled, he was admitted. Once paroled, he had to pay his parole officer $30 per month—even though with his prison record it was next to impossible to find a job. He had been convicted because of his skin color and the neighborhood where he lived. His gentleness and hushed voice humbled me.

Putting faces on the men in prison, hearing their stories, and witnessing their pain have motivated me to study the system into which these men have been thrust, sometimes by their own violence and indiscretion and other times as a victim of the wrong time, wrong place, wrong color, wrong class. I want to keep an open mind--to listen to the voices of prisoners (and victims), some loud and some barely audible. I want to give the careful attention and time required to explicate the complex systemic institutional power relationships dominating the direction of justice in our nation. I am glad to have some wonderful companions on this daunting but critical journey into the prisons of America, dubbed by *Prison Nation* editors, Tara Herivel and Paul Wright, as "warehouses for the poor."

--Margaret Eskew

Who's Going to Tell?

Who's going to tell me
The joyous news today?
They proved my son is innocent
By testing DNA.

Who's going to tell him
Everyone was wrong?
I will go tell him myself
And change the flowers on his stone.

Who's going to tell me
It only touched one life?
After two years in that Georgia clay
He was joined by his wife.
Who's going to tell me
This is the only way?
How do you exonerate a man
Lying in a grave?

Who's going to tell me
Who killed my son?
Nobody here to face the shame
When the deed is done.

Who's going to tell me
Where the justice is?
I need to fully understand
So I can tell their kids.

--Michael Ragland

Aint Marthey

"I see him, Aint Marthey, up there hanging from that tree. Right up there, Reba, a little farther to the left, right behind that chinaberry tree." Wendy yanked on Catherine's shirt and whispered to her to quit lying. She knew Catherine couldn't see anything. Why would she lead old Aint Marthey along like that?

Aint Marthey was getting more and more agitated. Finally, Reba piped up at Catherine's prodding, "Aint Marthey, I see him, too. What's he doing up there?"

"Chile," she says, "Dem bees some bad white peoples. Deys done gone an' kilt mah nephew. Deys done strung 'im up fuh nuthin'. He ain't done nuthin'. Jes woik his finguhs tuh de bone. He wuz allus so smart—got hissef a college edgication.

What dey done gone an' done dat fo? Gawd haf mercy. De debil done got in 'em." Tears were streaming down Aint Marthey's face. Suddenly the words flew right off Wendy's tongue: "Aint Marthey, don't cry. When I squint my eyes real tight, I can see him, too--way up there. We gonna help him. I'm gonna go git Mama."

"Ain't nobody can hep 'im now. He gone." Her eyes darting wildly around, Aint Marthey picked her way across her neatly swept front yard, trudged past the picture of *Ecce Homo* hanging on the wall to the right of the door, and lowered her heavy body onto an easy chair. It was Sunday afternoon, and the three sisters set the plate of fried chicken, mashed potatoes, green beans, sliced tomatoes, and red jello with a dollop of mayonnaise on the top onto the well polished table. Their mama sent them every Sunday to bring Sunday dinner to Aint Marthey. Today the girls didn't feel much like stretching out on Aint Marthey's floor to read the Sunday funnies.

Later they came and carried Aint Marthey off. Somebody whispered to their mama that she had been taken to the crazy house. For Wendy Sundays were never the same again. It was hard for her to enjoy the comics any more. Aint Marthey's stocky presence resiliently bled through "Blondie," "Dick Tracy," "Brenda Starr," and "Henry." Sometimes Wendy would find herself just staring up at the trees searching for a rope.

--Margaret Eskew

A Losing Battle

Carmen could not believe that he was gone. Chris was her first love, her hero, and one of her closest friends. She had met him when she was fifteen and he was seventeen. She still loved him–no longer a romantic love, but a love full of respect and devotion.

She wondered if there had been anything that she could have done to prevent such a tragedy. She asked God why Chris had had to die. Their life together flashed before her to memories spanning back to their earlier days–to the times they had walked to school together. He would walk her to her school and then hurry to get to his, three miles away. He had been a good boyfriend and a good person.

When she had first met Chris, he was working two jobs—a rarity for a high school student. She asked why he worked so much, taking so little time for himself. He confided that he was responsible for providing for his mother and sisters. Chris had grown up witnessing the physical abuse of his mother by the men she dated. He knew that she endured the abuse only because she lacked employment. The men she dated worked and provided a roof over their heads, so she made the necessary sacrifices for her children. Chris suffered silently, watching his mother take beatings. When he was old enough, he got a job to help with the bills, at one point challenging his mother's alcoholic partner to a fight that resulted in the man leaving. From then on, Chris assumed full responsibility for his mother and sisters.

A selfless person, Chris often did what he thought needed to be done. When Carmen became pregnant with their daughter at the age of sixteen, he joined the military to increase his ability to provide for her, their baby, and his mother and sisters. After completing basic training, he asked her mother for Carmen's hand in marriage. They wed and moved to Oklahoma. After only seven months of active duty his company was called up for deployment to Iraq in Operation Desert Storm. He had not expected to be leaving his new family so soon, but he followed through with what was required of him, assigning financial allotments for his new family, his mother, and sisters.

Their rocky marriage could not endure their immaturity or the separation and ended before his duty was completed. Upon his return, he was dishonorably discharged for illegal drug use that had begun while he was in Iraq. His drug use increased beyond his control. When asked what had sparked his drug use, he confided to Carmen that something had changed what he believed in during his deployment, but he was unable to discuss it.

He eventually returned to Mississippi, clean of the crack that had led to his discharge, but continuing to use marijuana.

No longer able to provide adequately for his family, he sought employment that would create greater financial possibilities. However, his military status prevented him from obtaining gainful employment. He made an attempt at education, but once again his military status barred his access. Disenchanted by how the country he had fought for treated him, he "settled." Obtaining a position as a store clerk and working as many hours as he could, but still not having enough to provide for those he loved, Chris turned to the streets. He began supplementing his income by dealing drugs, using the proceeds to help his mother pay her bills, to assist his sister with the expenses of college, to provide the basic necessities for his children, to help close friends, and finally to pay for his own education.

With the hope of quitting the game, Chris began and completed a course in barbering. To his dismay, he was declined a barber's license. His plan had failed. All the time he had spent in class was for nothing. In his mind, he had no other choice but to continue to sell drugs.

On April 12, 1999, Carmen received the call that changed her world. The frantic voice screaming in pain over the phone frightened her. It was her own child, but her words were frighteningly unintelligible. She finally recognized the words, "He's dead. My daddy is dead!" Distraught and wailing loudly, Carmen drove like a mad woman to get to their child, hoping against hope that her daughter had somehow made a mistake. The inconsolable child collapsed into Carmen's arms, crying: "Mama, my daddy is dead because he did not want to go to jail."

Chris had been pulled over by police, who had searched his car for drugs. To avoid detection and the imprisonment that would follow, Chris had quickly swallowed the crack-cocaine. Rushing home, he had worked to vomit up the crack. Having miscalculated the time that had elapsed and the amount of the substance he'd swallowed, he was unsuccessful in detonating the ticking time bomb. Always ready and willing to help others,

54

Chris had been unable to save himself.

My friend was gone. The man who had been a living hero to so many died fighting a losing battle.

--toyann daniel mason

The Children of Cain

Genesis 4:1-10
Matthew 5:43-48

Only a few days ago, in another college town not far away, the spring semester was drawing to a close. Thousands of students strolled across the lawn for their morning classes. In nine minutes, the fierce winds of human violence erupted leaving us–all of us–numb and bewildered by the senseless, tragic loss of the young and the eager, the gifted and promising lives of those who were destined to make a difference, destined to dance and to sing, to write and to discover.

In another place ten thousand miles away, 75 people, innocent and hopeful, were snuffed out by a suicide bomber. That same day, the American toll of soldiers lost in Iraq grew to 3,131. The toll for Iraqi citizens grew to more than 31,000.

In Kansas City, an elderly widow lay dead, her car stolen by an anonymous gunman to find his way to another killing field–a hamlet mall where people strolled into food courts and searched out the latest bargains. Three dead. It was an ordinary day that brought extraordinary trauma.

Violence upon violence--you and I are living in a world increasingly defined by violence. While we mourn the loss of life caused by natural disasters in Greensburg and New Orleans, human beings are taking a far more deadly and vicious toll in the whirlwind of terror and rage that is spinning throughout our world.

Violence reminds us that we are not only the children of

Adam; we also are the children of Cain. Exposing the ugliest strains of our human character, violence is not simply a phenomenon of 9/11 or in Baghdad. It is not simply a phenomenon in Blacksburg or New York, in Kabal or Sadr City. It's not simply a tragedy spawned by the Hitlers or Husseins, by Osama bin Laden, by Hamas, by Hesbollah or Iran or Kim Jong-il. The problem with human violence does not just exist out there in someone else's heart and soul. Our presumed innocence and our self-righteous judgment are mostly a way of washing our hands of the reality that we all, God help us--we are all children of Cain.

Today we have celebrated the achievements of the brightest and the best, students who are graduating with anticipation and expectation. As we launch these young to study, to labor, to make a difference in this tinder-box world, let us be candid about the fragile world that you and I have created. It has become a world where hostility and bitterness have exploded onto the human scene more dramatically and more destructively than ever before: killing in schools, killing in malls, massacres in our cities.

We often presume to establish the ways of peace by killing in return. We hope to end the killing with more killing. Yet, we suspect somewhere deep within us that military power and precision bombs alone will not be sufficient to overcome this reign of terror.

If we cannot be reminded here before the altar of God, where can we be reminded of the truth that there is no good violence? War is not good violence. Capital punishment is not good violence, and the notion of holy war is sheer nonsense, nothing more than a myth created to help us manage our guilt. War is never holy. Surely, there are moments in our tragic and broken human history when war has been and will be inevitable. But let us not deceive ourselves into believing that war--that people killing other people--is a good or righteous act. War always echoes our broken human condition, our failure to achieve God's purposes in creation.

The presence of violence has become so vivid, so naked, so expected, even so accepted. And violence is not 2000 miles away in New York or 10,000 miles away in Baghdad, or even 100 miles away in Atlanta.

Violence is closer to home and it is perpetrated not only with guns and knives. It wears many faces. Let us count the ways that we, like Cain, put Abel to the ground–the violence of power, the violence of prejudice, the violence of language, the violence of sexual abuse, the violence toward persons with a different sexual orientation, the violence of silence, and perhaps most pernicious of all, violent and hateful religion. Violence wears so many faces.

The violence of power: violence is power out of control, unbridled and destructive. It may be the untamed power in the workplace where one uses authority and position to demean and to ridicule.

The violence of sexuality is everywhere present. Sexual abuse victimizes more people than backstreet thugs on Saturday night: child abuse, spouse abuse, rape – using sex to control and to diminish.

There is the violence of economic peril where over half of the world's population lives on less than a dollar a day. While we can and should celebrate our economic progress, it is an act of violence to ignore the people who live on the margin, for whom poverty and economic hopelessness breed gang warfare and despair. If we continue to ignore economic injustice, it will finally burn our democracy to the ground.

And there is the violence of religion where devoted Christians, not just Muslims, kill and maim in the name of God. Whether it's Islamic Jihad, or Jewish Zionism, or the Christian's Army of God, it is all dangerous and violent religion. It is religion gone bad. Fundamentalism is the outcome of religion that has been hijacked by fear and anger.

I stand in the pulpit today to ask how we can come to terms with this explosion of inhumanity. Is our faith simply irrelevant in the rough and tumble of our lives? Do we have to leave our really tough questions outside on the steps of the sanctuary before we come in to worship? As we live here on the edge of such trauma and chaos, my conviction is that our faith may turn out to be our highest and best hope, perhaps our only hope. The truth is that violence arises from deep within us. We are wrenched and torn by fear and anger. Our inner turmoil breeds rage and resentment and malice and hostility. Wallowing in the tragedy of unbridled self-importance, we diminish, we dismiss, and we destroy. Like Cain, we kill because we are afraid.

But fear will not be stemmed by mindless brutality or raging conflict. Fear will abate and anger will subside only when we discover and commit to a new way of being together. If we are to escape the vise-like grips of violence, it will not be because we have grown stronger; it will not ultimately be because we have acquired more lethal weapons. It will be because we have been captured by a blazing new light, because we have the courage to hear a new voice.

So, we have come to this: Our eggshell world is broken to pieces–shattered, lying in crumbles, smoldering and jagged. What are we to do with the pieces?

As one who is deeply troubled by the darkness that is crippling human civilization, I ask that we, at least here in the sanctity of this hallowed place, turn our faces to see and to hear the presence and the voice of Jesus. Jesus himself, you see, was the tragic victim of human violence. So, for Jesus, violence was not abstract or remote. Jesus felt the sharp assaults as a dreadful, devastating, shattering avalanche of rejection that brought searing pain and a wrenching death.

You will remember that violence visited Jesus in Gethsemane where he was arrested in the presence of his disciples. Roman soldiers with their swords and paraphernalia of war marched into the Garden of Prayer, violating the night. Like us, the disciples had not learned. Peter, the most swashbuckling of all the disciples, did what we are always inclined to do. He confronted violence with violence. Peter's response was so contemporary. Peter drew the sword, defiantly cutting off the ear of the

58

approaching soldier. It is our human way–meeting violence with violence, confronting it head on, holding our ground, taking on the enemy.

But, can we learn from the violence that visited Jesus? If so, I offer these three words:

First, we have to pick up the pieces. We have to pick up the ear we have severed and put it back on. You see, violence will never be the cure for violence. And there is no easy or shortcut way to pick up the pieces. But that is what Jesus did. We have to rebuild what our violence has destroyed. We have to put the ear back in place. We have to heal the wounds that our violence has inflicted. We have to go through the rubble and rake up the debris. We have to rebuild the buildings, light the storefronts again, place goods back on the shelves. It requires sacrifice, investment, taxing our purses and our hearts. It is not enough to say, 'I'm sorry." When Peter acted with violence, Jesus' response was to redeem the violence. If we want to take Jesus seriously, retaliation can never be our last word. God's last word is redemption. Redeeming the violence is hard, brutal, painful, back-breaking work. Yet, if we follow Jesus, I believe we have to begin by redeeming the violence.

Second, we have to look for ways–specific and concrete– to respond to violence with compassion, compassion for the wounded and compassion for those who inflict the wounds. Jesus would teach us that there is only one cure for human rage. That cure is holy, deliberate, and willful caring, even for those who do us harm.

If Jesus is to be believed, and maybe it is just too much for us to believe, yet if Jesus is to be believed, unencumbered compassion, that is, love that has no conditions, is the only way out of this death spiral of human hatred. Hatred cannot drive out hatred. Only reaching out to the hated can do that. Violence will not end violence. Only love that has no boundaries or conditions will do that. It is a hard word to hear because compassion has not been our way.

It sounds so foolish, so naïve, so unrealistic as to be

absurd. But let us hear this word in all of its foolishness–for two reasons. The first reason is that our way is not working. In our irrational rage, we can kill until our planet grows deathly silent. Our capacity to destroy, even to annihilate, has reached epic proportions. Let the gospel teach us that fighting will never end wars, capital punishment will never abolish crime, hitting back will never make us even. Killing one another simply is not working. And the second reason we should hear this foolish word is this: It is the word of the Lord.

A final word: Jesus met violence with forgiveness. The Amish have it right: simple, unvarnished forgiveness--not forgiveness if you will repent, not forgiveness if you beg and humble yourself.

You and I, of course, have come to design our own brand of forgiveness. Our brand of forgiveness often sets out to cripple the one asking to be forgiven, to make that person walk with his head pitched low, "I'll forgive you this time, if you promise never to do it again."

Forgiveness? In all candor, we prefer to get even. Forgiveness, in the hard language of Jesus, means to embrace the hurt, and harder still, to embrace the one who brought the hurt. Forgiveness is about lifting up our enemies, for while they may be our enemies, they are not the enemies of God. The light of Jesus will enable us to see in the faces of our enemies, the very face of God. We may have to look hard, but God is there. If Jesus is our clue, it may be that violence can only be overcome if we meet it with forgiveness. It makes good political theater to track the enemy to the gates of hell, and in this immoral world, it may be the only way to be elected to political office. But it is not the gospel. God loves every Muslim and every Jew as much as God loves every Christian.

But lest we think that our meanness and incivility have created a mountain of regret too high for us to climb, I have a word of hope. I believe there is hope in the dark shadows of our anguish. That hope is that we, like Cain, also bear the mark, the imprint, of God. And, that mark means that God is still with us

60

and God will not leave our side. God will not leave the side of the neglected or those who neglect. God will not leave the side of the injured or those who injure. God will not leave the side of the victor or the victim, the violent or the violated.

God's revolutionary word in Jesus is to bring us to see one another, even our enemies, in a new and radically different way. God is calling us to pick up the pieces, to heal the wounds, to meet violence with forgiveness. Let us be clear: We will not win the war against terrorism with guns alone. Religious bigotry, which is simply another form of violence, will not be overcome by passing out tracts on how to be saved. Evangelism is a good thing. But bearing witness in a way that condemns and judges, that disrespects and treats people of other faiths with a condescending arrogance is a sinister force, seeking to manipulate and control. Whether in Muslim clothing or Christian clothing, bigotry is fueling the flames of hatred and meanness. And religious hatred is still hatred; holy meanness is still meanness.

I speak with a halting voice this morning, afraid of my own words, afraid of our own humanity, daunted by our own inhumanity. It seems more natural, more rational, even safer, to live like our brother, Cain – profane and vengeful, putting down those who threaten us. But I do know that both violence and our violent response to it are shrinking us, that our humanity is being diminished by our inhumanity. We can be certain that the moral high ground will never be claimed solely by military victories. No doubt, we will continue to wage wars, the conflicts in the Middle East are likely to go on for decades, but let us never begin to believe that wars will ultimately bring peace or disarm hatred.

I urge then that we try listening to the gospel. The word of the gospel is to let go of retribution and revenge as the foundation of our hope. It is a radically revolutionary word. The word of Jesus is that we are to love our enemies and forgive those who hurt us. Let us not dismiss loving our enemies as simply pious language. Loving our enemies is not a metaphor. It means to respect them. It means to hear their cry. It means to be kind to people you don't like.

Believe me, this word is easier to preach than it is to practice. But nevertheless, it was precisely this kind of radical revolution that Jesus set in motion. We will not know God's kind of world or experience what John called "eternal life" until that radical revolution begins to take hold in our own lives.

Pick up the pieces. Heal the wounds. Build back from the ashes. If we can find the courage to begin to live in the transforming light of unbridled compassion, and to begin to embrace the power of forgiveness--to paraphrase a great Baptist preacher named Martin Luther King--

We will be free at last, free at last.
Thank God Almighty
We will be free at last.
Amen.

--R. Kirby Godsey, Chancellor, Mercer University

Conversation on Race

Morgan Freeman

Hot, dusty Mississippi afternoon,
Neighbor kids laughing and lounging on the steps
As a black man approaches in a
Shiny blue suit, brown scuffed shoes,
On the way to Whittington's plantation.

"Hey, teacher," one of them shouts:
"What's two times two?"

I look away.

The black school principal, head down,
Pretends not to hear.
He hurries down the road to visit some children
Who have no school bus. He has no car.

Hot, dusty Mississippi afternoon,
Shouting kids jump into the swimming pool,
While rows of small black fingers twine through the fences,
Faces seemingly not envious, just watching.

I look away.

How did a famous black movie star come from such a place?

Look away, Dixie Land.

--Rosemary McKelvey

*Sophisticated Brotha:
Answer to Dr. Maya Angelou's
"Phenomenal Woman"

I am tall, short, light, dark, small, big and handsome,
My style and appearance were not chosen, but given at random.
I've been called the greatest creature to ever walk the Earth,
That title was not self-given, but all started at my birth.
For many years now, I've been belittled one way or another,
No matter what they say to me, I'm still a sophisticated brotha.
I've been oppressed, beaten, bruised and scarred,
I've been treated like an animal and placed behind bars.
I've been hurt for so long, because of my skin color,
No matter what they do to me, I'm still a sophisticated brotha.
I may not have a big ole' fancy college degree,
But I will walk with my head held high, because I'm me.
They pass me by as if my face were covered--
No matter how they act towards me,
I'm still a sophisticated brotha.
I think before I speak, and my actions show you so;
I reason within myself about things I already know.
My style and class together resemble that of two true lovers:
Some call me "Rico Suave,"
The epitome of sophisticated brothas.
Brown is my skin tone; deep and smooth is my voice.
"What kind of man is this," they say, "that even angels rejoice?"
My strength is unlimited--like the love of a mother.
"My talents, unspeakable," so say I, the sophisticated brotha.
I may be complex, obscure and subtle to some,
But make no mistake about my genuine charm.
Roaming the Earth like me there is no other,
Because I'm the one, the only – sophisticated brotha.

* Sophisticated – very intellectually appealing; subtle: finely tuned, experienced and aware.

--Johnny Solomon, III
Recipient, Young Georgia Author of the Year (2003)

66

Reflection on King's
"Letter from Birmingham Jail"

In history there is often a coming-together of circumstances and time that calls for the right person to bank in on the moment. The time has to be right for people to want to listen to that person, who will lead the way to a better future or a new solution. Martin Luther King, Jr. was such a person. Time had run out on the segregation era. Time had run out on the status quo of the Negro. In his letter from the Birmingham City Jail, a letter written in response to a letter to him from seven ministers and a rabbi that had appeared in the newspaper rather than in his mailbox, Martin Luther King pointed out to a set of white ministers that the time had come to actively call for change.

Martin Luther King, Jr. proved to be a formidable verbal strategist in this letter. He introduced his own importance and his equality to those he addressed, regularly calling them "friends." He used the Bible as common ground to explain their concerns, addressing each item point by point and concluding that there was only one option left: direct, nonviolent action.

King maintained that there is never a good time for justice--that "freedom is never voluntarily given by the oppressor." He registered his frustration with the timetable of the white moderate who "paternalistically believes he can set a timetable for another man's freedom." He identified the misconception of white moderates about time, observing that time will NOT take care of the problem: "Time itself is neutral; it can be used either destructively or constructively." He so rightfully insisted that NOW is always the time to do what is right.

Martin Luther King, Jr. asserted that it was time for the white church to stop making excuses, such as "Those are social issues, with which the gospel has no real concern." He reflected on a time when the early Christians took pride in being the "disturbers of the peace" and he prayed this same spirit would overtake the white Christian Church, lest they become "an irrelevant social club."

King calmly regarded the events of his day as inevitable—
a time when it all came to an end and a new beginning had to
be made: a time to "do or die." He spoke eloquently of a time to
come, hopefully soon, "that the dark clouds of racial prejudice
will pass away." A man of God, King knew that there is a time
for everything under the sun. He was the right man at the right
time to lead this nation forward toward greater citizenship.

--Yvonne Gabriel

The First Day of School

The long hot days of summer were finally over and all
the chigger bites and scratches from blackberry bushes and
briars had cleared up as Katherine jumped the high, salty waves
that crashed against the jetties. This year she would get to tag
along with her four older sisters to the big yellow school bus
that would carry them to school, where she would get to start
the first grade. She wasn't particularly looking forward to sitting
still even though her sisters had thoroughly practiced her, forcing her to await their permission before getting off the wooden
bench their daddy had built as seating for the long kitchen table
where they all ate. Katherine was worried about talking out of
turn even though she had been admonished over and over again
always to raise her hand. The justification for this rule was
beyond her understanding--her daddy's friends had paid her to
talk for them. Why, she had overhead Johnny Solomon tell her
mama it was worth a hundred dollars just to listen to her. The
one consolation she had was that she and Sonny Boy would be
starting school together—and she couldn't wait to learn all those
new things so she could be smart like her sisters.

Katherine's sisters had played school with her ever since
she could remember, using the Bible and the funny papers as
their books, Elsie the Cow cream can labels for their paper, and
whatever was on hand to illustrate the principles of addition,

subtraction, multiplication, and division: fiddler crabs, blackberries, Cheerios, pine needles, and even the lead weights for hanging in shrimp nets.

Joan and Doris had been in charge, sternly admonishing Katherine to sit in her chair, raise her hand, and ask for permission before saying anything. They were particularly strict about the proper form of any request: "Can I?" accomplished nothing; "May I?" ruled the day. Once when they couldn't find any pencils, Joan pondered for a few minutes what to do and then triumphantly led them all out the back door into the yard, selected an appropriate stick, and proceeded to set up math problems, lecturing them all the while on how Jesus himself had written in the sand. Convinced they were all following the example of Jesus, they wrote on their tablets of sand: "He who is without sin should cast the first stone" and "Love thy neighbor as thyself."

Katherine thoughtfully considered her neighbors and how she was going to accomplish loving them as she got dressed for school that first day. Wilhelmina was always so mean--Katherine didn't think she could stretch her love that far. After wolfing down her grits and eggs, she informed her mama she was heading off down the dirt road to meet Sonny Boy.

Sonny Boy, Wilhelmina's grandson, was Katherine's best friend. Together they had made great plans about what they would do on the way to school and back, and maybe even at recess, if they were lucky enough to get the same teacher. They had stomped through the woods together, picked blackberries, and even caught stray pigs in bushel baskets. A faithful friend, Sonny Boy was game to do whatever Katherine dreamed up— he had even let her cut his hair with Mama's scissors one time. Starting school for the first time, a girl needed to have a friend like Sonny Boy to count on.

Katherine was taken aback when her mama informed her that she and Sonny Boy would not be going to school together. She stamped her foot hard, demanding to know why. It didn't matter that it was the first day of school. Her mama reached over and got her switch. Afterwards Katherine went on to school, the evidence of "spare-the-rod" discipline streaking up and down her skinny white legs.

School was not the fantastic adventure Katherine had imagined. Assigned to Miss Lowe's class, she didn't last long before Miss Lowe shifted her over to Mrs. Wiltshire. Not quite five feet tall, Miss Lowe had a round, wrinkly and white-powdered face framed by thin, dark hair twisted around her head. Hard of hearing, she had heard only the "sht" of Katherine's one allowed interjection, "shoot." Thinking Katherine had used the "s" word, Miss Lowe became livid and threatened to wash Katherine's mouth out with soap. Her earnest attempts at clarification yielded only further remonstrations. Katherine was not having a good first day of school—first the switching and now the threat of having her mouth washed out with soap—for no reason. She couldn't seem to win. She reasoned that things really couldn't get any worse, but the transfer to Mrs. Wiltshire's class didn't signal a turnaround.

Tired, old, and orange, Mrs. Wiltshire had a big, thick neck and a prominent nose that punctuated her face like a giant question mark. Her orangey hair was curled in stiff ringlets and she was big enough to play tackle football—kind of like an elephant with the coloring of a lion. The classroom was already filled when Katherine arrived. Mrs. Wiltshire wanted Katherine in a different spot, grabbed her by the arm, and sailed her over two sets of chairs to the desired location. The second day of school Katherine came down with a bad stomachache, which disappeared as soon as the school bus passed. By the time Mrs. Wiltshire broke her leg, Katherine had already logged 60 absences in the first grade.

--Margaret Eskew

Interview with Joan Godsey

Barack Obama, the first African American President of the United States, was elected on November 4, 2008. I spoke with Joan Godsey right after the election. She is a remarkable figure in Macon who did her share in the sixties to help make such a day possible. She got emotional: "I just can't believe that I would see this in my lifetime. Barack Obama as President is a wonderful thing for the country and for the African American community."

Days before the election I met with Joan in her warm and welcoming home to discuss her role in the integration of education in the sixties in Alabama. Joan is the immediate past First Lady of Mercer University, where her husband, Dr. R. Kirby Godsey, served as President for twenty-seven years. Joan greeted me with her signature hug--warm and genuine. Her green eyes sparkled with enthusiasm. Auburn hair swept up in a French twist added to her already regal appearance.

Would you tell me about your circumstances during the Great Depression?

We did not suffer much, but we had lots of beggars coming to the door. My parents were caring people and gave them food and money. My father was in the grocery business. Both of my parents were extremely conservative with money. If you could not pay for something within that same month, you did not buy it. I think I inherited that from them; I can't stand to see anything go to waste.

When you were a child, how did you perceive the black people in your surroundings?

Well, my mother always had help that was black and she made it clear that they had their own place and they needed to stay there. On Saturdays, we used to go to town in the car, and I would watch the black people in their ill-fitting clothes and poor circumstances. Our church did not question the inequality. I went with my parents to church every Sunday and I learned about Jesus and his message to make things right. My mother was kind. The blacks in Hattiesburg lived between two rivers and the rivers would flood. My mother would go out there and help them with clothes and food.

I did not go to school with black people; we lived under the "separate but equal" law, which was not equal at all.

Who taught the black children?

Black teachers taught them in separate schools. These schools were set up by churchwomen from the North under an initiative of Eleanor Roosevelt. This was not very well liked by a lot of Southerners who believed the blacks should not be educated--that they should stay in their place.

Joan graduated from the New Orleans Baptist Theological Seminary with a master's in church music and a master's in religious education. She was invited to join the faculty. Kirby Godsey was a student of ethics at New Orleans Seminary when they met.

Who are three people who have influenced your life?

My mother: she was strong and nurturing. My father: he never knew a stranger; he talked to everyone. My husband: he liberated me.

Can you elaborate on how he did that?

I never questioned anything. I never questioned my faith; I always wanted to please everyone. I shared my parents' political views and I never disobeyed them. Kirby changed all that. He had a different background. He had a vision of many things, and his study in ethics supported that. That year he was probably the only person on the whole campus of New Orleans Seminary who voted for Kennedy. The rest of us wouldn't have dreamed of voting for a Catholic. It wasn't just the blacks--we rejected anything that was different.

I had two opposing voices in my life: my strong mother with her conservative, traditional views and Kirby, whose new ideas agreed more with my faith.

After Joan and Kirby were married in 1959, they accepted teaching positions at the Judson College for Women in Marion, Alabama.

How did racial tensions manifest themselves in this town after the Brown versus the Board of Education law was passed?

In 1966 a Head Start program was started in Alabama. The program was designed to prepare disadvantaged children better before they went to elementary school. This was a nationwide initiative. To get started, three white people had to be involved. I agreed to do the music, while Lynn Huckabee did nutrition, and a white Judson student got involved. It was a summer program.

Did you anticipate that you had stepped into an ant bed?

No, not until Kirby was called into the office of the Vice President of our college, who also happened to be the mayor of Marion. He carried a lot of weight. He called Kirby in and told him to "do something about his wife." He was very much against the Head Start program and expected Kirby to tell me not to get involved in it.

What was Dr. Godsey's answer?

He said: "First of all I could not tell her what to do if I wanted to and, secondly, I don't want to."

It felt like the whole world had gone mad. John F. Kennedy, who was sympathetic towards the plight of the black people, was assassinated. In the public high school in Marion, Alabama, some white teachers even stood up and cheered! It was just heartbreaking.

Then in 1965, there were the marches from Selma to Montgomery as part of the movement for voting rights. White people and black people and many people from the North came to support. But they were met across the Edmund Bridge by police on horses with billy clubs who forced the demonstrators to go home. Several people were killed. Martin Luther King led one of the marches. This was only thirty miles from our house. I really wanted to be part of it, but I had two small children. We were glued to the TV.

The march really inflamed my desire to be part of the Head Start program. I felt so committed to it that I was not going to let people around me scare me out of it. I went to work on my bicycle so they would not damage my car. My biggest fear was that something would happen to my children. Oh, yes! In those days terrible things happened to people who supported the rights of black people. A few college students worked with us in the Head Start program; someone put a burning cross in their yard: the symbol of the KKK.

Tell me about the Head Start program.

There were about a 100 kids in the Head Start program. We met in a black church where Martin Luther King had spoken. The program was comparable to a kindergarten. My mother still did not understand why I would work there and expose myself to danger. I told her that I felt the black people were equal to us, and they needed help. She was concerned about my safety more than anything else.

Was she aware that the actual danger came from the white people?

Yes, and my parents certainly did not approve of that. They were very kind, and the black people who worked for them loved them. Sometimes the people from the North did not understand that many black people were not being mistreated. Some white people just did not want the black people to rise up in society and become "uppity"--a term reserved for black people pushing for change.

I had hired a black lady who helped me with my children. There were restaurant sit-ins at that time. Black people went and sat in places in restaurants and buses normally reserved for whites. My housekeeper was doing just that in a restaurant where I went for dinner one night with my family. She was concerned that I would be upset with her, but I was so proud of her!

Were there any repercussions for working with the Head Start program?

Yes, our neighbor shot our dog--we believe he did it because he was a racist. While I was giving a devotional in my

74

Sunday School class, a man in the class stood up and tried to convince the rest of the class to get up and leave, because "she is nothing but a nigger lover."

I was very active in that church. I played the organ and was involved in many areas. It was painful. I dropped out of church for a whole year. The pastor never came to see me; nobody said anything about missing me. Nobody called. Nobody asked me anything about the incident. There was no support whatsoever. Even in the college, there was no support. The sole supporters I had were Kirby and the Huckabees, who had started the program with me; they left at the end of that summer. That whole year, people would not speak to me. Even the florist who delivered flowers held them out to me and simply could not look at me. He was very much a segregationist.

So there was nobody in that whole town who wanted to change things?

Nobody. I cried every night. I will give you an example. Before all this happened, Kirby and I had both been in the hospital, and people had stood in line to come see us. Everybody was so kind and considerate. Then after Head Start, I was in the hospital again for something, and nobody came to see me. Nobody. And the nurses treated me very coldly. It was so, so different. Even the man who pumped the gas for my car, who had always been so friendly, now did not care to speak to me. The town had only 3800 people in it and everyone knew everything. I did not even want to go to the beauty shop. I started to avoid people. I became very sensitive. I felt that every reaction from people was connected to how they felt about my work with Head Start. It was a miserable year--I cried a lot.

We moved after that year. Kirby and I went to Tulane for him to get his Ph. D. So that next summer we left. I was very relieved--glad to get out of that town. My children grew up in integrated schools. Hunter told me he had three girlfriends: one white and two black. My son Raleigh's best friend was black. It seemed that integration was working. We felt that if they would all grow up together, racism would disappear. Unfortunately, it

75

is not that simple.

Joan worries about President Obama's safety: "You have no idea how strong racial hatred is." Yet she is full of joy that America has made such great strides. She is one of the brave, courageous people who helped make that happen. There is a price to be paid for standing up and speaking out against injustice. Joan certainly paid that price in effectively being ex-communicated by the people she considered her friends and fellow Christians. Joan chose to side with those who needed her help.

--Yvonne Gabriel

The Other Dollie

Mr. Lang lived across the marsh from Wendy's house, a little beyond Aint Marthey's on the way to New Berlin. If you didn't mind the fiddler crabs or happening upon a snake, you could take a short cut across the marsh and be there in ten minutes. It was the place where the rope had come down out of the sky and picked up some houses and whirled them around like doll houses and set them down again in a different place all broken up. A wiry little old man, Mr. Lang reminded Wendy of a caterpillar turning into a moth, changing colors and textures right before her eyes. White skin was erasing the dark brown from his face, neck, and arms in big splotches. Looking down at the freckles that had appeared on her arms over the summer, Wendy wondered how long it would take her to go completely brown. She wondered if she would turn pink again when she got old like Mr. Lang.

Late one night Wendy, awakened by hushed voices, heard her daddy say: "Dollie, if that mother dies, I'm gonna bring that baby home for you to take care of. There ain't nobody else. We can't just let that baby die."

Wendy's mother already had eight children to care for. The newborn baby belonged to another Dollie, who lived across

76

the road from Mr. Lang. Lying there in the pitch darkness in between two sisters, Wendy could sense her mother's apprehensions. As she carefully inched upward to escape the warm breath on the back of her neck, she pondered who this other Dollie could be. This other Dollie had never been to their house. Wendy hadn't ever heard of her before. What did she look like? Why were Mama and Daddy so secretive? A shiver of fearful anticipation rippled the tiny, almost invisible blonde hairs on her thin arms. She instinctively snuggled closer to her sisters.

For a while, Wendy watched vigilantly for someone to deliver a baby to her house. After a while, she surmised that she had simply dreamed the whole surreptitious late night exchange until she chanced to see the other Dollie for herself. As she and her sister Reba rounded the bend in the road across from the "Jook Joint" one evening on their way to spend the night with a friend, Reba pointed to a young black woman and furtively whispered the name "Dollie." Seeing headlights from an oncoming car, the two sisters sprang like jack rabbits into the tall weeds and lay as flat and still as they could until the car passed, fear of it surpassing the healthy respect they ordinarily accorded the snakes and other varmints native to the north Florida marsh. In awe, they watched as Dollie, lithe and beautiful, moved her sun-tanned body sensuously to the syncopated beat blaring from the jukebox, her perfect skin the color of café au lait. Wendy knew without ever being told that Dollie's mesmerizing dance was not meant for her greedy eyes. Excitement pulsated in jazz rhythms in every limb of Wendy's body, alternately whispering and shouting for some physical manifestation.

In the clandestine darkness of the tall grass, Wendy whispered to Reba the big secret about the baby Daddy was going to bring home for Mama to care for. Two years older and much wiser, Reba didn't give any credence to her sister's disturbing revelation, warning her that there were strict rules about "niggers" and white people living together. Jumping up from their hiding place in the bushes, the two sisters, now covered with beggar lice, began to run toward their destination, the falling darkness momentarily threatening to envelop them.

Confusion clouded Wendy's head, erupting breathlessly as they slowed their pace. "Reba, are we whites or are we 'niggers'?" implored Wendy, her blonde hair now matted with sweat as she turned her green eyes upward toward the deep brown of Reba's irises, separated from the night only by the white rings about them. The light from a post projected weird patterns on Reba's unfreckled olive brown skin, creating patterns of white and dark brown, eerily reminiscent of Mr. Lang.

--Margaret Eskew

Bateman & Wade

You have to understand the circumstances to know why I loved that little neighborhood grocery store, Bateman and Wade, and why I started to shop there. After all, it was more expensive than the big chain stores. I was a young dentist's wife trying to manage my "house money" frugally while my husband struggled to establish his fledgling practice.

Shortly after moving to Macon, I presented my check for a week's groceries at the old Colonial store in Ingleside Village shopping center. The clerk refused to take my check! They did not know me, he explained. I promptly left the store and drove around the corner to the small Bateman and Wade store. There I shopped for the next twenty years. I had heard friends talking about the wonderful meats and produce Mr. Bateman and Mr. Wade procured for their store, but I had been reluctant to go there because of my limited budget. They, of course, took my check without question and won my heart.

This unique little store hovered on the edge of the black neighborhood with Pleasant Hill on one side and the white affluent Vineville neighborhood on the other side. Pig's feet nestled next to prime rib roasts in the meat counter. Collard greens vied for space with artichokes and asparagus in Mr. Lewis's produce section. The minute I walked into the store, I felt as if I were back home in Greenwood, Mississippi. Mr. Wade greeted me with a smile and a "How are you, young lady?" If I had my babies with me, everyone stopped to admire them. The attention was a magic elixir to a homesick young mother far from home.

While shopping, I observed the well-dressed matrons of Macon sipping their cokes at the front of the store while their cooks strolled the five short aisles and stood in line to order the week's best meat and chickens from Mr. Bateman. Some of the older ladies dropped by every morning for a coke and purchased some small item to justify the trip. Lonely for my mother, I hung on their words as they chatted with each other.

Many of the "Bateman and Wade ladies" had never cooked, always having a cook in the house six or seven days a week. One day an elderly matron, a retired dentist's wife, confided to me in the checkout line that she and her husband had lived in a boarding house when they returned from their honeymoon. This was necessary, she explained, until Dr. Farmer could buy her a cook.

Mr. Lewis, the produce manager, constantly catered to his well-to-do customers, spoiling them as a parent spoils a child. I observed more than once the behavior of his "spoiled progeny" when his produce did not please them. When the sweet onions from Vidalia became famous, they were in short supply in town. Mr. Lewis knew to save the ones he received for his ladies. They were told to "drive round back" to get a bag. No other customers ever saw those onions!

One day I found myself alone at the meat counter exchanging pleasantries with Mr. Bateman. It was that day he related the tale of the Thanksgiving "rebellion." It was the custom to place turkey orders with Mr. Bateman well in advance of the holiday. But this particular year, the ladies began calling to cancel their turkey orders. After lunch that day Mr. Bateman had a few quiet moments to count the cancelled turkey orders. There had been so many calls that he was sure something was going on with his best customers. A few phone conversations later, he learned what had happened.

While the ladies were chatting by the coke machine, their cooks had been whispering to each other in the aisles, plotting a quiet rebellion. On the appointed day, each of the women informed her employer that she would not be available to cook and serve Thanksgiving dinner. They would be in their own homes celebrating Thanksgiving with their families. That year the local country club had the largest reservation list ever for the Thanksgiving buffet.

Ah, I loved those stories as I shopped, forgetting for an hour or so how far away I was from home and from those who loved me and knew who I was. In those young days, I warmed myself in the glow of that little store's intimate surroundings. The store was my good friend in a new town far from home.

--Rosemary McKelvey

The Alex Reid, Jr. Store in South Macon & "The Phenomenal Woman"

My grandmother, Miss Bay, ran the local general store in South Macon, nestled within the heart of a black community. The store was not bigger than five hundred square feet, but the contents could rival any Super Wal-Mart aisle. There were not aisles upon aisles of produce, only an open space in the center with shelves lining the walls. The store was constructed completely of wood, including the floors. Although the floors sank in where the wood was worn thin from foot traffic and occasionally bounced customers gently up and down like a small trampoline, the building was basically sound. At the all-but-grassless entrance to the store, customers inevitably tracked in the dirt, their shuffling creating its own characteristic sounds and a constant source of work for the resident sweeper, the dutiful grandson and heir apparent. The store was adorned with a great white sign, which hung from the center of the apex of the structure, proudly proclaiming the "Alex Reid Jr. Store," deferentially named for Miss Bay's only son.

The shelves were full of all the essentials necessary for maintaining a store in a black neighborhood: crackers, sardines, and loaves of Colonial bread, delivered weekly by the bread company. Ample supplies of vanilla cookies, cans of Spam, and ginger snaps were regularly stocked. The pickled pig's feet and ears occupied a prime location next to the old-fashioned cash register, strictly used for storing money--it didn't perform the functions of a modern day cash register, adding and subtracting, and displaying the sum of money owed. The human brain did all the calculation--and Miss Bay was a whiz. To the right of the cash register, the Coca-Cola machine faithfully dispensed bottles of Coke or Seven-up upon the deposit of 25 cents, the thirsty customer being required to lift the lid and slide the cold bottle along a track until the machine released it at a pre-ordained point.

Mornings between the hours of eight and noon, the store radio blasted out the gospel music of Mahalia Jackson, the Five Blind Boys of Alabama, Shirley Caesar, or any other gospel great. Afterwards Miss Bay silenced the radio for the rest of the day, disdaining the contemporary fare offered in the afternoon. The volume of the radio gave testimony to Miss Bay's deep devotion to gospel music—she always felt compelled to sing along with whoever was singing at a particular time. She knew the words to every gospel song by heart and sang along effortlessly, her voice traveling beyond the walls of the store out into the main street. Often her voice was perfectly in tune with whoever was performing on the radio program, but there were memorable times when she led the neighborhood dogs in a chorus of howls.

Miss Bay did not permit interruptions during the broadcast of Reverend Ike. She clung to his every word echoing through those radio speakers. Her grandson, wise beyond his years, developed a personal dislike for Reverend Ike, who always seemed to be asking for money. He wanted desperately to voice aloud his humble opinion of the Reverend but intuitively understood that his feet would feel Hell's flames if he deigned in any way to impugn the minister. With difficulty, the clever grandson remained silent—and safe. His hunches were confirmed later in life when he discovered that the good Reverend had indeed become wealthy through the contributions of hardworking people, including the feisty Miss Bay.

This grandson was always an employee of the store due to proximity alone. Often the elderly would come into the store and purchase groceries that were too heavy to carry home. The "chosen" grandson would then carry groceries all over the neighborhood for whoever could afford a dime. Distance was not a factor, although there were certain customers who paid more than others. Mrs. Jefferson always paid a quarter, or higher, which would trigger a spending spree: four vanilla cookies and a drink could be purchased for making the Mrs. Jefferson run. As the grandson grew older, Mrs. Jefferson's pay level increased. She paid top dollar for the upkeep of her yard: five dollars versus only three dollars for Miss Lily Mae's yard. Miss Lily Mae just happened to be Miss Bay's neighbor. Her yard was much smaller than most in the neighborhood, so she enjoyed a price break. It consisted mostly of dirt, partially ground tree stumps, and rocks, increasing the cost of maintenance, but the grandson felt compelled to cut her yard as a necessary means of maintaining the peace between her and Miss Bay.

With a generosity seldom matched, Miss Bay would lower the price on goods, so that everyone could afford her prices. Sometimes she would even give away groceries, knowing full well that she wasn't going to receive any payment for them.

Any Alex Reid Store employee learned several invaluable and practical lessons about commerce. None, however, was more important than the lessons Miss Bay taught indirectly: She love and kindness--to treat others as you wanted to be treated. She summed it all up with two simple words: "Be lovely." Unbelievably, this was the advice from a woman who carried a gun. She modeled the value of giving to the less fortunate. She implicitly trusted in God to sustain her in every situation.

The once dubious grandson now testifies:

I didn't fully understand as a young boy how she could listen to hours of gospel, but now that I have become a man, the same gospel songs can be heard blaring through my car speakers as I travel to and fro. Life has come full circle for me. I find myself firmly embracing the values and traditions that my grandmother, Miss Bay, the matriarch, manager, and might of the Alex Reid, Jr. Grocery Store, taught me over four decades ago. Maya Angelou must have used her as the model for her poem, "Phenomenal Woman."

--Kevin Reid

Miss Bay

Dark and weathered from years of working in the Georgia sun, my grandmother was small in stature, standing about five foot one and maybe weighing 135 pounds. Belying her small frame, her powerful voice thundered authoritatively throughout the neighborhood. She was a force to be reckoned with. Teddy Roosevelt might have spoken softly and carried a big stick, but Grandma, known all over as "Miss Bay," bellowed as she wielded her stick. Adjacent to their house, Grandpa built her a grocery store, from which she would reign supreme.

Before there was Oprah, there was my grandmother. She used the store as a hub for dispensing advice to the locals and she wasn't shy about giving it. If you were in need of marriage counseling, or if you had money problems, Grandma's store was the stop for vanilla wafers, a cold pop, and advice. I remember Grandma dispensing her wisdom to a young lady who had come into the store: "Marriage ain't easy. You just have to work at it and pray a lot." Years later I found her advice to be true, but she hadn't warned me that I would have to work my butt off.

Quite the businesswoman, Miss Bay served the neighborhood well long before the days of Wal-Mart. Constructed of pine planks, the store emitted a very pungent fragrance after a good rain. The only time the pine scent was overruled was when someone opened a can of sardines. Depending on the traffic, the wooden floors required sweeping several times a day--and that chore often fell to me. The store was very much like a scene from the television show, "The Waltons." Unlike Ike Gotsee from "The Waltons," my grandmother was available day or night by simply calling out: "Miss Bay?" However, everyone in her neighborhood knew that she wasn't available before 8 a.m. and certainly not after 8 p.m. Though never posted, those were the unspoken rules of her store.

I learned many valuable lessons from Miss Bay as I watched her conduct business. For example, she only issued credit to those she knew could repay her within a reasonable time. However, she frequently extended charity to others who could not afford to pay--mainly me.

I also learned lessons of survival. In Miss Bay's neighborhood lived a local bully named Sammy Thomas. When Sammy was eleven, he and I had a physical altercation on the way home from school one gloomy afternoon. I ran to my grandmother's house, almost tearing the door from the hinges, and interrupted her while she was cleaning collard greens for the evening meal. She just looked at me and demanded: "What's the matter with you, boy?" I returned her gaze, replying, "Sammy." She snorted, "Sammy what?" I answered in a wimpy voice that Sammy and I had just had a fight. Grandma just laughed and teased: "Boy, is that why you are crying?" Sensing that she was about to issue me some advice, I drew closer to her. She laid out an ingenious plan that would not fail to restore my street credit.

"Boy, you can't fight Sammy fairly because he is bigger than a grown man." I edged even closer and listened more intently as she unhatched the details. "Kevin, I want you to hide the biggest stick you can find along the path on the way back from school. When you reach that point, pull out the stick and wear Sammy's ass out. Don't let go of it, no matter what."

Why hadn't I thought of that? "A good old fashioned ambush–that's what Sammy needs." I had learned how to set up great ambushes from watching Bonanza, but I got the distinct impression that Miss Bay's ambush had a greater chance of success. Was it possible that she had personal experience with this particular kind of ambush? Maybe this was how she had captured Granddaddy.

I did exactly as my grandmother had instructed. I gave Sammy Thomas such a beating that I am sure he awakens in a cold sweat even today. When I carried the stick into her kitchen to boast of my success, she admonished me sternly: "Boy, get that stick out of my house." My street credit restored, the next day I received the nickname, "the Bull." Yeah! I liked that. It sang. "Mean Guy," my cousin, would now think twice before challenging "The Bull"!

I was thirteen before I ever heard my grandmother's given name, Lucille. I've often wondered how Grandma became "Miss Bay."

--Kevin Reid

Miss Bay Goes to Vegas

I pulled into the dirt driveway of my grandma's house and parked my '73 LTD as close as I could to the side entrance. I waited in the car for a couple of minutes hoping that she would come to the door and voluntarily let me in. After a few minutes of mental preparation, I let myself into the house. Upon entering, I called out to my grandmother–it was necessary to identify myself as friendly or risk being filled with lead. My grandma was a Glover–and they were notorious for shooting, and not being shot. As long as I can remember, I have always carried a gun of some sort—beginning with cap pistols as a young child. Later– around the age of eight, I graduated from cap guns to a more lethal form of weapon.

As I made my way to the kitchen, I breathed in the aroma of bacon cooking. The warning sounds of Reverend Ike addressed to sinful souls blasted from the radio. Grandma was still packing her leather suitcase. It looked like something Moses had carried up to Mount Sinai. I sat patiently and waited until

Reverend Ike had gone from preaching the gospel to soliciting for money. Grandma had finished packing and moved on into the kitchen where she was putting biscuits and bacon into aluminum foil for her journey. Always courteous, Miss Bay turned to me and inquired: "Boy, have you ate yet?" Not hungry, I declined her offer of food. "I'm ready," she announced imperiously. I grabbed the old leather suitcase–it felt like it had a dead body in it, rather than a week's worth of clothes–and summoned all of my strength to pick up the bag. I wondered how Miss Bay would be able to maneuver the suitcase herself–and instantly remembered that she was indeed an incredibly resourceful woman.

On the way to the Greyhound station, Miss Bay didn't hold anything back in her running commentary on my driving habits: "Slow down! You are going too fast. Put both your hands on the wheel! Stay off that shoulder!" Here was a woman who had never learned how to drive giving me instructions. Luckily for me, Miss Bay couldn't read my mind–I valued my life too much to voice my opinions aloud. We finally arrived at the bus stop where my aunt Catherine--Aunt Cat--stood waiting in the lobby. Both women were dressed in their Sunday go-to-meeting outfits: floral dresses with hats and gloves. Of course Cousin Lizzy was notoriously late. However, it wasn't long before she arrived in the mandatory floral attire. The Golden Girls trio was now intact. The three women immediately huddled in a corner of the lobby, going through their purses. Curious about the huddle, I gingerly approached the group, finding a weapons' check in full swing. Every one of these sweet little old ladies was packing heat on the Greyhound. In vain, I voiced my concern about the trio breaking the law. The three boarded the bus and sat directly behind the driver. Unbeknownst to him, the bus driver was in for the trip of his life.

A week later my worst fears were confirmed as I waited patiently at the bus terminal for Grandma's return. I soon heard the bus racing through the terminal and come to an abrupt stop. The doors of the bus flew open and the bus driver shot off the bus, as if his pants were on fire. Predictably, Grandma and her gang were sitting directly behind the driver's seat. I arose from the comfort of my secure seat and assisted Grandma with her bags. As we loaded the bags, Miss Bay erupted spontaneously in a stream of molten commentary: "The driver was always speeding. He drove with bugs all over the windshield. I am amazed that he made it here alive. Praise the Lord, we didn't have an accident." I bet that driver was himself erupting in spontaneous prayer: "Praise the Lord that I am now free from these gun-toting old ladies." I am sure they had threatened him with bodily harm. That was their MO.

The ride home was a repeat performance: "Slow down. You are going to kill us both." Death would be a welcome relief from this. Grandma proceeded to tell me about the trio's Vegas experience. An unlucky guy had made an attempt to mug them, while the trio was walking back from a casino. He had definitely chosen the wrong group to prey upon. Cousin Lizzy pulled out her .32 revolver, while the other two scrambled for their weapons. Amazed and bewildered, the mugger managed to escape with his life—but only after they had tortured him verbally. What the poor bus driver had had to endure, the mugger had received, raised to the tenth power. Oh, yeah. There were varying degrees of the verbal abuse they had refined to an art.

As we finally reached Grandma's house a little before sunset, a welcoming committee of the neighborhood faithful had already gathered in front in anticipation of hearing firsthand the adventures of Miss Bay in Las Vegas.

--Kevin Reid

Race

Such a small word with a big impact:
It separates the Whites from the Blacks
And the Asians and the Hispanics.
It seems to me
That we ought not to worry so much about
What we look like or from whence we came.
Does it really matter?
In the big picture of life or the long run,
If we want to win it, we have to forget
What it is
But agree that we are all in it;
And if we all want to finish, let's join hands,
Forgive and learn to love each other,
Put on our armor and shoes,
Run together,
And finish
This thing called race.

--Elnora Fluellen

This Is My Story

Are We There Yet?

Oh, no! I am looking at the calendar with only a week left of school before summer vacation. Lovely, I think to myself. For some people, the beginning of summer symbolizes an escape into carefree days of sleeping late, watching television, and escaping from homework, science fair projects, and all that horrible agenda. For others it means the family vacation season has officially opened for business. The time is rapidly coming to embark on another adventure of a lifetime.

Every summer without fail the family vacation commences with a new destination for me to plant my feet upon, usually some distant soil for which I could care less. I am at the will of my father, Larry, whose mission it is to personally check off all the states of the union. My mom and sister are also co-captives in the good old family station wagon out here on some two-lane cow- infested highway.

"Are we there yet?"

"No, son, be quiet."

"But are we there yet?"

"No, son, now be quiet."

"There is nothing to do or see in the car. I'm bored. I'm hungry."

"It is not time to eat, son."

As hard as I try, nothing I can do or say can parole me from increasing my collection of cross country miles.

"Quick, everyone look over there! That's an oil derrick pumping oil from the ground. "

"Yeah, dad, who cares about some silly stick going up and down, up and down? Hey, mom, try finding a station on that A.M. radio again. Please?"

I suppose my father was not so different from most men who elect to torture their families by closely examining every roadway with potholes--along with the total boycott of any restroom facilities. Darn that large sweet tea I had.

"Dad, can we stop now?"

"Not for another couple of hours."

"Come on, dad! We kids need a bathroom break. Please? Mom, talk to dad. I gotta go bad. "

"We are almost there, son."

"Larry, the kids have had enough, and I am getting a little tired, too. See if you can start looking for a place to stop."

Finally, the rolling nightmare ends, and we arrive at a stopping point for the evening. *Oh, this is lovely.*

"Dad, Barbara and I think this place really stinks." My inner voice reminds me that the outdoor temperature must be about one hundred degrees out here in the shade with no breeze in sight. *Those are not flies—they're mosquitoes.* I am not sure which is worse after a long car adventure: hiney numbness, weak knees, or a relentless need to relieve myself. *Ah, relief at last! My rear side is no longer numb.*

The sun is retiring in the west as the meal is prepared.

"All right, soggy peanut butter sandwiches from the bottom of the cooler again!"

"I'm sorry, children. The sandwiches fell into the bottom of the cooler and got wet. We will have to make do. Cliff and Barbara, quit fighting."

After a *lovely* evening in an Arkansas rest area, it is time to get some sleep for the night. Tomorrow is another long travel day, so everyone needs to get some shuteye. The hands on the clock appear to be rotating slower than molasses. Gee, it sure is hot and I am awake here in the middle of nowhere. After a joyous evening of nourishing the local mosquitoes, I eventually doze off into the zone.

As the easterly sun enters the sky, an inescapable "Bang! Bang! Bang!" shakes us rudely from our slumber. Well, what do you know? It is a police officer knocking on the window.

92

This is a great opportunity to convince Dad that all this travel is somehow against the law, and at home is where a child should be during the summer. My, he's a big man and looks ferocious.

"Is there something we can do for you, Officer Johnson?"

"Yeah, you can tell me what you know about the bathroom facilities over there? The bathrooms were vandalized last night."

"Sorry officer, we were all asleep and didn't hear anything. We are on our family vacation and I stopped here to get a quick nap."

"All right, you need to go ahead and get moving out of here before I give you a citation. The signs say, "no camping." You know you are not supposed to be here."

"Yes, Officer."

Wow, now that is what I call entertainment: good old Larry getting awakened by an officer of the law and then receiving one heck of a lecture. Priceless! Now I have something cool to tell my friends.

"You heard what the officer said. Let's make the bed, repack all our stuff, and get moving down the road."

"Mom, I'll put the middle seat up, if you can raise the tailgate seat."

"Barbara, can you repack the cooler?"

"Hey, Dad, we all need to use the restroom and brush our teeth."

"Not a chance, you heard what the officer said. Now get back in the car with your sister so we can get moving down the road."

Back in the car we go. As we were pulling back onto the highway in the family station wagon, I fondly remember asking myself why I had had to drink a full glass of tea this morning. As we left the rest area, the big blue sign announced the next rest area in 320 miles. *Oh, say it isn't so.*

"Hey, Dad, are we there yet?"

--Cliff Brown

Vacations from Afar Again

Twenty years later the nightmares of my past vacation travels are still squarely etched into what little I have left of my mind. Last November I found myself on a two-lane blacktop, basically in the middle of nowhere. I had laid down the law that the family needed to take a day trip.

Fall, one could argue, is the best part of the year for outdoor activities. I would certainly be foolish to argue otherwise. As a child, I had the great displeasure of traveling on yearly family vacations throughout this great country, which my father was steadfastly determined to explore every summer. Funny how, as I progress in years, roll reversal has slapped me from behind.

"Time to get up, boys! The time is five a.m. We have a long day ahead of us. Let's get up, get dressed, eat, and hit the road."

My oldest boy looked at me with the same facial message of disgust that I had shared with my father at the onset of a family outing when I was his age. Nevertheless, we sneaked out of town with only the moon and stars as our guide. With a chain of green lights greeting the windshield, the minivan rapidly whisked down the deserted local roadways en route to the expressway.

Oh, how words cannot begin to express the absolute joys of quiet children in the backseat of the car who are still in a state of sleepiness. It was a peaceful ride with the radio turned down just enough to hear the music. My wife Becky and I were having a nice quiet conversation, when it happened: that great ball of fire in the sky began its upward ascent. Why do kids always rise with the sun on the weekends? My youngest boy awakened from his slumber with a warm greeting for his parents.

"Are we there yet? How much longer until we get there, Daddy?"

Hmm . . . Where have I heard those words before?

Could it be history is playing a cruel joke on me as I recognize a clear reflection of my youth in both of my boys? I remember as a child driving my father's patience to the edge of insanity, constantly inquiring when we were to arrive along with just about any other thing my warped little mind could think of to assure him I was not having a good time. My father Larry would consider this payback for all of the years he had to put up with my sister and me on those long car rides during summer vacations.

"Where are we going?"

Great. Now my oldest son Darrin has joined the daddy interrogation. They say paybacks are heck. I must agree.

"Daddy, we're hungry. Can we stop now?"

The radio clock displayed 7:10 a.m. The north Georgia Mountains were still several hours away. Fast-forward three hours and the minivan pulled into a burger restaurant for a pit stop. Thankfully, this establishment had a playground, to which I gladly exiled both boys. Peace had returned temporarily. Forty-five minutes ticked off the clock and back into the minivan we went. The outside scenery was more radiant with every forward mile up the four-lane black top roadway. Georgia is truly a beautiful state with oceanfront and mountaintops and forests in between. In November varieties of trees parade their intense colors against the backdrop of mountains and valleys.

"Are we there yet?" "What? Oh, no, boys. Dad was just thinking about some things."

Meanwhile the family minivan had entered one of Georgia's most northern counties. The view was spectacular.

"Stop the car, Cliff!"

"What's wrong, Becky?"

"Get your camera and check out that beehive behind us."

Behind us? I walked about a quarter mile down the side of this road. No disappointment here. Above me attached to a twig was a large beehive. I snapped a few pictures and made the journey back up to the van.

"What took you so long?"

As if I had expected any other greeting. As we continued up the road, a sign ahead advertised: "Fish Hatchery, Turn Right." The van descended a narrow roadway for about a mile. Suddenly the pavement ended and the dirt began. Becky and I gave each other "the look" and onward down the path we drove. The path was extremely narrow. Turning the van around was just not going to happen. In another two or so miles we reached the hatchery: "Closed on Saturdays." Of course it was.

My luck continued. Meanwhile, I noticed a car coming from the opposite direction. I figured we had come this far, so forward the van continued.

"Dad, I've got to go number one."

My only consolation was "one" was a whole lot easier to offer a solution for than "number two." However, as I found myself gaining elevation on the bumpy path, any sort of facilities was out of the question. I stopped the van near a creek side.

"Pit stop, boys."

Out went the boys to mark new territory. Thankfully, a forest ranger was not lurking around the corner. My boys were successful in marking a couple of trees. After dipping their hands in the flowing water, they made a dash for the van.

"Dad, that water is ice cold!"

Smart boys: cold outside van, warm inside van--boys chose warm van.

None of the paths had any names posted. We happened upon a local who was kind enough to steer us in the right direction. These two fine gentlemen looked like they had just ventured down the mountain from tending to their moonshine distillery. You could certainly get misplaced there. I was a living example.

Up the hill further the van traveled.

"We're hungry."

"Boys! Stop hitting each other. I told you two to be nice to each other."

At this junction I felt confident that even a bullhorn pointed directly at my boys would have been ineffective in achieving harmony between them. Finally, the top of the mountain came into view. The view from there was breathtaking. If I had had binoculars, I could have seen the path the van had traveled a few minutes earlier. Hemlocks, elms, and other species of trees were on display with the sun's light complementing the brilliant colors surrounding our van. I stopped in the middle of the path and we all got out for a breath of fresh air. As I paused to experience the quiet gentle breeze, I envisioned what paradise must be like.

"I'm tired daddy. When can we go home? Trent hit me."

"Alright, Darrin, I heard you."

Correction: As I paused to experience the not-so-quiet gentle breeze shattering any experience of peace with nature, I really did not know what I could have been thinking: quiet and obedient children--Not!

We all gathered back into the van for the downward trip to the bottom of the mountain. The great ball of fire was beginning to retreat behind the horizon. My immediate question was, "How in the heck do I get out of here and rediscover civilization?"

"Ouch, he kicked me."

Ladies and gentlemen, remember: what goes around comes around. All those years of nagging my parents on family vacations have come full circle.

The sun was setting and we were somewhere in the range of 250 miles or so from the final pit stop.

"We're hungry, Daddy. You need to stop."

Oh, does anyone have an aspirin?

--Cliff Brown

Does Anyone Understand That Formula?

"Ouch!" Another bite. I must be made of something really sweet. At a time when the outdoor sauna continues to push the Fahrenheit scale further north, the calendar on the wall is announcing the welcome arrival of cooler temperatures along with the seasonal suspension of the "all-you-can-eat buffet." With the approach of the fall season, my faithful book bag is beckoning me to evict all the dust bunnies that have enjoyed a summer of free rent, courtesy of my dormant academic schedule. On this cool morning, as I travel along this two-lane roadway, the smell of diesel fuel, coupled with the familiar sight of the yellow cheese mobile reflecting off my sunglasses, reinforces in my mind the end of summer. As a rising college student, I cannot for the life of me come to a logical understanding as to why I would want to expose myself to the torture that some college classes impose.

This academic term I am a willing hostage of this crazy subject where the letter x seems to be the key to successful achievement. He pals up with his good friend, the letter y, whom he calls his variable. All I can decipher is a bunch of mixed-up letters. Apparently the author forgot that a is the leading letter of the alphabet and not x. All these letters and formulas may be great for some math number-loving genius, so why in the great name of writing am I even dignifying this brain-warping topic?

Until now I had never really contemplated how much those letters have influenced my life. I can fondly reflect on the days when my hair was more plentiful and a bit darker--I was just a y floating around without a care in the world. I had collected enough monetary funds to solve for the letter c. After sticker disbelief, I settled upon a basic four-cylinder model.

I guess it was during the high school years that the idea of actually liking a girl entered my mind. So there is that letter g. If you were to ask, I am certain my math instructor would remind you that the letter g is just a y in disguise. Remember students, you are trying to solve for the variable y. After checking out some formulas, I finally found one that would solve my equation and provide me a function of m. About three years later, I was served notice that in nine months I would successfully solve for the term b. Yes, indeed, my math instructor would be comically amused at the relationships of life that have been carved out of these maddening math formulas.

By the way, watch out for b squared. Has my life become a quadratic function? What is the function of life? Is there a simple answer to such a mountain of a question? In solving for l, there will always be ever-changing variables--such as when the next time c will be replaced. Several variables may be substituted to determine what model of c will serve the function. In plugging in the variables b squared, $c,$ and m, we can determine that b squared will cost the most to maintain.

One of the critical variables to solve for will be d. This requires a complicated formula that cannot be solved in quick fashion. As I follow behind the yellow cheese mobile with my dustless book bag, the process of solving for d is one day closer to completion of the final answer. Hopefully, in one year the letter d will be solved for. The reward will consist of a little sheet of paper from a house of higher education enclosed in a frame with an answer that will obviously be displayed in simplest form.

--Cliff Brown

Every Woman

I hate doing dishes. I don't mind the buying, the cooking, and the serving--although a glass of wine is welcome in these phases--but I just hate cleaning up. "Now if you had trained your husband and children right, you wouldn't have this problem," I can hear you smugly comment. Yeah, yeah. Well, *you* don't have to read this tirade. This is only for loser moms like me who buy into the homework pretexts and the working spouse pleas.

Now that we've got the right crowd around us--back to the sink full of dirty stuff. I do not like to see how little my kids eat of a meal I considered five star quality. I'm not exactly invigorated by their remarks at the dinner table: What is that? Fish again? You know I don't eat green beans! Did you do something different to the salad? Not to mention the never ending poop jokes that my food apparently never fails to inspire--those can be quite funny, I have to admit! After dinner, everybody scurries away like a mouse from the cat. I sigh and drag my feet back and forth between the table and the sink, soaking the potato pot, digging crap out of the sink--you know that soggy stuff. Well, it all changed when my wise teenagers, who know a lot more about everything than I do, bought me an I-Pod. At first, I received the gift with hesitation: Too expensive. What am I gonna do with it? How does it even work? My little techno wonders fixed me up with some of their stuff that I had been forced to listen to over the past five years.

One day they pissed me off royally and I just wanted them all to go away and leave me alone with my dirty dishes. I did not even want to hear them. "Where is my I-Pod?" I demanded. I selected some "high school musical" and stuck the thingie under my bra strap. A chorus of joyous young teenagers burst out singing "We're all in this together." The music was surprisingly fun and lively! Before I knew it I was singing along looking at my pots that I was in it together with and realizing life wasn't always that great for them either. I danced and sang to my pots and had a blast. Instead of feeling my aching legs, I felt my brain being flooded with some good kind of endorphins. My kitchen transformed itself into a dance floor, the tiles being perfect for my eighties' moves in white cotton socks.

I've now graduated from "high school musicals" to masters like Marvin Gaye, Chakakhan, Maze, and Jocelyn Brown, for starters. I do my laundry belting out "I'm every woman" at the top of my lungs, folding those towels with a snap. I swing my broom around effortlessly with Mariah Carey. I relive Whitney's glory days while washing the windows. Good memories, youth, parties--I still have it. That girl is still alive!

"Go do your homework. Get out of the kitchen--unless you wanna dance! The floor is mine after dinner."

Hmm, maybe I'll change some of those light bulbs into a different color.

"MOM! Can you be quiet!"

--Yvonne Gabriel

Windmills: An Anti-Hero Story

To break all the rules in sweet revenge or to become a millionaire after having been a geek—you're still all winner. In the end you overcame--you conquered. Veni,Vedi,Vici, right? Not my stories. Forced through assignment to relive these small but sharp little injustices, I'll share with you the story of the one time I made an "F" in elementary school.

Growing up in Holland was idyllic—the school was in the center of a small village surrounded by farm fields with the most beautiful, clean, black and white cows you'll ever see anywhere in the world and small homes, close to each other with neighbors competitively striving to make their little yard the prettiest, adding good humored gnomes and windmills to the abundant variety of flowers already there. With fondness I recall the soothing drone of our timetables we recited each morning. The large windows in our classrooms allowed the Dutch skies to compete with the many famous paintings that depict those billowy clouds. I can still feel the clay, the paintbrush, and the hammer we used in the enormous attic above the school that was used for our art classes. I remember the approving smiles of my parents as I proudly showed them my excellent report cards that were never a surprise.

In all of those six years, I never made a "B." One day, however, I was caught off guard with a test about the map of Holland. We had filled in many rivers, cities and provinces in the course of a few days. For some reason I was totally oblivious to the fact that our teacher, a middle-aged man with a middle-aged temper, who was also the headmaster, expected us to know that map on that particular day in history. Panic stricken, I sat at my desk, staring at the paper in front of me. So horrified I was that I could not even remember where the city of Amsterdam was, a fact I would know without studying had my brain not been saturated with a venomous sort of adrenaline that prepared me for flight or fight--but not for calm recollection of already long-known facts.

My brain raced for a way out of this situation, but there was none. Half an hour later I received my grade: an "F." I had never heard those words pronounced in association with my-self. It was too much to handle. What did I do? Make a plea for another chance? Offer a passionate explanation? No, I burst out crying. I had no handkerchief and soon a combination of snot and tears fell into the lakes and rivers of the Netherlands, the red ink from the burning "F" turning them red like the cursed Nile.

My teacher, cranky as he was, looked at me with disgust. I could not stop crying. Sympathy would have probably made it worse. A darker shade of red joined the mess on my map that by now looked like the Vikings had murdered the whole population: my nose was bleeding. Oh, my God. With nothing to shut it off, the warm blood dripped through my helpless fingers onto my clothes, the desk, and the God-forsaken map.

"Teacher, Teacher!" The boy next to me cried urgently, his arm stretched out to catch the teacher's attention. The teacher had already seen me and was approaching rapidly.

"Get out of here!" he thundered, red in the face.

I looked at him helplessly, not understanding where I should go or what to do with the ongoing stream of blood com-ing out of my nose.

"Get out of here!" he repeated, louder this time as if it were possible I had not heard him the first time.

"Go to the bathroom and clean this mess up after you're done!" he screamed in Hitler style.

At least this time he had given me some indication of where I should go. I got up quickly and got away from him, leav-ing a trail of blood on the floor behind me. I had seen that man hit a big sixth grader so hard the boy had fallen with his head against this teacher's desk. He had a foul temper and enjoyed an unquestioned authority.

In the bathroom, the cool, clean tiles and the cold water helped to get me settled. My nose finally stopped bleeding, but I had to get back to class. From the little kitchen adjacent to the bathroom I grabbed a rag and went as quietly as possible back into the classroom.

I was a mess--blood on my clothes, my face all red and splotchy. Now I had to get on my hands and knees and wipe up the blood. The drops had already dried to the floor. It was a slow and painful procession, from the door to my desk, which of course was all the way in the back—with me being the tallest and all. Blood from my nose, sweat from the dread of the test, and tears for my "F"--there is no happy ending other than that the floor was clean after I finally reached my desk.

No hero ending. End of story.

--Yvonne Gabriel

Just Swingin'

"I can swing higher than you," Emily taunted.
"No, you can't," I yelled back, pumping my legs harder.
"Yes, I can, Barb," she triumphantly crowed.

No matter what I did or how hard I tried, my five-year old legs couldn't get that swing to the heights my sister Emily reached. After what seemed like an eternity of trying, we both jumped down to get something to drink.

Back at the swings after our quick break, Emily ordered me to hold one swing out of the way while she turned flips on the high bar of the other swing. Obediently, younger sister pulled back the metal swing by its chains and stood there hold-ing it for what must have been a year. Suddenly, something bright and colorful caught my eye. I ran to investigate, finding a beautiful butterfly on one of Granny's roses.

Instantly, Emily started screaming: "She killed me! Owww! It hurts! Help! Granny!" I turned around and there was Emily, hanging upside down on the bar, blood pouring out of her forehead. I had let go of the chains without a thought.

She kept on screaming: "It hurts! Help me!" I stared at her. I knew my carelessness had caused this. Mama, Granny, and Granddaddy were going to kill me for sure. I had hurt Em and she was dying. Possible forms of punishment for my crime passed before my eyes. I began screaming and crying that I hadn't meant to kill her. I ran and hid behind Granny's house.

Granny was too busy taking care of Em to worry about me. She calmly took Em inside the house, cleaned the wound, and called Mama. It was bad: there was a hole in Em's head. When I had let go of the iron swing, it had popped Em's forehead so hard that it had busted it.

Mama rushed home to find Em still screaming that she was dying and it was my fault. Mama rushed her to the doctor's office where they put 12 stitches in her head. I stayed in my hiding place a very long time, alternating between crying and praying that God would save me. I began feeling very tired, so I crawled out from underneath the fig tree where I had been hiding. I wasn't sure where to go. Granny had been out several times trying to coax me into coming inside, but I knew I'd get a spanking if I went in. I really hadn't meant to hurt Em. It was an accident.

Finally, I decided to lie down on some of the pine straw around Granny's roses. I knew Granddaddy would find me there when he came for his medicine. Alone and scared, I closed my eyes to rest for a few minutes. I awoke to the sound of Mama's soft, sweet voice telling me that everything was all right. Emily was going to be fine, although she might be grumpy for a few days. The doctor had warned Mama that Em was going to have quite a headache.

Mama picked me up and carried me inside. We went down the hall to Emily's room. Em was lying down with a huge white bandage wrapped around her head. When I saw her, I burst into tears again: "Oh, Mama! They wrapped her up like a mummy! She's going to die, isn't she?"

Mama assured me that Em was fine. Em opened her eyes and looked at me, a big frown covering her face. In a loud voice, she began to scold me: "Barbara," she screamed. "Why did you do that? You let go of the swing. My head hurts. I am really mad at you! Just wait till I get you back for this!"

--Barbara Sellers

The Opera Lover

The gray-headed gentleman and the attractive young lady at his side left bohemian Paris, made their way through the lobby, and, along with several hundred other members of the audience, walked out of the opera house. He had an appearance of thoughtful satisfaction, while she displayed a dreamy expression in her bright blue eyes.

They proceeded down the sidewalk, past brightly lit store windows and restaurants filled with elegantly dressed diners, toward the parking lot where they had left the car. Before they reached the first corner, he asked her if she would like a little something to eat before they headed back home. Of course she agreed, so they went into a fancy restaurant, where the maitre d' seemed to know the gentleman and showed them to a table for two in a quiet nook against the back wall. After they were seated and he had ordered for them, the gentleman looked at the young woman with interest.

"Well, Elaine, how did you like your first experience with an opera?" he asked her.

"Oh, Granddad, it was just wonderful! I had no idea that I would enjoy it so much. I always thought that opera was dull and boring, with lots of screeching noise. But it wasn't that way at all. I'm so glad you asked me to come with you!"

"I'm really delighted you enjoyed it," he said. "I thought that *La Bohème* might be a good introduction to opera for you.

It has many of the qualities that characterize the best operas." He paused, and then asked, "What did you like most about it?"

The young lady looked thoughtful for a moment, and then she looked up with a serious expression. "Well, it was really sad. I know that I shouldn't say that I enjoyed feeling sad, but I guess I actually did. I mean, it was touching to see how much Rodolfo and Mimi loved each other. I don't know much about being in love, but I've certainly seen a lot of romantic movies, and I've seen how Mom and Dad really love each other. And you and Grandma, too! But seeing Mimi and Rodolfo declare their love for each other so beautifully, and then for Mimi to die . . . Well, it just doesn't seem right, does it?"

Her grandfather smiled at her attempt to express her response to the opera, and he said, "No, it doesn't seem fair. But as you can see, sometimes life is that way. Somehow, life doesn't always give us what we want or what we think is fair. I'm not sure that I can explain why life is like that, but anyone who has lived as long as I have can vouch that that's the way it is sometimes. Anyway, this particular opera is one that is called a 'verismo' opera—since it is 'realistic' or 'true to life.'"

"Is that why the other couple—what are their names? Marcello and Musetta, or something like that?—were always fighting?" Elaine asked.

"Exactly," said Granddad. "Musetta is a woman who seems to be looking out for a man who can provide her with material pleasures. Things. That's why she took up with that wealthy old man we saw in the second act. Marcello is a poor painter and certainly can't compete with a wealthy rival. But deep down, Musetta actually loves Marcello, even though she doesn't want to love him. So they have to work things out in a raucous sort of way. That's what we saw them doing in the third act. Sometimes it takes people who love each other a long time to find out for themselves how much they really do love each other. By the time Mimi dies, this other couple seems to be firmly united, perhaps because they see how fragile life and love can be. This, too, is realistic."

106

Their conversation was interrupted briefly by the waiter, who brought their dessert, along with coffee for Granddad and a cola for Elaine. They savored their chocolate pie for a few minutes, but eventually Granddad asked Elaine for another reaction to the opera.

"What did you think of the music?"

"Oh, it was beautiful," she gushed. "I don't know that much about music, but it really had a lot of melody. Not at all dreary and noisy, like I thought opera might be."

"Do you recall any particular bits of music that especially struck you?" he asked.

"Well, I loved those two songs in the first act that Mimi and Rodolfo sing to each other when they first meet. And then a few minutes later at the end of the act they sing a beautiful duet. At least, I thought it was beautiful."

"Yes, indeed," Granddad agreed. "That duet is among the most highly regarded romantic duets in all of opera. I'm glad you were moved by it."

"Oh, I think I was moved by the whole thing, Granddad. As I said earlier, I don't think I knew how wonderful opera can be." After a thoughtful pause, she looked at him and said, "Tell me something, Granddad. I've seen you sitting in your chair time and time again, listening to some opera on the stereo. How did you get started? When did you first become interested in opera? Did someone take you to see an opera in a theater?"

"Well, when I was about eight years old, my father bought an old—well, it would be old now, although it was the latest thing then!—phonograph record player and some single records. These all played at 45 rpm. That means revolutions per minute. I expect it's hard for you to visualize the kind of music equipment we had in those days. Some of the first records he bought were opera arias sung by some of the greatest singers of the previous decades. The names of these singers meant nothing to me, although I do recall liking the sound of them as they rolled off the tongue. Ferruccio Tagliavini, for example, had what I thought was a wonderful name. And he was a great tenor.

Rodolfo was one of his most famous roles. I became familiar with some opera arias just because we had a few opera records that my father played fairly often.

"And then when I was about eleven years old, maybe two or three years younger than you are now, I had what you could call my first real introduction to opera. My father took us all to the old Peachtree Arts Theater in Atlanta. It was a little movie theater on Peachtree Street up in what we now call Midtown that played mostly movies that were imported from Europe. It must have been in 1951 that I went there with my parents and my sister to see a new film entitled *The Tales of Hoffmann*. It was an English film based on Offenbach's opera of the same name, and for all I knew it was an exact representation of the opera. I've seen it several times over the years, and I know now that it is not an exact representation of the opera, but it is pretty close.

"And it's one of the most attractive movies I've ever seen. I've seen it several times since that first time so long ago. I've even gone out of my way to see it in some of the cities I've found myself in from time to time.

"I suppose what really grabbed me about that film is the fantastic story that the opera presents. It's about a poet who tells the stories of his three love affairs. He fell in love at various times with three different women, but in the end they all turn out to be three aspects of the same woman. And he is never successful, because in each story he is challenged by a rival who always defeats him. And these three rivals turn out to be three embodiments of the same rival who blocks his way to the real woman he loves—or thinks he loves.

"Offenbach's music is so romantic, and the film makers did such a truly great job of presenting the fantastic events of the opera, that I must have been turned on to opera when I was eleven. And I've been turned on to it ever since. I would say that *The Tales of Hoffmann* is still my favorite opera."

Elaine sat listening attentively as her grandfather reminisced about his early acquaintance with the world of opera. "Well, when did you see your first opera on a stage in a theater?"

"Oh, I remember that quite well. I had listened to the Saturday matinee radio broadcasts from the Metropolitan Opera for years, and I was pretty familiar with a lot of operas, but I didn't actually get to see one on the stage until I was twenty years old. A friend of my father's had a ticket to one of the performances by the Metropolitan Opera when they came to Atlanta on their annual spring tour. I guess this person couldn't get to Atlanta that evening, so I got to go to the Fox Theater to see *Madama Butterfly* performed by the Met as my first experience with 'live' opera. I'll try to take you to see that opera sometime. It's also by Puccini, who wrote *La Bohème*."

"Have you seen many operas since then?" Elaine asked.

"Well, not as many as I would have liked, that's for sure," laughed Granddad. "But the following year, when I was twenty-one, that same person gave me tickets for all of the Met's performances in Atlanta. So I drove down to Atlanta every day for a week in order to see six more operas performed by the world's greatest opera company. I don't think I was quite aware of it then, but looking back at those old programs, I know now that during that week I saw and heard some of the greatest opera singers of the twentieth century. I also saw the Met give several performances in Detroit a few years later. And then I went for a long time when I had little opportunity at all to see an opera—just every now and then. But in the last few years, your grandmother and I have been fortunate to have season tickets to the Atlanta Opera. It's not the Metropolitan Opera, but it's a very good regional opera company, and it gets many singers who have already established themselves in their operatic careers. Some of their productions have been most impressive, and we've seen some very good performances during the last five or six years. Now that I know you're so interested, I'll see if we can arrange to include you on our opera expeditions from time to time. Would you be interested in that possibility?"

"Well, you know I would!" Elaine exclaimed with excitement. "When's the next one?"

Granddad laughed and said, "Well, we'll have to see

about that. . . . But it looks as if the folks here would like for us to move on. They seem to be ready to clean up so they can get home. Are you all set?"

The two of moved through the restaurant out onto the sidewalk and strolled on to the parking lot where they found their car. As they traveled down the highway, Elaine said, "I wish this evening didn't have to come to an end."

Her grandfather smiled happily to himself as he thought triumphantly, "Ha! I have just increased the audience for live opera by one young enthusiast!"

--Rick Thurman

Jezebel

The small tidy, well-kept house seemed out of place in the surrounding environment. The pots of geraniums and chrysanthemums lining the steps of the porch were an inviting presence to visitors. The immaculate lawn was another contradiction in this otherwise unkempt neighborhood littered with beer bottles, fast food wrappers and bags, and the occasional condom lying on the sidewalk.

Drucella Johnson had lived in this house since she was born. Her grandmother had bought the land long before. The previous owner had thought he was selling it to a nice white lady whose husband was off fighting in the war. No Negro would have had the cash necessary to pay for the land, so Mr. Fred sold the property, not bothering to investigate, sure that the highly refined light-skinned woman of color could not be such.

Drucella lived in this beautiful home with her granddaughter, Jess, a 12-year-old precocious child who would do anything to please her grandmother, the only person in the world on whom she could depend. Jess's mother, Deborah, had chosen a life much different from that to which she had been accustomed. Drucella had sacrificed to send Deborah to private school and provide piano and ballet lessons. She had been proud when Deborah was presented as a debutante at the Cotillion Ball.

Going to Burston's Department Store had been a weekly ritual for the two as Deborah grew up. There had been the weekly brunches where they had dressed up so Deborah could practice the etiquette skills Drucella had lovingly taught her. Deborah and her young friends had often gathered at her house for tea and a game of bridge. Having the right connections was important for a young lady of character and sophistication.

Their family had been very close. Outsiders viewed Drucella, her husband Calvin, and Deborah as the ideal family. Both employed in good jobs with the government, Drucella and Calvin realized that their lifestyle and luxuries were the envy of many. Each year they had enjoyed vacations--traveling across the continent to the Grand Canyon, visiting Disney World, rafting in the Colorado River, and exploring the San Diego Zoo. Hearing the Reverend King speak at Ebenezer Baptist Church in Atlanta was an annual treat for the entire family. Deborah had been but a small child when in 1963 her parents had taken her to the March on Washington. Family conversation frequently centered on the civil rights movement.

Unbeknownst to Drucella, each opportunity she had conscientiously provided for Deborah became one more step in a direction that Deborah had firmly resolved not to take. While she gladly accepted the indulgent pampering, an insatiable desire to experience what lay beyond the boundaries of her much guarded inner circle grew incessantly within her. At a friend's house, Deborah experimented for the first time with marijuana, slowly widening her circle to include people who lived on the other side of the tracks. The large amount of money that Deborah always carried caught the attention of her newfound friends. Naive, she felt honored that they wanted to include her in their circle.

Experiments with crack cocaine soon followed. Although Deborah had been able to convince her mother that everything was all right, Drucella had inadvertently discovered the drugs on Deborah's dresser. Two visits to an outpatient rehab clinic failed to still the desire that burned within Deborah, leading her to do anything necessary to satisfy her craving. The day she was discharged from the second clinic, she methodically scoured the house in search of valuables to sell to support her expensive habit. Jewelry, silver, crystal and coins that had been in the family for generations were packed into suitcases, which Deborah slipped out of the house one at a time. When Drucella returned home and found Deborah and her valuables missing, she blamed herself for failing as a parent. Depression set in.

Deborah had smoked and snorted drugs, gradually depleting the money from the sale of the stolen family treasures. Drucella and Calvin, and then just Drucella after Calvin had parted company, expended many years and large sums of money in efforts to support Deborah each time she had vowed to turn over a new leaf. During one of her bouts of drug usage, Deborah had turned to prostitution to support her crack habit, becoming pregnant when she failed to use protection. Delusional about the consequences of her actions, Deborah had thought only of the money. Having no idea of the identity of the father of her unborn child, she completely avoided her mother during her pregnancy, not even communicating her situation. While in labor, Deborah confided to an overly judgmental nurse the circumstances surrounding her pregnancy. Deborah was hung over from a day of drinking and using drugs. Clueless about what to name the child, Deborah took the sarcastic suggestion of the nurse, naming her daughter "Jezebel." Not in a state of mind conducive to good judgment, Deborah failed to consider that such a choice would surely condemn her daughter to a life of ridicule.

In the year since Deborah had absconded with her mother's possessions, friends and relatives had reported seeing Deborah walking the streets, but no one had known that she had gotten pregnant or had delivered a beautiful, bright-eyed brown baby with a head full of curly dark hair. Jess was several months old before Drucella learned that she was a grandmother. Social Services had called her late one night after Deborah was arrested for soliciting an undercover policeman. The policeman had subsequently found the child nearby, sleeping in the back of an abandoned car. Drucella had had to go to the precinct and take Jess home with her. Jess, undernourished and suffering from several medical problems including HIV and Fetal Alcohol Syndrome, was still experiencing drug withdrawal symptoms at the time. Deborah had never bothered to get prenatal checkups or even attempt to stop using drugs and alcohol during her pregnancy in hopes that she would miscarry.

The sudden appearance of Jess might have been just the answer to many of Drucella's prayers. As she climbed the stairs to her house, she clutched Jess tightly, reflecting on all the things she needed to do to get the baby settled: doctors visits, medical bills, and social services. Raising an infant at her age, especially one with such tremendous needs, was a lot to contend with. Yet Drucella had been so lonely. She had loved and lost Deborah, and then Calvin. Maybe this child, this innocent child, would love her back. Bitter and lonely, Drucella had nevertheless always put on a "happy, successful face" with her friends and family to mask her pain.

Drucella's mother had always taught her that family was all that you had: you stick together through the good and the bad. Maybe Jess was what Drucella needed. She would love this child unconditionally and treat her like the princess she would grow up to be. There would be no expenses spared--no shortcuts taken. This was Drucella's grandchild. She would be a proud grandmother who would go to the ends of the earth to protect this child. There would be love and laughter, and all would be well. After all, appearances were everything.

--Elnora Fluellen

Another September

Lois Stevens pulled her white Mercedes slowly around the accident. She saw muscle-toned firefighters standing next to the handsome emergency technicians who were putting a stretcher into the back of an ambulance. "Finally!" she thought, as she accelerated to ten miles an hour over the interstate speed limit. Minutes later, she reached the parking lot and pulled past five empty handicapped spaces, searching for the closest available parking spot, irritatingly several lanes from the front entrance. She jumped out and hurried across, dressed smartly in a navy skirt and jacket and strappy light blue high heels complete with rhinestones on the front.

The doors swung open as she approached the main entrance of the hospital. A short pudgy man of about forty-five passed her and smiled. She returned the smile as she hurried past the crowded waiting area with some people chatting in small groups, some reading, and others trying to sleep sitting up. Magazines covered with the airbrushed faces of smiling young Hollywood actresses lay strewn about on the tables. Down the corridor lined with empty wheelchairs, she strode purposefully toward the doctors building adjacent to the main hospital. The elevator doors opened, revealing a tall handsome man with a full head of gray hair, who nodded and smiled at Lois as she stepped on. "How are you today, young lady?" the gentleman asked in a warm southern drawl, speaking with familiarity even though he did not know Lois. Far from offended, she smiled as she courteously replied.

Dr. Bledsoe's waiting area was plush and softly lit. Rod Stewart was singing a ballad in the background. Lois glanced at her watch, signing in five minutes late. Quickly scanning the room, she selected a corner wing chair next to an overweight woman and directly across from a young man in blue jeans, reading a sports magazine with a sprinter on the cover. He smiled at Lois, letting his eyes linger over her, pausing momentarily at her long brown legs as she crossed them. She returned the smile, visibly pleased at the attention she was receiving from an attractive man almost as young as her son.

It was September, marking two years since her husband had left her for a woman half his age. But he had not gotten much else--Lois had the house on the lake filled with expensive

114

antiques, the cars, and a comfortable monthly alimony check. After the initial shock, she had shed forty pounds and toned her body by walking five miles a day. She updated her wardrobe and began to travel, reveling in the looks and comments her new body elicited from men of all ages and sizes. But she wouldn't date them, preferring their admiration from a distance.

"Ms. Stevens?" the nurse called as she opened the reception door. "How are you today?"

"I'm really great," Lois answered with enthusiasm.

"You look wonderful. You're healing nicely," she commented as she led the way to the door of the examination room. It had been four weeks since the face-lift, and the swelling was gone. "What do you think of the results?"

"Even better than I had expected! I don't know why I was so nervous about it."

There was a soft knock at the door, and in walked Dr. Bledsoe, who looked more like a schoolboy than a plastic surgeon. "Well, hello, Gorgeous! How 'bout a date?"

"Sure, Doc, as long as your wife doesn't mind!" Lois chided him good-naturedly.

"Aw, she's used to it. Keeps me busy and outta her way, she claims." Dr. Bledsoe turned the lamp toward Lois and, holding her face, pulled her blond hair aside to reveal the stitches. "Your sutures are healing nicely. Is the soreness gone?"

"Yes. I feel as good as new. And I sure don't miss the wrinkles."

"You look at least ten years younger," testified the nurse from behind Dr. Bledsoe.

"Okay, Lois." He flipped off the lamp and stepped back, opening the file on the counter. "We will see you in eight weeks to take your 'after' pictures. Take care," he smiled and patted her shoulder as he was leaving.

Lois took the elevator back to the main level, retracing her steps past the wheelchairs and the waiting area through the automatic doors toward her car. She walked with confidence and security, certain that every man and boy she passed was looking her way approvingly. Her long, suntanned legs had attracted a lot of attention in the months following her exercise and diet regime, and now her face had made the transformation complete. As she strolled across the parking lot with the soft fall breeze caressing her face, comments from her children floated into her thoughts and caused a smug smile of satisfaction to spread unbidden across her face — her ex-husband with his teenybopper girlfriend had also noticed the new Lois.

Lois situated herself in the luxurious white leather seat of her sports car and inserted the key in the ignition. A remake of the old Hank William's song "Hey, Good-lookin'!" was playing on the radio. She rechecked her make-up in the rearview mirror and smiled with pleasure at her reflection. Singing along with the radio, she exited the parking lot and turned left at the intersection, heading toward the interstate access ramp. She never saw the truck.

Drivers slowed their cars as they passed the scene of the accident. Lois lay unconscious on the stretcher that two handsome emergency technicians were loading into the back of an ambulance. A white cloth covered everything but her face, which miraculously had sustained only a slight cut above her left eye.

"It's a good thing we're this close to the hospital," one of them exclaimed, "or she wouldn't make it."

"She'll live," commented the second tech, as he gazed at the mangled Mercedes. Blood covered the leather seats, now exposed after the muscle-toned firefighters had cut through the roof to free Lois. Something glistened brightly in the sun, catching the technician's eye. He leaned over and picked up a blue high-heeled shoe with a rhinestone buckle on the top, mutilated and saturated in blood.

"Dammit!" he swore, shaking his head. "I wish we could have saved her legs."

--Terri DeFoor

116

The Boy behind the Couch

The boy was terrified. He was listening to the familiar sounds of his parents arguing--only this time was worse. Their screams made him wish for deafness. As he cowered behind the sofa, tears began to run down his face. Silently, he begged his parents to stop.

"Please listen to me. You must stop this. I can't take much more of it."

"Shut up, you stupid bitch. You don't know what you're talking about. I'm only trying to talk some sense into that pea-brain of yours. If you would shut up and listen, you might learn something. Look at me when I'm talking to you!"

It hadn't always been like this. He could remember when his parents were happy. They smiled, talked, and even took family vacations together. Then something happened. His father started drinking and the fights began. Over the years, it grew worse, going from an occasional argument to daily fights.

"You and that idiot son of yours – I can't believe I got stuck with the two of you. What the hell did I do to deserve this miserable life I'm living?"

His mother was crying. "Nothing. You didn't do anything. We love you. We want you to love us like you used to. Why can't we be a family again?"

" I told you to shut the hell up. Where is that boy?"

He tried to crawl deeper into his hiding place. He didn't want to be found. At times his father would begin taking out his frustrations on him. Careful not to leave marks that would be visible to others, he often used the boy as a boxer might use a punching bag. Bruises and pain were constant companions of the boy. He tried hard not to let anyone know what was going on. He knew his father would end up in trouble if he told, and that would be even worse for him.

One day he overheard his mother talking to her sister on the phone one day, telling her that money was short. Her boss had called the office a while back and told her that she might be laid off. Eventually she lost her job, and unable to find another, she stayed home and took care of him and the household chores. He was surprised to hear her say these things. He thought she had chosen to stay home.

The shortage of money caused his father to drink even more. There would be times when he would pass out in his recliner. The boy relished the peacefulness of those times. Other times, like tonight, his mother and father would spend what seemed like countless hours yelling and screaming at each other. On some occasions, they would fling household items at each other during the heat of the argument. One day he barely missed being hit by a drinking glass his mother threw at his father. He began taking refuge behind the sofa. The space was perfect for his small, ten-year-old frame.

His father had temporarily forgotten about him. "Woman, will you stop that damn insane crying?" He heard the sound of a slap, and his mother screamed.

"Shut up! What do I have to do to make you shut up?"

As he huddled there, the voices escalated. Words were being said that he didn't recognize, but he knew they were bad. Suddenly a plate of food hit the wall just behind the sofa. It fell beside the boy, landing upside down on the carpet.

His tears became sobs. He tried unsuccessfully to stifle the sound. He could hear his father stomping down the hall towards the bedroom. His mother followed closely behind, screaming that she was going to take the boy and leave forever. His father taunted her that she would never leave.

The boy began to think about leaving. If only he could go and be with his grandfather, but he had left the boy several months ago. He desperately wanted to be where his grandfather was, but his mother told him it would probably be a long time before he saw him again. Grandfather had gone to heaven.

He still loved his parents. He wanted them to love him and be a happy family again. In his nightly prayers he used to ask God for help. When no help came, he had stopped praying. Suddenly he realized that he was whispering the prayer he used to say at bedtime. He thought he felt a touch on his shoulder. Grandfather used to lay his hand on the boy's shoulder while they talked. The boy always took strength from the touch. It made him feel safe and loved. But when he looked up, there was no one there. Startled and afraid, he hid his head again in his arms, crouching even further behind the sofa. He stayed there for a long time, listening as the fight raged on.

He didn't remember leaving his hiding place. He didn't remember going into his parents' room and crying for them to stop. All he remembered is hearing a loud sound, like that of a firecracker popping. A few seconds later, he heard another.

There was an uncanny quietness in the house. The shouting had stopped. He went back to his hiding place and stayed there a very long time. When he began hearing voices, they sounded far away. He heard someone say that his parents were dead. When they found him, he had blood splattered on his clothes, and in his hand was a gun.

--Barbara Sellers

The Sideshow

"Ladies and Gentlemen, gather 'round! Come and see for yourselves the beautiful Leonora being beheaded under the guillotine! Heads will be rolling. YES, ladies and gentlemen, come see the man who hammers a nail in his head! A ten-inch nail!"

Tom got in line. His Sunday loafers, reserved for his visits to the South, were pinching his toes. Why had he let his Mom talk him into coming home this weekend? His papery grandmother had kissed him on the cheek in her regal manner, the bluish hair swept in a French twist for her 90th birthday. Tom had escaped in his father's car before she could ask him to play that God-forsaken piano she had tortured him with his entire childhood. She would die on the spot if she knew he had burnt all his piano books on the first night he had arrived in New York.

Tom entered the dimly lit, dusty tent. Several velvet

curtains worn with too much trickery hung to hide the monstrous and the hideous. A boorish young fellow with happy eyes grabbed the microphone. His earlobes had big round holes in them and a dark ornament in his nose curled up from each nostril. Tattoos covered pale, chubby arms that would have looked harmless without them and his hair stood up in an angry ridge. His armor could not hide his good cheer.

Following an elaborate welcome to the greatest show on earth, he lunged forward and cautiously stuck a lighted torch in his mouth. He consumed two more torches with careful, gentle gestures. Obviously relieved he had not burned his face, he announced the sword eater. An older man, his face lined with warning, sauntered onto the stage. His glasses accommodated his aging vision while his protruding naked belly, complete with tattoos, dared all assumptions. Virgil told the audience he was the oldest of the perhaps 65 sword eaters still around in this country and that he had taught a good many of the younger ones. He casually picked up a sword, positioned his worn Birkenstocks, and stuck the sword halfway down his throat as if it were nothing but a french fry. Tom's tie was starting to bother him.

Virgil was obviously the Chief, "The Godfather" of the sideshow. He moved slowly, like a big lazy cat, defying death with swords that had cut all fear out of him. He commanded the audience to direct their attention to a cabinet covered with a glittery curtain.

"*Be* amazed by the woman with the body of a snake!"
A leathery looking pirate of a man glared at the cynical crowd from under a slap of black dyed hair. "Ladies and Gentlemen, I introduce to you Samora, the snake with the head of a woman that we captured for you in the rainforests of South America!" He grabbed the curtain, almost tearing the fragile cover with his claw-like hand. In the box were some plastic plants with the body of a big, toy snake wrapped around it. The fabric of the reptile was worn at the seams, revealing its polyester intestines. The snake's head, however, was that of a breath-takingly beautiful young girl, standing up behind the curtain, her body out of

120

view. Her skin was pale ivory, her hair an angel's gold cascading down in generous curls as a waterfall on the desolate plants. Her eyes were wide and innocent as they searched the audience. She fixed her gaze on Tom.

Is she looking at me? Tom looked away. The curtain fell. The audience was quiet, digesting the stunning beauty of that face in the middle of the smelly tent, filled with decay and deceit. Tom wondered if he would see her again: it must have been his imagination. He looked at his watch; he should be heading home soon and face the music. Another young lady appeared on the stage. She was pretty enough. Tottering around on scuffed, patent leather boots, Sheila explained the history of the sideshow: "Back in the days when people had no television, they came to the show to be entertained, to laugh, to have a good time. Some aspects of the show are just illusion and others are real acts performed by trained entertainers."

Tom thought the girl needed a good bath. Her thin bleached hair was plastered to her head. Brown patches peeked out from under her armpits. Skin softly bulged through a big hole in her fishnet stockings, right where her legs came together in a purple pair of booty shorts. Still her face was pleasant and calm. Her unshaved armpits disarmed Tom. As she babbled on, the young boar walked back on stage and took his shirt off. Firm white fat hung heavy over his belt. Silver studs decorated his pink nipples. He lay down on a bed of nails, his head and bottom supported by a greasy pillow. Undisturbed, he shot a grin at the audience, while Sheila sat down on top of him. She crossed her legs and re-positioned herself, casually checking her cuticles. The hole in her stockings tore further. Her skin touched fat. The nails dug in deeper into the young performer's back and into Tom's hands. With another flash of the armpit hair, Sheila disappeared. Tom removed his tie.

On the right side of the tent a curtain opened. First he saw her face--it was that girl. The pirate had called her Elnora. The promise of her face was fulfilled in her body. Long and slender, dressed in a black tutu that was gathered by a strapless corset, Elnora radiated a pale natural grace. She could not have been more than seventeen, her girlish chest rising softly above the tight brassiere. Her innocence and beauty transformed her whorish outfit into a garment of virtue. As the man scurried through another jungle story, her eyes sought out Tom again. There was no mistake about it.

Slowly, smoke began to fill the cage, caressing her ankles, creeping up her legs. Bright lights blinded Tom, condensing the smoke to an impenetrable layer, enveloping her lovely shape. Her eyes, however, seemed to burn through the smoke in a continued, desperate plea to him.

--Yvonne Gabriel

The Void

At least I got to go to summer camp–away from the village, in the south of the Netherlands that was considered farmland by most. This little town where I was born and raised had a Catholic Church firmly planted in the center. The weekly Sunday mass was the best attended event of the week–beautiful in the eyes of a tourist maybe, and paradise for me when I was a young child, but a source of endless boredom for the blossoming teenager, who had read too many books and knew better. The cows standing in the pasture with no other wish than to chew the grass and look at the world with a stupefied expression from behind the barbed wires filled me with despair. The milkman, who came every Monday, exasperated me, dousing my mother with his village gossip, emphasizing the fact we knew everybody and their cousins. High school was in a small city five miles away, but I was just a visitor there. I spent endless hours on my bicycle, going back and forth–the wind, the fields, the rain. There was no way for me to stay in the city; I lived in a village.

The teen camp close to Belgium brought together young folks from all over the country. Mauringh immediately caught my attention. Like a young, aristocratic prince, he stood in the middle of the grassy campground, quite out of place. He was very tall and thin, but graceful. His black wavy hair almost covered dark brown eyes that twinkled with intelligence and good humor about his present surroundings. He was ill-equipped for the outdoors, the wet muddy fields and crude walking paths penetrating the surrounding forests. His funky and fashionable but worn shoes protested the long hikes as did the rest of his urban wardrobe. Gradually, we found each other's company.

Mauringh was amused by my wide-eyed "countryness" and my ease with the elements and nature. I was too shy to say much in the presence of such refinement, which suited him fine because he talked nonstop about subjects that mostly went over my head, such as Dadaism and Jazz musicians. Despite his apparent intelligence he attended a school far below his abilities. He was rebellious, but knew he was going to have to conform after this summer. Mauringh gradually persuaded me to tell him about my life in the village and he listened, in disbelief and with a fascination I did not understand, to my little illustrations of the village, stories of my two sisters with whom I fought constantly, and of my uneducated, strict parents. Talking to him made me realize that his world was like another planet, unattainable.

After our summer camp was over we each returned–I, with much regret–to our vastly different lives. We wrote each other; his letters were always filled with stories of exciting concerts or fantastic parties. Mine usually consisted of drab reports about another Friday night spent at home on the couch. I was so happy to receive letters in the mail from "Mauringh Franssens, Ltd." I did not know what 'Ltd.' stood for but it looked so cool.

On Saturday evenings, my parents went to church, thank God, which gave me an hour of freedom on the phone–my lifeline to that other world. We would talk and sometimes he would play one of his own compositions on his saxophone for me or read one of his newest poems that I hardly ever understood, but gushed over profusely, determined not to betray my total ignorance about such matters.

I visited Mauringh once. I lied to my mother about

spending the night with my best friend and took the train to the big city, feeling like a criminal. His home was in the heart of historic Utrecht, full of abstract art, the walls covered with books. A psychologist, his mother looked at me critically; it was clear she did not share her son's enthusiasm for the country girl. I shrank under her sharp scrutinizing eyes; I felt she could look right through me. I did not blame her; I actually shared her opinion. I also met his girlfriend. Of course she was beautiful, although somewhat chubby. She smiled at me forgivingly.

In his room Mauringh had a party for his friends, who laughed at my solid Rockport shoes and snickered at my southern accent. They convinced me to smoke some pot, which almost choked me to death. They hung me out of the window, roaring with laughter. Mauringh presided over all like a permissive prince in his court, smiling benevolently, but his friends knew I was his protégé and they could only go so far. He put his arm around me and looked proud—completely genuine in his friendship towards me. He talked to me as comfortably as if I lived next door.

When his friends left, we looked at everything in his room: his abstract, somewhat gloomy paintings, his music collection and all sorts of oddities. His creativity was dazzling. I looked at his long, skinny nose while he talked; I had never seen a nose like that. I tried to make a copy in my mind of his vibrant eyes, framed with those unusual eyebrows. I memorized the movements of his long, slender hands, playing with that eternal cigarette. Everything about him was beautiful, ethereal, detached. I hugged him at the train station, breathing in the scent of patchouli and Gauloises that permeated everything he wore, knowing I would not see him again, because "we" had only existed, the acquaintance of our searching souls had only been possible on that neutral campground and the unseen space where the telephone wires meet--in a sort of no man's land, where our lives temporarily lost their claim on us.

My kids are at school and I'm trying to get some writing done for my college classes. I probably won't graduate until

I'm fifty, but I'm filling such a deep void. I am answering a voice that's been calling me throughout my years of working as a nurse and a flight attendant. I quickly check my email to see if my transcripts have made it yet from Holland. No, a Mr. Franssens apologizes for the delay. Mr. Franssens–I keep looking at that name. My mind is reaching back into history and slowly the wheels turn in motion. That was Mauringh's last name. From deep in the archives of my mind the image of Mauringh surfaces.

I haven't thought about Mauringh in ages and had actually forgotten about him. How old had we been? Maybe thirteen or fourteen? Thinking back, I realize that he already knew most of what I am now learning in college. I recognize some of the subjects and names he used to talk about, Tolstoy among them. I marvel at him all over again, realizing the poise and the sheer intelligence he had already possessed at that age. I am lost in time and remember the shy, blushing child I used to be. I smile at my small town naiveté and my reverence for Mauringh, who was for me the embodiment of potential realized--shining brightly in my memory, a beautiful memory.

I decided to google Mauringh. The last name brings up a "Jean-Paul":

"The art of living, theater, opera, composition. A flamboyant appearance, a bohemian with aristocratic characteristics." It sounds like Mauringh, but this must be his father perhaps. I switch to "images" and the nose takes my breath away. This has to be his father. I continue to read with fascination about this apparent genius and famous author. I had never heard of Jean-Paul Franssens and Mauringh had never told me. All I knew was that his parents were divorced and I did not dare ask about that--at the time, divorce was still a big taboo in the village. Still, I wonder why he had never told me anything about his father.

The author quotes Mulisch:

"This is the story of a man who was in love with life and art, and he tried passionately to unite these two, without wanting to compromise either one of them—until he himself became the arena of those two, lethally competing parasites."

I sense the truth of these words, but about the son . . . . I intentionally read slowly, restraining myself not to rush ahead:

"Finally he arrives at Franssens personal drama, that most likely connected to his later drift towards death: the psychosis and suicide of his oldest son Mauringh (1964-2002)."

No! No . . . . Please, God. No!

In shock, I stare at the screen. I am scared to read those words again, because then it will be true. Tears stream unbidden down my face. *No, not Mauringh, not my beautiful Mauringh, who knew everything at thirteen and was more of an apparition than an earthly human. How could this be? What had the world done to him?*

I know it's been hard. Life is hard. Once again I see him standing in that field. His shoes were not made for trudging the soil. His hands, useless for labor, were only made for creation. His tall, skinny limbs were almost beyond the grasp of gravity. Our world eats divinity alive. Rockport shoes are needed to keep us grounded, to help us to plow away–to get up every morning and lift our yoke, to take care of the mundane, to make money, to compete. A lower awareness serves us to tolerate these pointless occupations, our dirt, the mess we make.

As ignorant as I was at thirteen, I knew intuitively that it was a privilege to have been around Mauringh. Words fail me:

"Father and son embrace each other dancing, with the slow motion of swimmers in a giant wave. Jean Paul Franssens' last wish appears to be fulfilled. In an interview he had said: 'That boy is dead and I want to go as well. . . . We belong together'" (Van der Heijden). Vullings, J. (2008). Jean-Paul Franssens herdacht. In *Vrij Nederland*—a monthly Dutch magazine.

--Yvonne Gabriel

Espero a Esperanza

"Papi! Papi!"

I can still hear Esperanza's voice calling to me. Usually

I would hear it just before she launched herself at me. I think I was able to turn and catch her each time. It's true that she called every grown man who visited the orphanage in Huehuetenango "Papi."

Like the other children there, Esperanza was starved for attention, and attached herself to any and all comers. Still, I like to think that, for the three weeks I was there, Esperanza sought me out the most--even if it was mainly because she delighted in jumping at me from surprising directions, riding on my shoulders, and being turned upside down.

Esperanza's mother lived there in the orphanage, as well. She often gazed, unseeing, at whatever was in front of her, and she rarely spoke. The unspeakable horrors of her past (which were nevertheless learned and spoken of by the "service" group I was a part of, with much head shaking) seemed to be gripping her still, holding her captive.

Sometimes, though, it would be as if she had awakened. One afternoon, just before the daily late afternoon rain, she joined me in playing tag with Esperanza, their beautiful smiles mirrors of each other. The mother, perhaps not entirely freed from her past, still could not laugh along with her daughter. But Esperanza laughed enough for them both.

I sometimes wonder why Esperanza's mother named her that. The verb esperar sometimes means "to hope" and sometimes it means "to wait." When Esperanza's mother gazes, in silence, without focus, at the world in front of her, is she waiting for something? Can she, in the grip of her past, have hope?

It has been almost two years since I said goodbye to Esperanza. She was nine then. This summer, when I see her again, she will be eleven. She'll be less of a child, and more of a young woman. Her deafness, which hardly entered into our relationship at all when playing tag, will likely be more of an issue. I doubt she'll remember me, but I wait, impatiently, and with hope, to see her again.

--Tim Craker

The Cat That Lives by the Road

The engine strained against the cold. I rapidly rubbed my hands together to stay warm as I waited for the windshield to thaw. As little pieces of ice started to slide down the windshield, I peered out toward the drainage ditch at the end of my driveway. She was still there, peering out with big eyes like yellow saucers. She'd been out there now every morning for a few weeks, but I hadn't gotten a good look at her. She was wild and skittish, always running back into the ditch when approached.

My daughter, Megan, had been putting cat food out near the road for her but I'd given strict instruction not to name her because we couldn't take in another cat. When we talked about her, we referred to her as The Cat That Lives by the Road. I'd seen her scoot out of the garage on cold mornings and from what I could tell, she was a grey tabby. She was tiny but her large eyes indicated that she was a grown cat. I suspect that someone had put her out. I hoped that she would just be passing through.

Driving home one night in the pouring rain, I wondered about the little cat in the ditch. The windshield wipers slapped back and forth in a losing battle with the sheets of cold rain. The ditch would be flooded. I hoped The Cat That Lives by the Road had found a dry spot. Finally with a sigh of relief, I spotted my driveway. As I pulled into the garage and turned out the lights, I saw two yellow eyes peer out from a box of old clothes in the corner. The eyes sank deeper into the box when I opened the car door. As I walked toward the house, I looked back over my shoulder and saw her peering out over the top of the box. Her yellow eyes seemed suspended in the darkness as I pressed the button to close the garage door. I whispered secretively to her, "It's okay, girl. You're welcome to stay in the garage tonight, where you can keep warm and dry."

It rained throughout the night. The morning light revealed a layer of ice covering everything. The newscaster announced that the roads were hazardous and recommended that everyone stay indoors. I welcomed an excuse to stay bundled up

128

inside. I put on a pot of coffee and threw logs into the fireplace before settling into my chair. Over the noise of the TV and the coffee pot, I heard a faint cry from the garage. Oh, I bet The Cat That Lives by the Road is eager to get out. I pulled on my robe and went to open the garage door just enough to let her slide out. As I opened the door, I could see the top of her head in the box. She showed no inclination to leave her warm bed. I left the door open just enough for her to get out if she changed her mind.

With sleepy eyes and uncombed hair, Megan came into the living room and asked: "How's Libby?"

"Who?"

"Well, Mom, we can't very well keep calling her The Cat That Lives by the Road if she doesn't live by the road anymore. I'm going out to check on her."

"Now wait a minute. Just because I let her stay in the garage doesn't mean I've changed my mind. No more cats!"

I had already taken in three stray cats. It was easy for me to get overwhelmed with all the creatures that need homes. I decided that three was my limit. We just couldn't afford another animal. I heard Megan open the door and go into the garage. Within seconds she came back inside.

"Uhm, Mom. You need to come see this!"

"What is it Meg? Is Lib . . . Is she okay?"

"Yeah. she's 'okay,' but this is definitely a situation that requires your attention."

Great! A "situation." I was hoping to have a quiet day at home. I put on my slippers and followed Meg into the garage. The tiny little Cat That Lives by the Road was curled up in her box with three even tinier kittens. She licked their heads while they nursed. She stopped and looked up at me as if to say, "Please let us stay here for just a little while. I promise we won't take up much space."

With the arrival of the kittens, The Cat That Lives by the Road officially became "Libby"–and we became the owners of not one new cat, but four. When the weather cleared, we took Libby and her kittens to the vet for a checkup.

The vet asked me how old Libby was and whether the delivery had gone smoothly.

"Well, I'm not really sure. She wasn't officially our cat until the day she had the kittens. Why? Is something wrong?"

"She's an old girl. That's probably why she only had three kittens. She's undernourished and covered with fleas. I also think she's blind."

Blind! My stomach twisted with guilt and dread as I thought of all the cold nights Libby had spent in the drainage ditch. As I loaded Libby and her kittens back into the car, I promised her that she wouldn't have to sleep in the cold again. I wondered what kind of person would have put her out knowing she was pregnant and blind. Would she be able to take care of her kittens? How does a blind cat survive? The other cats would just have to deal with the changes. I couldn't turn her away now. Mere proximity had made her my responsibility.

When we got home, Libby was flea free and her coat was shiny for the first time. I was relieved that she preferred the garage to the house. It made things less complicated for me and for my other overindulged cats who had never known a day's inconvenience. Libby proved to be a good mother keeping her babies clean and well fed.

The next six weeks went by quickly, and I set out to find homes for the kittens. The little orange and gray kittens scurried around while Libby patiently waited in her new bed in the garage. It didn't take long to find homes for them. One by one they left for their new lives. Libby took it pretty well. I wondered if she was relieved or sad for them to go.

Libby seldom left the garage. In the spring she would venture out into the garden to lie in the sun. Over the next few years we fell into a routine. She had become a member of our family. Then one day I got a phone call at work. The man across the street had killed a coyote and Libby was nowhere to be found. It seemed like my worst fears had come true. She was blind and defenseless. I hated for her to die that way.

When I got home, we went out looking for Libby hoping to find her alive or to find her remains for a proper burial. As the sun started to go down, I told Megan we'd have to call it quits for the night. We were both teary and tired as we walked back toward home. My flashlight caught a glimpse of something yellow coming from underneath the cover of the drainage ditch at the end of our driveway. Libby had retreated to her former sanctuary out by the road–a place she felt safe. We scooped her up and took her inside. She lay in my lap as I scratched her head. Her eyes were dull and cloudy. She purred with contentment.

Spring gave way to the summer heat and the morning air was hot and sticky. Each morning when Libby greeted me, I'd sit down on the steps to spend a few minutes with her before going to work. One morning she seemed particularly friendly and I spent so much time with her that I was almost late for work. I hated to leave her, but there'd be more time when I came home.

When I got home from work Terry was standing in the driveway with Megan. I could tell something was wrong. "Libby's gone, Mom. We found her in the garden."

"Looks like she just went to sleep and didn't wake up, Honey."

I bent down to examine the little cat. She had always been so small and fragile. Terry had wrapped her in a towel and placed her in a small box. "What do you want me to do, Honey? Do you want me to take her out back and bury her?"

I kneeled down and put the top on the box. I told him that I'd like to bury her in the place that she thought of as a safe haven--out by the road. A large stone marks the spot today.

The Cat That Lives by the Road had taught me that there is always room for one more. She is the inspiration for my favorite quote, fittingly, a quote from Helen Keller:

> I am only one, but still I am one. I cannot do everything, but still I can do something; and because I cannot do everything, I will not refuse to do the something that I can do.

--Janet Allen Crocker

The Harvest

The department store was decorated with beautiful autumn colors for the beginning of the school year. Five-year-old Megan admired the bright colors as we made our way back to the children's section to shop for new clothes for kindergarten. While I looked through a rack of sweaters, she carefully examined a colorful row of rubber rain boots, lined up neatly with the toes right at her eye level. Mesmerized by their hues and their smooth, shiny surface, she walked slowly down the row gently squeezing the toes of every boot. The first pair was bright green, the second a jonquil yellow, the third pair sunset orange, and the last pair a brilliant fire-engine red. Finally reaching the red ones at the end of the row, Megan studiously considered them. Obviously having arrived at a conclusion, she reached over, tugged firmly at my shirt, and announced loudly: "Mommy, the red ones are ripe. We need to pick them and take them home."

--Janet Allen Crocker

Dividing Ditch

To say my Mom was overprotective is an understatement. She didn't let me out of her sight until I went to kindergarten—except for one warm summer afternoon, a month before my third birthday. I begged her to let me ride with my Dad down to my Pa Pa's house. My Dad talked her into letting me go, reassuring her that it was just right down the street and we wouldn't be gone long. Mom stood on the porch, wiping her hands on her apron as she watched us back out of the driveway.

As Daddy and Pa Pa worked on a car with their heads under the hood, I spied a grasshopper and began to follow it across the yard. I forgot about the grasshopper when I came upon a bridge that went over a small drainage ditch separating my grandparents' yard from their neighbor's. I reached up to hold on to the cool steel of the handrails as I walked out onto the bridge. Leaves and sticks in the ditch pushed the water into a twisted path that swirled off into the distance. It was a small alien world, brimming with activity. Fascinated by the water as it found its way around the obstacles and made its way down the ditch, I grabbed the rail with both hands and leaned out over the water to get a better look. My hands slipped and I fell headlong into the cement ditch.

After that point, all I know is information I've received from others. I had a huge gash on my forehead. I lay there unconscious and face down in the shallow water. By the time my Dad and Pa Pa realized that I was gone, I had been lying there long enough for the entire length of the ditch to be tinged with my blood. Sighting me, my dad scooped me up and administered CPR. He jumped into his car and drove to the hospital, with me draped over his shoulder. Speeding, he caught the attention of the police, who gave chase. But their vehicles weren't as fast as Dad's 1964 Sports Fury. He was getting out of the car at the hospital, before they pulled up behind him. Seeing that his clothes were covered in blood and a bleeding child in his arms, they rushed with us into the hospital. In the emergency room, Dad helped the nurses hold me down while the doctor sewed ten stitches in my head with no anesthesia.

I wasn't privy to the conversation my parents had that night, but the looks that Mom gave Dad through the years when someone asked about the scar on my forehead told the story. She never ever entrusted her little girl to him again.

--Janet Crocker

To Grandmother's House We Go

My grandfather took great pains to hide his "medicine" from my grandmother. My sister and I would see Granddaddy slip off behind the house and dig in the straw around Granny's rose bushes. He would retrieve his stash, take a hearty swig, and return the bottle to its hiding place. He never realized that we had followed him. We always wondered why his medicine was outside. We always went inside to take our medicine, and the fact that Granny personally gave it to us made us curious as to why Granddaddy would hide his in the rose garden. When we asked him about it, he told us that Granny didn't think he needed any medicine, but it sure made him feel better. Granddaddy could do no wrong in our eyes, so we had no problem keeping his secret.

Occasionally, Granny would spy him from inside the house and make a beeline to the roses. I remember hearing the screen door slam and the tone of her voice as she told him that he had better quit before he got himself into trouble: "Jim, you need to quit this mess. One of these days you're gonna get yourself into a fix that you can't get yourself out of, and you better not think I'm gonna bail you out." She would then take the bottle and empty the contents onto the ground, well away from the roses. I guess she didn't think they needed "medicine" either.

My husband's grandfather worked in the fields. At the end of a hot day, he liked to make the trek to Mr. Rainwater's to purchase homemade brew. The Rainwaters lived down a path through the woods near the grandparents' house. Like my grandmother, Brian's grandmother did not approve of her husband's drinking and one day tried to talk him out of his "visit." Not persuaded, he took off down the path to make his purchase. The precious elixir procured, he couldn't resist sampling a few swallows on the short journey home. He settled himself comfortably under a spreading oak, took several pulls from the bottle, and closed his eyes to enjoy a few quiet moments.

Back at the house, Grandmother had become worried and not a little angry. She set out to look for him. Coming up on the oak, she spied him passed out on the ground beneath the tree, clutching his bottle. Perturbed, Grandmother weighed her options, deciding it was high time to teach him a lesson.

Her task accomplished, Grandmother returned home to take up another round of her endless chores. Hearing a knock, she opened the door to find Mrs. Burgess, her neighbor from an adjacent farm. As the two settled down on the porch swing to attend to the latest gossip, they looked up to see Grandfather staggering toward the house. He climbed the steps, tipped his hat, bid them good day, and went inside. Mrs. Burgess, not wanting to embarrass Grandmother, didn't miss a beat in the conversation. However, she soon hastily retreated home.

Grandmother went inside and confronted Grandfather: "How could you embarrass me like that? Comin' home in that sinful condition and actin' the fool? Sashayin' around in front of my friend in your drawers!"

Grandfather quietly retorted, "You thought I was asleep under the tree when you took my britches, didn't ya? Ya thought you was gonna teach me a lesson. I guess I done showed you up. Miz Burgess is gonna have a story to tell 'bout how I came home wearin' nothin' but my boots, drawers, shirt and hat. Now go git me my britches, woman."

Without a word, Grandmother went into the bedroom, got Grandfather's pants, and obediently brought them to him.

--Barbara Sellers

I Can Handle This

He knew it was coming. But he didn't want to know. Or maybe he just did not want to believe it. He sat with his brother in the living room of his father's house. The room was different: new floors, furniture, and decorations, not what had been there when he was a child. The changes, however, did not make the memories any less distant. The central part of the room, the massive rock fireplace that had emitted so much warmth, was still there. *Mom loves that fireplace.* As soon as the temperature lowered to fifty degrees in the fall, she would start begging Dad to make a fire. He stared at the television.

That room had witnessed countless hours of movie watching, game-day parties, Christmas mornings, and indoor roughhousing. *How many of Mom's porcelain decorations and pictures had we broken playing indoor football?* Some of her precious treasures were still on display, glued together in a desperate attempt to salvage them. His older brother, a law student, was sprawled across the couch on the other side of the room. They had sat there that same way a thousand times before, staring vacantly at the television.

Everyone else was milling around in the kitchen, making nervous conversation. It kept their minds off the pesent situation. He and his brother chose the TV as their companion–it seemed easier than trying to carry on fake conversations. *This whole situation was so messed up.*

"Jerry! Jerry!" She was yelling for his father, her son. "Jerry, she's gone. Oh God, she is gone!" She disappeared into the hallway. He didn't even realize that he had jumped up from the couch. He looked across the room and saw that his brother had done the same. They looked at each other with expressionless faces. His dad sprinted from one of the back bedrooms through the living room in the direction that his grandmother had come from. His brother followed his father. He slowly walked behind. He stepped into the kitchen, where several people were standing–apparent shock on their faces.

Everyone is stunned by something we all knew was going to happen. Why? He stopped for a moment, turned, and saw his grandmother, shoulders slumped and tears streaming down her face. She had just watched a woman 20 years her younger take her last breath. She reminded him of a little girl who had lost her parents in a crowd of strangers and needed comfort. He wrapped his arms around her. She began sobbing and crying out. Over and over again, he told her that he loved her. He had no tears. He would cry later, when he was by himself.

It was his mother who had died, but he had to be strong. *I can handle this better than anyone else. This is why I'm here. Not to show the pain that is eating me up inside–so everyone else can be okay.*

--Zach Wells

A Call to My Mother on Her Birthday

My Mom should be turning 55 years old today. She's not, and I've been sitting here wondering what today would be like if she were still here. I would have given her a phone call first thing this morning to wish her "Happy Birthday." I would then ask her how she is doing and we would spend the next twenty minutes talking about me, because she craved information about her children. She would hit me with a slew of seemingly innocent questions: Have you met anyone? Are you going to church? How are your knees? Do you have any REALLY good friends? Are you happy with where you are and with what you are doing?

I would answer all of her questions, probably divulging more information than I should. When I tell her that I don't have a girlfriend, she will worry that I haven't met anyone "special," but tell me that God has a purpose for everything. When I tell her that I go to church sometimes, she would tell me that I need to be more consistent, and to get involved in a Bible study, because only God can bring peace to my heart--and that's also where I should meet a girl. I would tell her that my knees are fine, and she will tell me with absolute honesty that I am the greatest athlete in the whole world, and she wishes she could see me play intramurals. When I tell her that there are a few guys I hang out with, she would tell me that the people I choose as my best friends will have a lasting effect on my life, and that I should be careful: "Dare to be a Daniel, dare to stand alone, dare to have a purpose, dare to make it known," she would tell me for the millionth time.

I would tell her that I am happy, but she would be able to hear the slightest discontent in my voice; she would encourage me to run the race that is set before me, and trust that I am in God's will. She would say something like, "You know that I love you, Zach. God has a great plan for your life, you have so much talent and God is going to show you how to use it. I am so proud of you. You are precious."

I would tell her that I love her--that I miss her. I would say not to feel any pressure, but a care package, with some hot chocolate mix, and whatever else she could come up with, would be nice. I would tell her to have the best day ever, and that I wish I could be with her, not considering the fact that she could ever not be there for me . . .

--Zach Wells

A HIGHER POWER

Our Eyes Look to the East

We listen today. Our eyes look to the East and our ears listen. We listen for the silence that tells us no more lives will end and that no more of our children and their children will be buried today. Our eyes look to the East.

We cry today. We cry as families bear the burden of heavy hearts and loss. Spirits have been broken; lives have changed forever more. Our eyes look to the East.

We blame today. We blame those in high places for decisions not well planned. We sigh with disappointment, grief, and sorrow. Our eyes look to the East.

We wait today. We wait for miracles, which can only come from God. We wait on bended knees and with bowed heads. We pray without ceasing.

It is today we understand we have been looking in the wrong direction. It is today we turn our eyes from the East. Our eyes look to heaven.

--Gloria Jordan

Robin's-Egg Blue

In the last years of her life, Ellen Jamison decided that miracles probably happen in the lives of many people. The secret, she concluded, was finally to recognize a miracle even if you did not see it at the time. Her miracle was a tiny blue robin's egg that touched her heart in a place known only to her.

John and Ellen had been married twenty-eight years the spring she found her egg. Their four children were away at college or out working at their first jobs. Both of the girls were at the university, phoning her daily to dump their latest crises on her. Ellen would hang up with a knot in her stomach and sometimes a tear in her eye—only to learn the next day that the problem was no longer on anybody's mind but hers.

She had just hung up the phone after hearing the news of Allison's "no date to the dance" crisis. She stood at the kitchen window peering through the shutters at the bare branches of the crepe myrtle bush whose crooked limbs brushed against the window. Ellen found herself saying a little prayer for patience, though at this stage of her life prayer was just a habit. Her prayers seemed like a big rock dropping with a thud into a dark well—a well without water.

While she gazed out at nothing, thinking again about Allison's disappointment, a robin sailed into view and carefully laid a sturdy twig across the V where the branches of the crepe myrtle came together. Ellen laughed at the optimism surrounding the first-laid twig, but the twig held and every other twig the robin and her mate brought stayed in place. A tiny cradle formed in the V. The robins lined the nest with wisps of paper and straw. Ellen moved the kitchen step stool to a permanent spot by the window, allowing her to see down into the nest to watch for eggs. Four eggs were laid. "Miss Nan Robin"—Ellen always named everything—began her warm vigil, nestled low on the straw with only the top of her head showing.

After the first week, Ellen had almost forgotten about the nest. She had left town to visit her mother in Alabama, not returning home for two weeks. Climbing up on a stool to look inside the nest, she saw that three of the eggs had hatched. The chicks and Miss Nan Robin had flown away, abandoning a fourth egg unhatched in the nest. Ellen decided she would get the ladder out on Saturday morning and rescue the solitary egg.

Friday night a big rain and windstorm raged outside the

Jamison house. Saturday morning Ellen found the little nest empty. She ran into the wet and muddy yard, searching the ground for the tiny egg, finally spotting it caught in the hedge next to the patio wall. She gently cradled the tiny egg in her hand, staring at it—lost in the tiny sea of blue.

When her girls had been in scouts, they had learned to blow out eggs to decorate them for Easter. Ellen decided to preserve her egg. The little oval box she had bought at the drugstore after Easter for 75% off would be the perfect place for her blue egg. She carefully lined the box with cotton, tenderly laid her robin's egg on it, and hid the box in the back corner of her nightstand.

The egg became her touchstone from that day forward. When she was worried, sad, or just discouraged, she would take out her tiny egg and drop herself into that heavenly blue. No longer did her prayers seem to thud into that dry well—they meshed into the blue with her. Ellen could never have explained to anyone why the blue egg was a miracle to her. She never really knew the answer—it just was. Over the next thirty-four years it kept her silent company, especially through John's long illness and death when he was only 63, leaving her alone in that big king size bed with all the covers to herself—leaving her alone to finish what they had started.

On her 80th birthday, Ellen moved to the Covenant Retirement and Nursing Center, taking a nice single room in the section for residents who could still get around—"independent living" they called it. She loved the view from her window. In the distance a small lake twinkled and glistened in the sunlight on pretty days. Trees ringed the lake, and residents could walk on a little path around the lake if they were able. There were benches under some of the trees for visiting, but residents mostly kept to themselves at Covenant, except for meals. Everyone was required to eat in the dining room at least once a day. Some claimed that was how the staff kept up with whether the residents were still alive or not.

Ellen amused herself on those solitary walks, picking out

some part of her life like a smooth stone on the lake's edge, turning it over and over in her mind as she made her way along the path. One afternoon she decided to take a long look at her marriage of forty-one years to John Cain. It did not seem possible, but thoughts on her marriage ended at the second bench, halfway around the lake.

How could that be? she mused. How could marriage to a fine man like John not fill up the whole walk? She had known him since high school and married him as soon as she finished college. They worked well together, had a good family, and got along just fine. But what she thought would come of living intimately with a man all those years—some extension of her soul beyond herself–just never happened. Whatever the reason, what had been between them wasn't enough to fill Monday's walk.

On a warm Wednesday after lunch, Ellen walked the path, picking up another stone from the shore of her memory bank—her children, Mark, David, Elizabeth, and Anna. The girls had turned out better, she thought, shielding her eyes from the gleam of the lake. They had finally sorted through their problems, she guessed, with no help at all from her. That was one good thing about getting old. You could take that stone, motherhood, skip it across the lake, and watch it sink beneath the cold water. It had felt good to be a mother—nature had seen to that, but it had been nice to let it go, too. Other parts of her life Ellen had dismissed from her mind by the time she noticed Alice Jackson resting on the bench beneath the weeping willow. What had it all meant? she wondered, as she sat down with Alice.

On that Friday Ellen had a stroke. The head nurse told the family that she might recover, but after two weeks of therapy, they moved her to the nursing center. With a loss of movement on her left side, she could only lie in bed or be strapped into her wheelchair.

Though her thoughts were wonderfully clear, not a word could she speak. So this is it, she mused in bed—the last stone to pick up, turn over, and toss away, the end of her life. She had imagined she would be sad and maybe scared, but she was not.

She lay there wondering if there was some part of her life that she needed to think about that had not been covered in her walks around the lake. She had held each stone that made up the pile of her life and none had seemed to weigh what they should.

About 4:00 Ellen managed to get the little oval box out of the bedside drawer and cradled her blue egg in her one good hand. She held it up to the bed lamp, gazing into the beautiful blue. She imagined she saw the blue of her first-born's eyes, the blue of her prize-winning morning glories, even the blue of John's first car. The egg seemed so heavy tonight, so full, and so very blue that Ellen could not hold it any longer. She dropped it into its cotton nest and managed to shove it into the drawer.

She dozed with her eyes closed, but the darkness behind her lids still seemed tinged with the blue of her robin's egg, that wonderful blue she had loved all of these years. Ellen thought she must be dreaming, for just at that moment, her long ago robin, "Miss Nan," swooped down toward the dot of blue in her darkness, snatched it in her beak and flew off into the sky, a bright robin egg blue sky.

When Janie Sewell came on duty at 7:00, the day nurse, Betty, passed on the news that Ellen Jamison had died at 4:30 p.m. "Wilson's has already picked her up," she reported, "but you need to pack up her room. Sacks and boxes are in the supply closet."

Janie checked in and began straightening the desk, putting off cleaning out Mrs. Jamison's room. That was just part of working in a nursing home, but Janie always felt uncomfortable looking through people's things. I'll clean out the closet first and then the chest of drawers, she decided. At the back of the closet was a pretty, brown velvet coat. Janie tried to imagine Mrs. Jamison in that coat. Behind the coat hung a faded lace-trimmed satin gown and matching robe. That must have been worn to impress some man in Mrs. Jamison's life. Two boxes held all of Mrs. Jamison's possessions. Janie was soon finished.

Janie thought about Mrs. Jamison. She had really liked her a lot. Even though she had had a stroke, Mrs. Jamison had a nice gentle way still showing in her soft brown eyes. Her right hand had withered, but she could still pat you with her good hand when you fed her or held the straw to her good side for a sip of water. Janie looked out the window, reflecting on how pretty and soft Ellen Jamison's skin had been for an old lady.

Opening the drawer of the bedside table, Janie found it empty except for a small oval paper box covered with pictures. She opened the box and gave a little cry of surprise. Inside was a tiny bird's egg, bright blue, lying in a white cotton ball nest. She had seen Mrs. Jamison clutching the box to her chest with her good hand, but she had never even wondered what was in it. When a patient can't talk, you just don't ask a lot of questions. The little oval box made Janie laugh. She just had to sit down on the stripped bed and look at it for a while. A big brown rabbit covered most of the top. Around her neck was a flowered necklace. The rabbit was covered with little children jumping off her head and sliding down her paws. A Mother Hubbard rabbit—patient and resigned, Janie thought.

Someone called to tell Janie that she had a phone call, breaking into her reverie. She slipped the little box into her pocket and hurried off. When she returned to Mrs. Jamison's room, she was crying. Her daughter had called to tell her how mean the ex-husband had been to her when he brought the children back from their monthly visit. Janie decided to go outside and sit on the bench under the oak tree until she felt better. She reached into her pocket and pulled out the little box, took out the robin's egg, and held it up towards the setting sun. It was such a beautiful color of blue. Janie began to stroke the little egg with her fingertips. She started to feel much better. Somehow she knew that Mrs. Jamison would not mind that she kept the robin's egg. She would take it home and keep it on her closet shelf. She would not show it to anyone. It would be her secret.

--Rosemary McKelvey

Angel on Loan

We pulled into the parking lot and found a place to unload the bike. My husband, Damon, jumped out of the car and came around to offer to help me, but I waved him off. I knew it would take me a while, and I didn't want to be rushed. He went to the back of the car and tugged at the bike rack. I heard his bike tires hit the sand on the pavement. He sat down on the curb and started to put on his cleats. Eight months pregnant, I struggled to get out of the car—first bracing myself and then pulling on the top of the car door. A bicycle race in the heat of the summer would make for a long day.

We drove for three hours on two-lane roads through farming areas and small towns to reach our destination in a rural area outside of Athens, Georgia. Hundreds of cyclists were gathered for a large race that would last half of the day. Finding a shady spot under a large tree, I unfolded my chair. I had a bag of books and I planned to read most of them that day. I kissed Damon as he left to join the pack of bikers starting to line up for the beginning of the race. I tried to get comfortable, rubbing my stomach to comfort my squirmy, unborn daughter, Megan. I explained that it would be a while before her dad came back and she needed to settle down.

Almost an hour into the race, I lowered my sunglasses to watch the other spectators milling around. Something was going on. They were hurriedly packing their cars and scrambling to leave. I watched as an older man in bicycle shorts carried a mangled bicycle toward me. As he got closer I recognized Damon's bike. I pushed with both arms to stand up to meet him.

"Are you Damon Allen's wife? About twenty cyclists went down on a curve. A dozen or more are on their way to St. Mary's hospital in Athens with road burn and broken bones. They think Damon has a broken leg. Let me help you load the bike in your car and I'll give you directions to the hospital."

He strapped the parts of the bike that were still intact onto the back of the car and stuffed the rest into the back seat.

My mind was racing as he gave me directions to the hospital.

"Highway what? Turn where?" I wasn't familiar with the area and his directions weren't making sense to me. The hospital was about an hour and a half away so I should hurry. Leaving me standing beside the car, he went to help another family. Cars began to stream out of the field from every exit. As I opened the car door, it occurred to me that we had driven up in Damon's car–a straight shift–and I didn't know how to drive it. Now was NOT the time to learn.

My legs started to shake and my heart began pounding in my ears. I felt like I was going to pass out. Overwhelmed, I couldn't think straight. I didn't know how I'd ever find the hospital. I could feel panic overtaking me. The doctor had said I could travel if I'd be careful and take care of myself. I held my protruding stomach: "Don't worry, Megan. We're gonna be alright. Everything will be fine." I tried to reassure myself through the mounting panic. Taking deep breaths, I tried to gather my thoughts. Tears came to my eyes and began to stream down my face. I wondered if I should try to get someone's attention and just leave the car there. I saw someone approaching and turned around to see a beautiful young blonde girl standing beside me.

"Hi, my name is Megan. My parents are on their way to the hospital. I was wondering if you needed some help."

I broke down crying, relieved that someone was offering help. I explained the circumstances to her. She kindly handed me a tissue and helped me into the passenger seat, explaining that she was only 15 years old but her birthday was only a month away, on July 25th. Her dad had taught her to drive a straight shift. One of the wounded cyclists, he was on his way to the hospital as well. Her voice was soothing as she reassured me that she was a good driver and knew exactly where she was going. She made small talk and smiled when I told her my due date was mid July. Before I knew it we were at the hospital.

She whipped the car into a parking space near the hospital entrance. As I reached out to take the keys, she looked at me with the serenity of an angel. Holding both of my hands, she crooned: "Don't worry. He's okay. His leg is not broken. Everything is going to be alright."

About that time, several nuns, observing that I was in the last trimester of my pregnancy, swarmed me excitedly, bringing me into the hospital. When I looked back to thank Megan, she had already disappeared. The nuns realized that I wasn't in labor but put me in a wheelchair anyway. They pushed me down to where Damon was lying on a gurney having his wounds treated. He reached out, grabbed my hand, and explained: "My leg's not broken, honey. I've just got really bad road burn. I was so relieved when the attendant in the ambulance told me that you were on your way to the hospital. Her name was Megan. She was blonde and blue-eyed–just like our little girl will be!"

Damon was able to drive back to Macon and, as we settled back into our routine, I often thought of the young woman who was so kind to me at such a difficult time. Eerily, my daughter, Megan, was born late on July 25th.

I've thought back to that day many times. Her name was Megan; her birthday was July 25th. Why would a 15-year-old girl's parents let her volunteer to drive a woman she didn't know to the hospital? Where was her mother? Her father was hurt and on his way to the hospital. He had taught her to drive a straight shift. How did she know Damon's leg wasn't broken? How did the attendant in the ambulance know that I was on my way to the hospital? How could it be that the attendant in the ambulance and the young woman who helped me were both named Megan and had blonde hair and blue eyes?

--Janet Crocker

Vigil of Hope

The wide porch allowed a view far down the empty, painfully quiet road as another day inched steadily toward evening. The road would soon be dark, except for one spot where the streetlight shone every night, all night, until sunrise renewed the father's hope. Years passed, and he continued to close every day with the same ritual. Perched pensively on the weathered rocker, without rocking, he strained for movement down that road, refusing to wring his hands in despair. He also refused to close the door and just get on with life. His heart steadfastly held the middle of that road—empty, but filled with grace and possibility.

As the father waited for the sun to set, that stinging day of severance floated once again into his quiet heart. There was the son, insistent, impatient, ready for the road, his bags packed with stifled dreams. Through with the father's suffocating boundaries, the son opened his hand and stretched it demandingly toward the father. Life had passed him by for far too long. With tears, the father placed a leather bag into the son's hand. After an awkward goodbye, the son walked down the road to freedom. The father knew how heavy the chains of that freedom would be. He knew it with agony, with a heart that broke a little more with each skip in the son's carefree escape. He knew that day what was coming for the oblivious, elated son. He knew it still, sitting on the porch, with lingering anguish and mercy. The father loved the absent, squandering son, even if the son no longer knew it.

The father directed his concentration on the road where the streetlight illuminated quietly, eerily. This could be the day of reunion and grace. But if not, the vigil of hope would continue. This lost, dead son would return to the land of the living, or the father would watch the road forever. Not too far away, the growing evening orchestra of crickets and frogs was joined by the low, contented bellow of a well-fed calf.

--Terri DeFoor

Full Consent of the Will

To be a Catholic in a small Mississippi Delta town when I was a child was tantamount to heresy. Greenwood, Mississippi was firmly entrenched in the southern "Bible Belt." Being

Catholic was only a little better than being a Jew, and there were not many of those in town. Blessedly for the Catholic children, we had not the slightest inkling of this fact. It was only in the summer when the missionary nuns arrived in Greenwood to instruct the Catholic children for a concentrated two-week church school that I felt different from the Baptists, whose church was across the street.

The town just never could absorb the appearance of the black-habited nuns when they arrived each July. People would fall off the curb staring at them when they walked to town to buy school supplies at the dime store. The poor clerks in Woolworth's could hardly ring up their purchases.

The summer I was seven, the nuns came to instruct our Sunday School class in preparation for our first confession. I had dreaded this time the entire winter for I was convinced that I had committed a terrible sin the previous summer. I had sat on the steps across the street at Milly Wadlington's house and listened to a joke the boy next door was telling her. It was about a little boy who had begged his mother for a ride on the bus. She had refused because she did not have money for another fare. He promised he would hide in her underpants if she would take him. I had laughed along with Milly as he told the joke, but I knew I should not have listened.

The nun who was our teacher began to teach us how to examine our consciences in preparation for confession. Sister Anne explained the difference between a venial sin and a mortal sin: "A venial sin is a small sin, such as being disrespectful to a parent. For a sin to be considered a mortal sin, there are three points to consider. One, it must be a grievous offence against the laws of God. Two, there must be sufficient reflection. Three, there must be full consent of the will."

I comprehended the part about a grievous offence as well as a seven-year-old could. I had to skip over sufficient reflection, but I understood full consent of the will completely. I knew I was guilty. I had laughed and laughed at that bad joke. That I knew constituted full consent of my will.

I did not sleep well for the next two weeks. Every night I knelt beside my bed and prayed for an answer. If I confessed that I had listened to the bad joke, I wondered what I would do if the priest asked me what the joke was about. I decided then and there not to confess the sin at all. I cried myself to sleep.

"What is the penalty for concealing a mortal sin in confession, Maureen?" Sister Anne asked in class the very next morning. I held my breath as I waited for the answer.

"I don't know, Sister. What will happen to you?" Maureen asked in her careless, confident way.

"It would be another mortal sin to conceal a mortal sin in the confessional," Sister Anne replied.

When I heard the penalty for concealing my terrible sin, I was certain I could not do that either. That night I again knelt beside my bed and tried to find a way to confess the sin without mentioning the bad joke itself. I finally decided to confess that I had committed a sin of impurity. Maybe, just maybe, that would be enough and the priest would not ask me anything else.

All dreaded days finally arrive. Saturday afternoon from three until five had been set aside for those making their first confession. My family lived within walking distance of our church. I left home at 2:45, finally reaching the church at 4:15. I practiced confessing to an oak tree, mumbled my sin of impurity into the pink fluff of a crepe myrtle, and whispered my offence down the culvert as I lingered at the curb on Church Street. The town clock struck 4:30 as I entered the church. No one was in line in front of the confessional. I held my breath, parted the curtains, and knelt down, peering through the screen at the profile of old Father Clerico.

"Yes, my child," the priest said softly.

"I forget to say my morning prayers, Father. I forget at least three days a week."

I could see the old priest's head nod as I carefully re-counted each little fault I thought could be a sin. I went on as long as I could, but finally knew I had to tell my terrible sin. "I listened to a bad joke, Father," I barely whispered. My heart

152

seemed to stop beating as I waited for his questions.

"Is that all, my child?" he probed.

"What?" I whispered.

"Is that all of your sins?" he asked.

"Oh yes, Father, yes," I sighed.

"Make a good act of contrition and for your penance pray three Our Fathers and three Hail Marys," Father intoned as I slipped out of the booth.

After praying my penance, I floated out of the church as if I had angel wings. I jumped and shouted for joy all the way home. I was forgiven and would sin no more. It was the sort of thing a little Catholic girl could be certain was possible when she was only seven.

--Rosemary McKelvey

Good Christian Folk

Every Sunday my mother took me to church, where I was taught that the beliefs of our church were the only true beliefs and that people from other religions were separated from God, needing to be gathered like sheep back into the fold. The church services were emotionally charged television productions. Even after the cameras were off, the minister, gripping the pulpit and with beads of sweat forming on his forehead, would plead for members of the congregation to come forward and turn their lives over to Jesus. Waiting for some congregant to muster the courage to step forward, we sang the hymn, "Just as I Am," over and over again. One Sunday, I took the plunge, never sure whether I truly felt moved by God or if I just wanted to silence the minister's plea.

As I grew older, I noticed that people gathered in small groups and talked about one another. They discussed what they had and what they had done. Ladies compared recipes and talked about their housekeepers as if they were pets. They gossiped about the sins of others and recoiled in disbelief with their hands over their mouths at the mention of a divorce or an unwed mother—yet always eager to hear all of the titillating details. I had managed to avoid most of the gossip during my childhood, but during my adolescence I realized that I could no longer escape it. I overheard girls in my Sunday school class evaluating what I was wearing. Apparently I had chanced to wear the same dress two Sundays in a row–they couldn't believe that anyone could make such a gross social error.

Gradually, I came to see church as a social club masquerading as a worship gathering. The message of God's love stood in direct contrast to the behavior displayed by the majority of the people at the church. They wielded religion like a weapon used to pelt others who didn't measure up. Shame and intimidation were integral parts of the system used to manipulate and punish others. Instead of loving and accepting misguided Christians, these backsliders were condemned and marginalized. Rather than bringing these people closer to God, the church hindered their development of a meaningful relationship with God.

Wanting to provide the best for me, my mother sacrificed to send me to a private "Christian" school when I was 12 years old. The school shared the same doctrine as our church. Later I learned that the school had been built specifically to cater to the "white flight" of the middle class during the early years of integration. Their criteria were very clear: Good God-fearing Christians followed their rules without question; those who didn't were heathens, condemned to have their flesh devoured by demons. Their distorted beliefs co-opted the Word of God as a tool of discrimination and oppression.

In Bible classes I listened to the teacher explain why the races were not intended to mix and stress the importance of keeping ourselves pure. Their primary mantra seemed to be: "Do not question." Their narrow-minded belief system included a strict adherence to a negative set of rules: Don't wear dresses more than an inch above the knee. Don't wear makeup or jewelry. Don't listen to rock music. Any failure to adhere to these rules was met with violent corporal punishment, righteously

154

judged to be within the will of God.

By the time I was fifteen, the oppression had become more difficult for me to bear. We were like sheep being kept in seclusion. The church leaders viewed worldliness as the ultimate sin. Approaching sixteen, I wanted to wear makeup—just a little mascara to cover my blond eye lashes. Before getting on the school bus one morning, I applied a light layer of brown mascara just to the ends of my lashes. When we arrived at school, one of my peers ran straight to the principal's office to report me.

The principal and a female teacher subsequently dragged me to the bathroom and scrubbed my eyes with paper towels and soap, damaging my cornea and causing black circles to form under my eyes. My pleas of pain were met with more criticism for the vanity and worldliness I had exhibited by wearing contact lenses. They were convinced I was consumed with lust and wanted to wear makeup to entice young men, citing my boyfriend David as evidence. For them it was unnatural for a 15-year-old to be interested in a boy. I hated the school, but my mother forced me to stay.

One cool October afternoon as I was walking with my other classmates to the bus, without any warning I passed out and fell to the ground. As I slowly regained consciousness, my classmates gathered around me in a circle looking at me in horror. They reported that I'd said something about being on fire, implying that I must have seen the gates of hell. Weary of their attempts to fill me with the fear of God, I didn't pay them much attention. I was eager to tell David about the strange happening.

When I got home, my mother was on the phone. I could tell something had gone terribly wrong: "Jan, sit down, honey. I have something to tell you that's difficult to hear. There has been a terrible accident. David was killed in an explosion. He was burned badly by the blast and died at 3:15 this afternoon."

I felt like I was on a swing that had been tightly twisted and released. Images and emotions swirled around me until I was dizzy: Died instantly from an explosion? How did that happen? David would have been at his after-school job at a warehouse. My mother was explaining that David and a friend had been playing with a blank pistol near a drum that had remnants of diesel oil in the bottom. A spark from the pistol ignited the drum and caused an explosion, killing David and burning his friend. The police said that it was a freak accident that would probably never happen again in a thousand years.

Sick to my stomach, I locked myself in the bathroom in an effort to protect myself from the tornado raging around me. I curled up on the cool bathroom tile and pulled my knees to my chest praying that this was just a terrible dream. I struggled with the information I'd been given: Dead. Explosion. Freak accident. Burned. Never again in a thousand years.

My mom's voice sounded as if it were coming in through a long tunnel, the echoes of her voice drowned out by the loud chaotic thoughts in my head. Eventually I heard my best friend, Karen, talking quietly outside of the door, gently coaxing me to come out. I finally reached up and unhooked the door; she sat down on the floor, held me, and rocked me back and forth.

The days that followed blurred together. David's family allowed me to ride in the family car in the funeral procession. There were flowers and crowds of people. I was on automatic pilot, smiling and nodding at the right times.

There were so many questions vying for answers. Why had I passed out when David had died? Was he trying to tell me something? Was that possible? It was just too weird to be a coincidence.

It took me fourteen days to pull myself together enough to return to school. At the bus stop, I didn't wait in the car with my mom, preferring instead to face the blistering wind. When the bus stopped and the doors swung open, my feet felt like they were made of lead as I took my first step back into reality. The chatter on the bus stopped abruptly and kids scattered to avoid sitting near me. I stared at the floor all the way to school, knowing that it would take a while for things to settle down.

A professor and the school counselor were waiting for

me when we pulled onto campus. They escorted me directly to the headmaster, who demanded to know more about my experience of being on fire. He was convinced that Satan had finally overtaken me, dooming me to hell if I didn't own up to my sins and ask for forgiveness. I was given the choice of confessing my sins in front of my class or being expelled from school.

I chose expulsion. Still struggling to work through what had happened, I didn't need to have the experience scrutinized by people who saw Satan's hand in everything. I was escorted to a holding room outside of the principal's office to wait for my mother to pick me up. The headmaster and the professors openly discussed my "possession by Satan" and their eagerness to get me off of the campus.

I was fifteen, adrift and confused--confused by what had happened. I knew I wasn't possessed by Satan. I also knew that I wanted no part of God or of Christianity as manifest in that school and church. Eleven years passed before I could trust again. The day my daughter was born, I knew that my wilderness was over. I had felt the presence of God and I knew it.

--Janet Crocker

The Holdout

The fat lady wedged herself into the end of the pew, her knees so tight against the back that nothing could pass between them. Julie wondered if she would be able to extricate herself at the end of the service. She didn't recognize the fat lady--maybe she was from another church and had come out especially for the revival. Why did she have to sit on their row? There were plenty more seats where she could sit with people her own age.

All of eleven years old, Julie had led the group of kids into the pew. Too late, she had realized that she was stuck. Her end of the pew sat smack dab against the wall. The first in, Julie would have to be the last out. The spirited singing took her mind off the fat lady for a little while. She knew she would have to hunker down for the service. Southern Baptists didn't have a set liturgy like the Catholics, so those spontaneous prayers could ramble on forever. She memorized again the movements of some of the deacons who almost genuflected as they grabbed for words for the offertory prayer with their hands crossed behind their backs and opened upwards toward the congregation. She grinned to herself remembering how Mama couldn't help laughing out loud when she had performed that deacon imitation for the family. There would be no bathroom breaks tonight.

Julie passed notes to her buddies and circulated a crude drawing of the fat lady with her boobs lying like giant turtle eggs on a mammoth beach ball. When they all snickered audibly, the fat lady glared at them with rank disapproval from her station at the end of the pew. Try as he might, the visiting evangelist couldn't match the appeal of the born-again rapist who had preached the last revival. The youth group had listened spellbound as the rapist-evangelist had graphically recounted with a little too much ardor the sinful things he had done before God had redeemed him. Instead of moving her to make an early profession of faith, the evangelist had convinced Julie to get in some of the "fun" things in life before settling down to make a lifelong commitment to being good. There was definitely something to be said for delaying conversion—she would just have to be careful not to die and risk going to the devil.

The Catholic plan was beginning to look more and more attractive: do it anyway and go to confession—at least that's how the Catholic convert had once described it. Catholicism was so wonderfully mysterious and magical--the forbidden fruit for Baptists. Some of the Catholic kids got to carry burning candles down the aisle. Julie herself would have preferred swinging the pots of incense. She did wonder why the priest couldn't hold his own Bible. As she imagined breathing in the clouds of incense, she gratefully heard the stirring strains of the invitation hymn begin.

It didn't matter how many verses there were to the hymn—the congregation sang them all through two or three

158

times, while the pastor pleaded for decisions to be made. Before the last go 'round, the pastor had the people bow their heads and entreated them to get right with God. The pianist played the invitation softly in the background, the left hand hitting the keyboard slightly before the right, creating a kind of rhythmic tug of war. Sometimes the unsaved children felt a hand on their backs as devout members urged them to go forward, give the pastor their hand, and God their heart.

Julie savored the whispered prayers of Mrs. Newton, the only charismatic in the congregation, and tried hard in her secret hideout in the woods to recapture Mrs. Newton's fervent and ecstatic utterances. As she leaned forward to catch Mrs. Newton's words, Julie was relieved to hear the pastor go into the final phase of the call to repentance. If all else failed, he would ask those with prayer requests to lift their hands, assuring them that no one was looking but the pastor and God. In a private hymn competition, Julie kept a running total of the number of raised hands in the margins of her Bible along with the titles of the invitation hymns. "Just As I Am" was currently in the lead. There was a lot of pressure to walk the aisles and join the church, or at least for the members to go forward to rededicate their lives. Baptist churches competed with each other in the number of professions of faith, baptisms, and rededications.

Julie was a holdout. Most of her buddies had succumbed to the pressure for repentance at an early age and had already been baptized, some as young as four and five. She tried hard to be good, but it just didn't come natural. More than one Sunday School teacher had quit when she was promoted to her class. Her usually tolerant mother had even spanked her hard when at the age of five she had dramatically called out to God to show himself to the Sunday school class—even leading the other children in a search for God—opening the broom closet and the doors to the cabinets to see if God was hiding there. Maybe God was under the table? If they were going to bow their heads and talk to God, Julie explained that they needed to know where God was. She didn't understand what the big fuss was all about. Her

159

questions usually elicited from adults a rapid and audible intake of air: Why did Mary marry somebody she didn't know? What does "circumcise" mean? Why didn't God want a man to be part of the birth of Jesus?

"Oh, why not tonight? Wilt thou be saved? Oh, why not tonight?" The weary and berated congregation sang all four verses and then hummed through several times with the preacher now begging for someone to walk down the aisle, warning that the unsaved among the group were risking dying and spending an eternity in the flames of hell. Unless a lot of people came down front, the revival was a failure. Finally, the spent revivalist took out his giant white handkerchief and mopped his face, signaling that he had given up and was prepared to pronounce the benediction.

Julie was ready to shoot out of there, but the kids in front of her were not advancing at all. She leaned around the line to see if the fat lady had gotten stuck in her seat. In horror, she watched the fat lady methodically swing her ample body toward the advancing children, cross-examining each one before granting space to exit: "Have you been saved? Do you know Jesus? Are you sure you're going to heaven when you die?"

Julie was trapped. The fat lady's questions made her highly uncomfortable. She could visualize the fat lady's pleasure in cornering the holdout—a pleasure Julie was determined to deny her. Desperate, Julie quickly surveyed the possible escape routes. As skinny as she was, there was just no way she could squeeze between the wall and the pew. Sneaking past the fat lady while she was witnessing to another kid was not a physical option. Why did girls have to wear dresses? If she had been a boy, with her long legs she could have vaulted over the pew. Frantic, she scrambled underneath the pew, barely eluding the greedy grasp of the fat lady, her heart visibly pounding in her thin chest. She struggled to right her clothing before an observant church member could bear witness to her indecency.

Having learned her lesson well, the next Sunday Julie waited until the last minute before claiming an aisle seat. As the pastor vehemently decried infant baptism, she fingered her pearls and entertained the idea of becoming a Catholic like her best friend Mollie. With her Bible as a shield, Julie secretly practiced making the sign of the cross each time the pastor pronounced "God" or "Jesus," expecting at any moment that God would strike her dead or at least signal His displeasure with a bolt of lightening and a deafening clap of thunder.

--Margaret Eskew

Imago Dei

I am created in the image of God.
Created, Creating, Creative, Creator,
I am one, undivided--
Not a trinity of body, mind, and soul,
But one in creation:
Single, solitary, free, choosing, deciding.
My mind—a gift of God
To be used, exercised, expanded, enlightened, embraced, enjoyed, engaged--
Not put on a shelf
Saved for some future time, stored for posterity,
Stripped of its power, strapped to some set of rules,
Strangled of its vitality,
Stuck in a nightmare of limitations and age-old rituals.
My body is a temple of the Holy Spirit,
From which issue
Praise, proclamation, profession, profundity, power.
God chooses me--
Resides in me, acts in me, abides in me, enables me,
Empowers me, endows me
With certain inalienable gifts
To see, to feel, to smell, to hear, to taste community--
And to savor it;
For community is God's gift to the world,

Its protection my survival and yours.
I preach, I proclaim, I teach, I heal, I sing, I listen,
I commune with God
And with my neighbors:
Creators, created and creating
In the Image of God--
Women, men, and children,
Imago Dei.

--Margaret Eskew

The Little Blue Dinosaur

With dread inhabiting her mind and body, she ventured once again into his apartment, her eyes rebelling against the stark contrast of the bright summer sun to the utter darkness of the living room. Black towels stapled over the windows allowed only a broken sliver of light to filter through, where one of his cats had shredded a corner of the fabric. The new plastic blinds they had installed together a few short months ago hung broken and horizontal, serving now as toys for his cats beneath the makeshift draperies. Dirty, moldy plates and cups littered the room, mingling the stench of rotting food with the unmistakable odor of cat excrement, stale cigarette smoke, and pot.

On a bare mattress in the middle of the floor lay a young man, his head heavy on a filthy pillow. He was fully clothed, and from the smell she knew they were the same clothes he had worn for several days. In weary resignation, she shooed the persistent cats from the cushion and gingerly lowered her body onto the corner of a ragged chair. "Jason!" she called as the cats mewed. "Wake up, son." Although she could barely make out the little round burn on the mattress, she knew there were several more–she had seen them before–fear-invoking proof that he regularly passed out with a lit cigarette in his hand.

The old man in the apartment next door had once told her that he was afraid he would one day walk over to check on Jason

162

and find him dead. Jason's mother lived with the same dread. Her heart settled loudly in her throat every time she approached the front door of his apartment. The old man's wife brought Jason spaghetti and meatballs at least once a week.

Jason stirred. He had made it through another night of pills, pot, and alcohol. Or maybe last night it had been crack or even heroin–Jason had never met a drug he wouldn't try. He considered himself quite an expert concerning what goes with what and how to get the best high. The mother looked at her first-born son amidst this filthy squalor that he called freedom. He didn't even know she was there. Twenty-six years old, he had been traveling down this destructive path for almost nine years. Once again the tears flowed unbidden down her cheeks for this, her prodigal son. What else could she do but cry helpless tears and incessantly beg God to help him? He had already been through several long-term drug rehab facilities--the "star student" each time. He knew those twelve steps backwards and forwards. It all worked until he stepped back into the world and allowed it to overrun him once again, each time bottoming out the resurrected hopes of his mother desperate for his return.

Praying fervently, she pushed his dirty hair off his forehead and caressed his cheek. He opened his eyes, struggling to focus. He may have seen her—she couldn't be certain—but his eyes closed once again, and she cried harder. Struggling to fish out a tissue from her purse to blot her puffy eyes, her fingers accidentally encountered a small object--a sacred relic of a better time that she had tenaciously clung to. In the dark she couldn't see it, but she knew what it was. Trembling, she claimed anew the little blue dinosaur, holding it out for God to see. "Remember this?" she demanded, almost screaming the question through her choking tears. "Remember?"

Maybe God didn't remember, but she sure did. Her mind traveled back to that beautiful yesterday–that day among so many that were taken for granted. She was a young and busy mother of three; Jason was a loving, rambunctious nine-year-old, with a streak of seriousness that struck the adults around him as humorous. He liked to try out big words and feign a deep voice. And he loved his Mama like nobody's business. In the kitchen one morning, Jason had come around the corner as she was unloading the dishwasher. He gave his mama a serious hug, his arms reaching around her middle. "Love you, buddy," she hummed.

"Mama, I have something to give you," he ceremoniously announced. He held out a fist and opened it slowly. Cupped in the palm of his hand sat a rubber-textured little blue dinosaur. "I wanted to give you something to remember me by."

Deeply touched, his mother thanked him profusely and solemnly promised: "I'll carry it with me always."

"Put it in your pocketbook, Mama. That way you will always have it."

Jason went back to his play. His mother, overcome with his ability to declare his love in such a tangible way, called her husband at work to relate the beautiful experience to him. The two of them laughed at their young son's serious, grown-up demeanor, and that was that. But she faithfully carried that little blue dinosaur with her from that day forward, and it would later faithfully carry her through many difficult days. She would take the little blue dinosaur out of her purse, hold it in the palm of her hand, and allow the memories to wash over her—the memories of a little boy who loved his Mama so much that he wanted her to remember.

There she sat in his filthy apartment, tracing every part of that little toy and claiming for herself in the presence of God that surely something of that little boy must still reside somewhere inside the grown man lying passed out in front of her.

"I remember, Jason. I won't forget," she vowed softly to her son, fiercely and resolutely holding onto hope in the shape of a little blue dinosaur.

--Terri DeFoor

164

THE MILITARY

Everything Can Kill You

The room was lit by the bright natural light of the sun, penetrating through the many windows in the room. Some of the windows were cracked open to allow the flow of jungle air boundless access. The instructor stood in front of the class dressed in jungle fatigues with a floppy booney hat fixed on his head. The faded fatigues looked as if they had been washed one time too many. The large muscular figure of a man about six foot five and darker than the night loomed over the room. His complexion seemed to become even darker, when he smiled to reveal perfect white teeth. He spoke with a strong Southern accent, his voice clearly out of place in the environment. Nevertheless, Ryan clung to every word, for this briefing contained vital information needed for survival in the Panamanian jungle.

The jungle school instructor's name was Sergeant Hammer, which proved to fit his style: he deftly hammered the impression of jungle life into the memories of the entire squadron. Sergeant Hammer began his briefing with these words: "Everything in the jungle can kill you, so listen carefully. We have killer bees, snakes, and sharks in the river. As a matter of fact, Jacques Cousteau's son was killed in this very river by sharks during last year's hammerhead breeding season. There is also a poisonous frog that has a shelf life of five years. There are monkeys who love to harass soldiers on patrol and steal their gear when they aren't looking. Even the trees are dangerous: they have spikes called Black Palm. If you fall down, don't reach for a tree. The Black Palm will cause immediate discomfort."

Ryan listened intently and took notes on what to avoid in the jungle. There was an additional warning about the fruit bats that are notorious bloodsuckers. The following morning would be Ryan's first day in the Panamanian jungle. The Black Hawk helicopter whirled overhead as his squadron of eight soldiers hooked up to the SPIES extraction system. (SPIES is the Army's acronym for Special Insertion Extraction System.) The SPIES extraction system is used to put a squad into the jungle without landing. Normally the canopy of the jungle is too thick to land aircraft. Ryan hooked into the SPIES system and felt himself gradually being lifted off the ground until he was suspended in midair, his arms extended in order to control the spin associated with this kind of transportation. Gradually, the Black Hawk continued to climb as it moved forward. Ryan could see the jungle move under his feet and his adrenaline increased with the speed of the Black Hawk. The pilot turned the aircraft toward the river and proceeded to dip the crew into the warm shark-infested waters. The water hit Ryan squarely in the face. It caught him off guard, and his heart was beating like crazy. "I bet those pilots are laughing their asses off," Ryan yelled at the other squad members. Finally the helicopter came to a hover above the thick jungle canopy and the squad was lowered onto the *swelliton* floor below.

Upon hitting the jungle floor, the squad immediately organized into a patrol with several objectives along a given route. Because the sun does not permeate the triple canopy, the squad gratefully experienced some measure of comfort from the rising heat. Ryan continually reviewed the list he had formulated in class: watch out for killer bees, snakes, poisonous frogs and the dreaded Black Palm. Ryan identified Black Palm protruding from all the surrounding trees. The spikes of the Black Palm were like needle tips, black in appearance and sharp to the touch. Ryan ran his fingertips across one of the dark needles while thinking how dangerous the plant could be.

Night was drawing near, and the squad had to find a campsite. Sergeant Hammer would be waiting at the first assembly area, so the squad traveled quickly through the jungle, reaching their destination just before dark. Hernandez started assembling a hammock with a mosquito net. The rest of the squad chose to sleep on the ground with little protection. Ryan noted that the night was completely dark--he couldn't see his hand in front of his face. But the jungle came alive as soon as the lights went out. A loud howling sound seemed to rattle everything in the jungle. It sounded like someone had let King Kong loose and he was headed right toward their assembly area. Finding the sound very unnerving, Ryan asked Sergeant Hammer what sort of animal would make such a sound. Already sound asleep, Sergeant Hammer didn't respond to Ryan's question. The howling thankfully ceased after a couple of minutes and then the rain started to fall. The large drops came crashing through the canopy unobstructed. The rain was so severe that it seemed as if it were coming from the ground itself. Pools of water started to form under Ryan and thoughts of drowning entered his mind. The rain persisted for hours. Ryan didn't sleep a wink.

Morning arrived with a yell from Hernandez's hammock: "Hey, some damn thing bit me last night." Hernandez rolled out of the hammock holding his right hand. Apparently a fruit bat had penetrated Hernandez's sanctuary over night and found his hand outside the boundaries of his fortress. Medic Torres attended to Hernandez's wounds while not being fully aware of the injury he himself had received during the night: a spider had bitten him on the lip and it had swollen bigger than a baseball. Reyes laughed so hard at all the night's events that he tripped over a fallen tree and landed on the spikes of Black Palm. Almost immediately Reyes began vomiting and called out for the medic.

Ryan just stood there and repeated Sergeant Hammer's words verbatim: "Everything in the jungle can kill you."

--Kevin Reid

The Bugler's Song, Part I

The sunny day betrayed the solemn occasion that lay before it. Marjorie sat as the flag was carefully removed from

169

atop the casket of her husband, Brandon. The color guard meticulously made 13 folds in the flag to form the triangle, revealing the stars. As the senior ranking member handed her the flag, she remained composed, stunned beyond words. The baby in her womb stirred and she smiled slightly, remembering the last time she had spoken to Brandon. She was startled at the sound of gunfire as the drill team began their salute. She could see them as each of the seven members fired three shots. The smell of gunpowder carried the scent of death across the grassy knoll. The precision they displayed warranted speculation as the large crowd that gathered watched, many with glistening eyes. As Marjorie listened to the solemn song of "Taps," she reflected with sorrow, yet joyfully, on her short time with Brandon.

Theirs had been an intense relationship, strong enough to endure the stress of his frequent deployments. The joyous reunions were filled with heated passion that one reads about in romance novels. They had been married four years and Marjorie had suffered two miscarriages, likely due to stress, so this pregnancy was particularly precarious.

The trip to the commissary had been uneventful. Marjorie had stopped by the hardware store to look at paint colors for the nursery. She was due in eight short weeks and the obstetrician was cautiously optimistic that this baby would thrive and flourish. When she returned home, she saw the government vehicles parked in front of the duplex she shared with Brandon. She got out of her car and was met by two uniformed soldiers who offered to help her with the bags. Grateful for the help, she didn't consider the implications of their visit. After the men had followed her into the apartment and she had offered them a glass of lemonade, she finally sat down to listen to what they had come to say.

"Mrs. Hollister, on behalf of the United States Army and a grateful nation, we are sorry to inform you of the death of your husband, Brandon." The words reverberated in her head but they didn't make sense. It seemed as if she were listening to someone speak in a foreign language. She understood each and every word but couldn't fathom the construction or significance of the sentence. "Is there someone we can call for you? Is there anything we can do for you at this time?" All these sweet, sensitive words belied the reality of what Marjorie had to face. She stood and faced the men, too stunned to speak. She walked into the kitchen and quickly began putting away the groceries, humming as she moved.

Her family lived in California and she was over 3000 miles away in the little, hokey town of Hinesville. They had been stationed in Georgia for only eight months and she knew so few people. She had been so busy getting settled in the house that she hadn't taken the time to form many friendships. She hadn't attended the baseball or basketball games or gone to the movies or clubs on base. Other than the employees on the base she had encountered and a few neighbors, she didn't know anybody.

The night before Brandon was deployed, she had surprised him with a beautifully gift-wrapped box with two ribbons, one pink and one blue. It was a small rectangular jewelry box. Brandon had opened it apprehensively, wondering what the pretty package held. Inside was a long, narrow stick, similar to a thermometer, but with a plus sign. It took Brandon a minute to fathom the value of this weird contraption. He looked into Marjorie's eyes and saw the hopeful, yet fearful tears of joy. "Brandon, I'm pregnant." There was utter silence. They embraced and held each other for what seemed like an eternity. "Baby, please be careful, we need you to come back home." Brandon had confidently responded, "Marjorie, I'll be with you always."

--Elnora Fluellen

The Bugler's Song, Part II

Holding his famous jar of honey, Pooh Bear smiled brightly atop the beautiful birthday cake as all the adults oohed and aahed over Brandon, Jr. and how cute he was. Precocious, he already had four teeth and had started talking at nine months. He could say "Da-Da" quite clearly, bringing tears to his mother's eyes. He was the spitting image of his father and seemed to look more and more like him with each passing day. Both sets of grandparents arrived, bearing ever more gifts for the overflowing table in the corner of the kitchen. Marjorie jokingly complained that Brandon had enough clothes and toys to outfit a set of triplets.

BJ's first birthday was bittersweet. The whole house seemed to be set up as a memorial. In the foyer was a display of Brandon, Sr.'s medals, pictures, decorations, and awards. It was difficult for Marjorie to look at the picture of him with his unit. It had been taken the day before he died. When she had returned from his funeral, she had found the picture in an email from one of Brandon's friends. The friend had described how Brandon had motivated the entire group and had quickly developed into a fine leader.

Each day Brandon had insisted that they all read passages together in the Bible and pray. Even though some of the soldiers weren't religious, they had participated with the group out of respect for Brandon. The Fourth Infantry Unit was a closely-knit group. Together they had formed a survival pact. In the event anything happened to one of them, each soldier had shared contact information with the others, so that they could stay in touch with the soldier's family and friends. They had solemnly vowed that if the need arose, they would support the family of the injured or fallen soldier. It was ironic that in the last picture, they were all flashing peace signs.

For Marjorie it was a particularly cruel twist of fate that Brandon was killed in the attack the week before he was to leave Iraq. Their happy expressions recorded in the picture reflected the knowledge of their imminent departure. Their six-man con-voy was ambushed when they stopped for a person lying in the road. It appeared to be an injured child and they had pulled over to offer assistance. In the lead truck, Brandon walked toward the body. As he drew near, he saw the wires beneath the insurgent's shirt. He yelled "Bomb!" as he threw himself over the suicide bomber, heroically sacrificing himself as he gave the others a chance to gain cover.

The military was a welcome force to some Iraqis. The soldiers often shared their care packages from home with the Iraqi children. Brandon and his friends had asked their family and friends to send school supplies. The Fourth Infantry Unit had recently distributed a big shipment of crayons, pencils, and notebooks, garnering smiles, hugs, and appreciation from the local villagers. War was tough, but children were children. The men thought of their own families back home as they watched the lights come on in the children's eyes.

The morning of that call that every military family fears to receive, Marjorie had gone shopping for some of Brandon's favorite foods in preparation for his homecoming. He had missed the delicious peach cobbler she had finally learned how to make. She had imagined his delight in coming home to find his favorite meal of fried chicken and sweet potatoes on the table. Even though Brandon knew she was pregnant, he would be surprised at her once trim figure, now obviously swollen with child. Feeling a little self-conscious, Marjorie wondered if he would still find her attractive. That call seemed so long ago now.

Marjorie had questioned God's faithfulness. While Brandon was serving his country, each morning she had gotten out of bed, knelt down, and fervently asked God to protect him and all the troops. She had repeated this each evening before going to bed. Hadn't God heard her prayers? Where was God when Brandon got out of his humvee and was ambushed?

Marjorie's family came to Hinesville to help her pack some personal items for the trip home, where Brandon would be buried. Dazed and in denial, Marjorie allowed the military to pack up her household belongings and ship them to her in California. After the funeral, she had had to find a new obstetrician to deliver her baby. She had emailed Brandon constantly as she had begun to prepare the nursery in Hinesville for the arrival of their child two months after Brandon's scheduled return. He had been so proud of the way she had been able to manage the household and their affairs so effectively. He had been so excited about coming home and being there for the birth of his son.

--Elnora Fluellen

Son in Service

Do you remember where you were and what you were doing when you heard of the attacks on September 11, 2001? I was standing before my class of pre-kindergarten students reciting with them the words to our national anthem. Suddenly the door flew open, the principal rushed in with a strange look on his face and led me to the hall. There I was informed of the attacks on the Twin Towers. In numb disbelief, I returned to the children and we continued struggling with the words of the Star Spangled Banner. Summoned a second time a few moments later, I learned of the attack on the Pentagon, and the fear that still another plane had been hijacked, destination unknown. It was later determined to be Flight 93, the plane that crashed in a Pennsylvania field.

Confused and distraught, I needed to remain calm for the children. My mind raced to my son. What did all of this mean for him? Straight out of high school, he had joined the United States Army two years before. Almost instinctively, I knew the United States would retaliate against those responsible for the attacks. I reasoned that it would be necessary to let the terrorists know that the U.S.A. would not ignore what had been done. At the same time, I earnestly prayed that it would not come to war. I could not bear the thought of my eldest child experiencing the horrors of war.

As the months passed, my fears were realized. Troops were leaving for Afghanistan and Iraq, and Sergeant Phillip Smith was one of the first to go. Upon his arrival in Iraq, he and his men were instructed to go door to door, searching for insurgents. Later he patrolled the streets, riding aboard a tank or humvee, and shooting at any threat encountered. I was in agony.

Worry was my constant companion. Sleepless nights turned me into a zombie. Like so many others with loved ones fighting the war, I was inconsolable—bursting into tears for no reason. Now I realize there was good reason for my radical change in behavior.

I was not aware of all that Phillip was witnessing as he fought. I did not want to know. All I knew was my firstborn, my sunshine, my "little boy," was involved in a situation I could never have imagined. There was nothing I could do to help him. Feelings of frustration, anger, helplessness, despair, and sadness enveloped me. How could I, his mother, have allowed this to happen? What kind of mother was I?

A battle began to rage inside me. On one hand, I thought of all those innocent lives lost on September 11. We, the United States citizens, must seek to punish those responsible. Yet I did not want my son added to the casualty list. Could we fight a war with no casualties? Was combat the only solution?

William T. Sherman once rightly concluded that "War is Hell." It is hell for those on the battlefield and for those left at home waiting. While Phillip was going through hell in Iraq, my mind was a violent battleground endlessly playing out the possibilities.

Phillip called home when he could. One particular phone conversation lodged itself vividly in my memory:

"Hey, Mama."

"Hey, Baby. How's it going? Are you doing all right?"

"Yes, ma'am, I'm okay, but something bad happened today."

"I'm so sorry. Tell me about it, if you can."

"We were going into Baghdad, and the tank behind mine hit an IED. A good friend and comrade was fatally wounded. I was able to pull him out of the tank before he died, but he never spoke or opened his eyes. He died in my arms."

I searched for words, but none came. Wanting to allay my fears, Phillip assured me that he was all right, but my imagination would not let go of his words. How could he be okay after such a chilling experience? My mind calculated what he had said: "the tank behind mine." This meant his own tank barely missed the IED. This time Phillip had been fortunate to escape death. Somehow, I had to put this in perspective. My son was still alive while another mother's son would come home in a body bag. Phillip had barely escaped this time. There were still dangers to encounter at every turn.

During those long months of Phillip's deployment, his phone calls and emails kept me sane. His frequent contacts countered the uncertainty of what was happening. His fiancée and I leaned on one another to keep our fears at bay; she often forwarded his emails to me. An email requesting school supplies for Iraqi children made me surge with pride. Though heavily armed, Phillip realized that inspiring goodwill was essential to his safety and the safety of his buddies. Crayons, pens, pencils, and books could perhaps achieve what weapons alone had not been able to do. Phillip's response to the innocent faces of the children assured me that war had not changed his basic character.

Phillip's message forced me to think of the Iraqi children. They had mothers, too. Their parents were probably just as frightened for them as I was for my son. Was I being selfish by only thinking of my son and his safety? I began to realize there were many more people in harm's way than just Phillip. Innocent Iraqis were being killed along with our troops. We needed to do whatever we could to help them. In addition, it seemed as though sending items for the children might strengthen ties between the Iraqi civilians and our troops.

I asked for permission to put a box in our lounge at work, and sent out a message to everyone I worked with and explained my son's request. To my amazement, the box was full the very next day. Each time I emptied the box, the items had overflowed onto the floor. Kind gestures such as these helped to make life bearable while Phillip was fulfilling his duty to his country. I confess that I never stopped worrying and praying, but knowing how much others cared and were willing to help eased the burden. I did not feel so alone.

I am one of the lucky mothers: my son is now home after

three tours in Iraq. Now other mothers are struggling with the
same demons – fear, helplessness, and anger at what our children
face. What is the solution? Is war the answer? Maybe Phillip's
response to the Iraqi children models what our national strategy
should include: take care of the children, and their parents will
respond with friendship.

--Barbara E. Sellers

The Dance

It's pitch black outside.
I sit in the dark and wait. As a child I didn't understand why my
parents started their day before the sun came up. Back then I
believed if the sun wasn't up, then people shouldn't be up either.
Over the years and through many dark hours of mourning, I've
realized I can learn a lot–about life and about myself–during
those dark hours of morning.

It's dark gray outside.
At thirteen I learned death doesn't wait for you to put on your
makeup and fix your hair. I regret missing my last chance to see
Papa alive because I wanted to look cute for the male ICU nurse.
I still struggle with the fact that who I am has nothing to do with
what I look like.

It's a lighter gray now.
When I was seventeen I discovered life isn't fair. A teenager
shouldn't have a parent with a terminal illness–much less two
of them. At times I hated both of them for being sick because it
meant I had to take responsibility for running a home instead of
having a normal life. I try to remember that everything happens
for a reason.

The white is almost blinding.
At twenty-three I learned some people die too young. How do
you console your best friend whose only son, just two months

177

old, has died during the night from SIDS? I checked on my own babies, kissed their foreheads, and felt guilty for being thankful it hadn't happened to mine. I often wonder how she's doing, but can't muster the courage to find her and find out.

The blues in the yard become vibrant.
When I was thirty I realized you are never too old to not need your dad after mine lost his fight against Wagener's Granulomatoma and died during the night. I wondered how the birds could be singing when the sun rose the next morning. Didn't they know my world had just ended? I wonder if my own kids will miss me as much as I miss him.

The greens gradually peek through.
At thirty-one I discovered you have to make time for the important things. I felt empty, as I stood teary-eyed on the rim of the Grand Canyon waiting for the sun to rise. It was the anniversary of Daddy's death–he'd talked about coming here but had never found the time. I try to keep "important" in perspective. I'm not always successful.

The yellows begin to shine as they pick up the light.
When I was thirty-two I realized death can be a relief. It hurt that my mother hadn't known who I was for the past fifteen years. She was just flesh, bones, and a couple of vague memories. It has made me try harder to be a good mother.

The reds and browns slowly begin to take on color.
At thirty-six I understood I had an inner strength I could have never imagined. I awoke in the night and found the entire left side of my seventeen-year-old son's body hanging limp, like a marionette without a puppeteer, after he suffered a stroke. I was scared–this wasn't something I could protect him from or make right for him. I'm learning to "let go and let God."

It's like watching the world come alive in Technicolor.
At thirty-nine, and facing a divorce after twenty years of marriage, I learned I was responsible for my own happiness. At the

time, I felt an incredible sadness and sense of failure. I've since accepted that I've made my share of mistakes, but I did my best. Several months later, when we reconciled, I realized a marriage requires the ability to forgive and the fortitude to stay the course when things are rough.

And then, as if I blink the day into existence, the world as I know it comes into view.
Now, at forty-three, I am just beginning to understand the full implication of my vow "to have and to hold...in sickness and in health." After twenty-five years of an often tumultuous marriage, I'm becoming aware that the angry, hateful words coming from him were his disease, not him. I cling to all those times when things were good. I wonder if we'll ever make it back to those times.

I realize no matter what the day brings I will get through it.
I reflect on my life up till this point. I mourn for lost loves, for chances not taken, for the life I dreamed I'd have. I try to understand who I am, dream of who I want to be, and wonder what I'll learn today. I wonder if this is why my parents got up so early. I sit in the dark, quiet hours of the morning and wait.

II

No matter how many miles I've traveled, the world changes for me just past Chapman's Curve. The familiar curve, with pine trees jutting up from the depths of the steep drop-off on my right, and the clay embankment, with its various shades of red and orange, rising up on my left, mean I'm almost home.

I've traveled this stretch of road hundreds, if not thousands, of times without really paying attention. But when you've been away from home for a long time, or have traveled many miles to return home, you appreciate things you've previously taken for granted.

It had been ten months since we'd been home when we

179

started this trip from North Carolina. Despite the twelve hours we had been in the car with two small children, we took the long way home–just for the Chapman's Curve experience. We followed the curve and veered left at the fork. A stretch of road, I'd guess about a mile long, came into view.

This road, light gray asphalt with white and yellow lines barely visible, seemed narrower than the five hundred miles of road we'd already traveled. We took this road more slowly than the other ones we'd traveled. As was my custom, I popped the Atlanta Rhythm Section cassette in, turned up the volume, and let "Homesick" rock the car with its beat.

We continued over the small Tobesofkee Creek Bridge, down past the nursery with its Quonset-shaped greenhouses and on past the pale brick duplexes. The tree line of Bloodworth's Dairy was just ahead. I rolled down my window. The smells of Lizella permeated the air–the oniony scent of freshly mown grass, and the earthy smell of dirt mingled with cow manure. I breathed in deeply and felt my body relax.

We drove under the canopy of trees from the dairy: Sunshine. Shade. Sunshine. Shade. Sunshine.

We followed the next curve right, picking up speed. I rolled my window up, turned the radio down and began collecting the loose items in the car. I was home.

III

I sat at the corner of Fall Hill Avenue and Route 1 in Fredericksburg, Virginia, waiting for the light to turn green. I scanned the road. Two cars were ahead of me. The left turn lane was empty. The hour commute had my heart pounding; my knuckles were white from gripping the steering wheel, and my stomach was hurting. I'd taken the long way in to avoid Route 3. But there was no avoiding this two-block stretch of Route 1. Turn green! Turn green! Turn green!

I held my breath as I waited. James Monroe High School was across the street on the right. A gas station was on my side of the street to my right. It was a bad place to be, given recent events.

I caught a glimpse of the white van as it pulled up beside me in the turn lane. *Oh, shit!* According to recent news reports the Beltway Sniper drove a white van. I couldn't move: cars in front of me, cars behind me, and the white van beside me. My heart felt like it would beat out of my chest. My hands were sweaty on the steering wheel. I kept looking straight ahead—not left, for fear I would see the muzzle of an assault rifle, and not right, in the event it was the sniper and he shot someone else at a gas station. *Hurry up and turn green, dammit!*

The light turned green. The van slowly made a left turn, heading north towards D.C. I made a quick right turn, heading south to work.

IV

dis·tract (dĭ-străkt´)
-- *To cause to turn away from the original focus of attention or interest; divert.*

If I had just ignored my sister, things would have turned out differently. But I didn't ignore her. And I've gone from writing about how the word "ma'am" makes me feel old to about why my writing isn't about my original topic.

I was online researching the word "ma'am" and didn't realize I was logged on to Yahoo! until "Realshortwoman," my sister, popped up on my screen. I didn't think chatting with her for a couple of minutes would be a big deal—until she reminded me about the time she had tried to mail chicken bones back to Church's. The chicken story was quickly followed with her latest "God I'm getting old" tale of receiving Kroger's senior citizens' discount and how she was pissed off about it, but not enough to demand a refund because it was such a substantial savings. I became engrossed in the conversation and completely forgot about my research.

I thought I'd try to work the chicken story into the section about being forgetful. I wrote in detail about my sister eating the chicken, throwing the bones back into the box, and then deciding she should throw the box in the dumpster. Yet when she got outside, she saw the mailbox and decided to check the mail. I wrote about her walking up the driveway to the mailbox, putting the box of bones in it, flipping the flag up and how she was halfway back down the driveway before she realized what she'd done.

As I finished typing the story, I remembered telling Toni, a seventy-something volunteer at the hospital where I worked, about my sister's chicken story and her concern about it being early-onset Alzheimer's. Toni's advice: "Show her a key. If she knows what it is and what it's used for, then she's just stressed out. If she knows what it is, but doesn't know what it's used for, then she's got Alzheimer's." Not exactly a scientific method, but Toni swore it worked.

Thinking about Toni had taken me back to Virginia. I'd met Carmel in Virginia. I remembered the hours I had spent listening to her tell stories about performing on Broadway, about traveling around Europe during World War II setting up USO's, and dancing with the soldiers to help boost morale. In her eighties, Carmel was full of wisdom about growing old. Her only advice, however, was to mow your own grass.

The memories made me smile but they had nothing to do with the topic at hand. As I tried to focus on my writing I remembered I hadn't paid the bills yet. So I paid the bills and pondered how I could work the chicken story, the Kroger story, and the Carmel and Toni stories into my writing. I was beginning to think I should select another topic. But what would I choose?

As I frequently do when I get stuck with my writing, I started cleaning house. I dusted Granny's old pump organ and considered writing about the organ and my love for music, but that wouldn't fill two pages. I could write about how my gambling great-grandfather had won (and lost) a town in North Carolina, a plantation in Virginia, and two Coca-Cola bottling companies in North Georgia. Or I could write about his father's collection of ten or so wooden arms he'd carved for himself after he lost one of his arms during the Civil War. But I couldn't think of anything connecting me to them and their stories and I really didn't know much else about them.

That reminded me that it had been several years since I'd talked to my cousins. So I spent several hours on the phone talking to them. The conversations took me back to my childhood. I could vividly remember Uncle Henry laughing at me after I had gotten my finger snapped by his pack of trick Juicy Fruit gum. I could remember the expression on my Uncle J. H.'s face when I finally realized that the Cool-Whip bowl I'd been holding on the ceiling with a broomstick didn't really have any water in it. I remembered the Sunday I noticed that "the blood of Christ" I had at communion tasted exactly the same as the Hi-C my momma served me at lunch the same Sunday. And when I realized that the fried chicken my Aunt Della served me for lunch had been running around in her yard earlier that same morning, I wouldn't eat chicken for years.

I was still mulling over "ma'am" and debating the merits of changing topics when I checked my email and found my cousin had emailed me four or five old family photos. That reminded me I needed to sort through my own pictures for our upcoming reunion. As I did, I ran across one I thought I'd seen online. So I got on the Internet and went to deadfred.com to see if the pictures were indeed the same. Halfway through this the computer turned itself off–a fairly frequent occurrence these days–so I decided to do research to try and figure out what was going on with it. The web pages wouldn't load and I discovered my browser was several versions behind, so I decided to update it. Once the update was completed I clicked on three or four pages to make sure it worked. I saw an advertisement about checking your credit score, which I clicked.

I was getting increasingly frustrated. I was just about out of time. I hadn't finished the "ma'am" story and wasn't sure I could. I couldn't find anything else on the list we'd been given in class that really piqued my interest–I'd already tried a couple of times to write about my experience eating Lemon Pledge and just wasn't up to trying to tackle that topic again. I reviewed my own list and remembered I still had one novel unfinished–another one still needed revisions–and several other unfinished projects. I resisted the urge to open any of them because I knew if I did, I would never return to my paper.

Throughout all this time I had made progress on the assignment–if you consider writing a couple of sentences or paragraphs and then deleting them progress. I didn't know what I wanted to write, but I definitely knew what I didn't want to write. I was chatting (read whining) with my brother about the fact this paper was taking me everywhere but where I needed to be. He reminded me of his catch phrase for jumping around or off topic: "Look! There's a chicken."

Determined to finish the assignment, with or without "ma'am," I put my headphones on and turned the music up loud. Normally this works, but it seemed every song took me to another time, another place, or another memory. And if it didn't, then it had me singing along and dancing around in my chair as I stared at the screen.

I began to wonder whether I had adult ADD/ADHD. So off I went in search of information. I found a test designed to tell you if you are attention-deficit, started taking it but got bored, and decided I should make a doctor's appointment.

But back to my story: according to one Internet source, the word "ma'am" is an abbreviation of mammary and . . . Oh, Look! There's a chicken.

V

The manila-colored unfurnished earth surrounding me was in stark contrast to the green, tree-dotted landscape I was used to. This piece of the earth, halfway between L.A. and Vegas, would be our eighth home inside of ten years.

Barstow, California. I hated the small, sand-colored Mojave Desert town nestled among the gray San Bernardino Mountains. Houses in the city were so close you could reach into your neighbor's home without ever leaving your own. Front yards were either paved or made of baked earth; I remember one yard filled with green gravel. I was shocked that people actually lived in the black- and rust-colored train cars littering the outskirts of town.

It was the land of devils. The whirls of dirt spinning around reminded me of the Tasmanian devil. The frigid air of the Santa Anas, or Devil Winds, made me bend over double and fight my way to the car against the invisible forty-mile-an-hour force. *I thanked God we wouldn't be here long.*

My first memory of Barstow is of the heat. I was welcomed with a blast of 114-degree air that singed my nostrils. It reminded me of opening an oven door and inhaling the heat instead of the aroma. It was a month before the hot, dry air no longer bothered me.

It rained only once while I lived there. I couldn't have caught a teaspoon of water during the five minutes it lasted. People stood under shelters watching the tiny drops christen the forsaken land–I chuckled and wondered how they'd react if they saw the rains that had recently flooded Macon, Georgia. The tiny drops formed puddles on the parched earth. Arroyos filled, rushing the liquid sunshine to parts unknown, and flooded the roads. It snowed once. A light layer of frosting covered the caked earth.

Throughout our first summer in Barstow we spent many hot days exploring the scorched desert, digging for opals in the side of a mountain, exploring the silver mining town of Calico, and romping around Rainbow Basin with its palette of pastels – never once breaking a sweat, despite the hundred-plus degree temperatures. I liked not sweating. I was beginning to think I could live forever without humidity or rain. We took our jackets with us on these hot summer days so when night fell, and the temperature plummeted–sometimes as much as forty degrees-- we could continue exploring.

They say you can see up to ten miles in the Mojave. I believe that's true. There are no pine trees to obscure the view, just scrub strewn about the desert floor. I scanned the miles of desert floor in search of the Desert Tortoise. I was fascinated by this reptile that could go a year or more without water. I wondered whether actually touching them would cause them to die, as I'd heard.

After four years in Barstow we were nearing the time we'd be moving on to our ninth home. I began thinking about Georgia pines, about air "so thick you can cut it with a knife," and about the sweltering heat. I looked at the golds, reds, yellows, and pinks that glistened on the side of the mountain. I dreaded the day I'd have to leave here.

VI

It's funny how you don't miss some things until they're gone. It had been years since I'd thought about Woolworth's when the July 18, 1997 announcement came that they were closing all of their American stores. Just the name took me back to another time and another place: the time of the five and dime.

I remember going to Woolworth's in the Gainesville mall with Granny when I was a child. As I entered the plate glass storefront, there were no shelves to block my view so I could see from one off-white end of the store to the other. There were aisles upon brightly lit aisles of stuff: plastic bowls and other household items, fabric and thread, cheap plastic framed religious prints, and an assortment of doilies hanging on hooks. It was always the doilies that intrigued me. Granny had them all over her house, but hers weren't as interesting as the ones in Woolworth's.

A grill was to the left of the store entrance from inside the mall. I ate there only once–a grilled cheese sandwich, I think it was. Granny let me spin around on the stools at the counter, something my parents never let me do. There were wooden phone booths with benches inside and doors that closed that made me think of England, but I don't know why.

VII

"I've changed my name to 'shit' and the first one that swears will get a spanking." Stunned silence filled the van. I can't recall, in detail, the first time I said this to my children. I know we were living in California because that's where I met Sandy Worthy, and she's the one who gave me the idea about changing my name. I know the kids would have been about eight and ten. I know I was driving a van because that's what we drove when we lived in California. I don't remember what had pushed me to the point of saying it except I was tired of the constant litany of "Mom," "Mom?" and "MOM!" But I do remember the blessed silence that filled the air once I said it.

"Hey, lady that's married to my dad," my daughter piped up. "Hey, lady driving the van." "Hey, Diane," one of my children boldly ventured. The list went on and on although I don't remember them all. I do remember the laughter as the kids tried to get my attention without saying "Mom" or without swearing.

I've changed my name many times over the years since that day in the van. "Do I need to change my name?" has become much more effective than "knock it off" when they're driving me crazy.

Although they are now nineteen and twenty-one, they still fight like they did when they were younger. On occasion they fight over things that matter, but most of the time it's for the sheer pleasure of irritating the other—or me. After a recent squabbling match, my son came into the kitchen, smiled at me and asked: "Ready to change your name yet?"

VIII

They hit the deck at zero dark thirty. They stand in formation in their cammies, blouses on, and trousers bloused, with covers on their grapes. They wear dog tags around their necks.

187

Some wear high and tights; some wear BC glasses. Some of them are salty; some of them are short–all of them green and squared away.

Ground pounders, grunts, air wingers, flyboys, chaplains and the occasional Devil Doc: when colors sound, they all stop and stand at attention or salute. It doesn't matter whether they wear stars, butter bars, or chevrons or how many hash marks they wear on their sleeves. It's their duty.

They are all about duty–on duty, standing duty, active duty, reserve duty, and PCS'ing in POV's to new duty stations. They show they're prepared for duty by displaying their 782 Gear during a J.O.B. They don't have jobs; they have MOS's.

Only those in trouble have Office Hours. Serious trouble may get them a six, six and a kick. The XO at the bottom of the disciplinary page in their SRB doesn't mean the boss likes them.

They sleep on a rack. They use the head. They go to Mess Night. They clean on field day. They go to the PX, the commissary, the package store, or sickbay. Sometimes they go TAD, AWOL, or out of CONUS.

They stand at ease, at parade rest, or corrected. Ask them a question and they'll respond with "roger that," "say again," "that's a negative," or "oorah!"

Known as Devil Dogs, Leathernecks, Jarheads or Gyrenes, they live in their own world. They speak their own language.

IX

I'd never really given much thought to feminism. I did agree if a woman could do the exact same job as a man, then she should be allowed to do the job. I didn't agree that a man opening a door for me meant he thought I was weak. That was the extent of my thoughts on the subject–until I took an English class in the late nineties.

When Dan Brown went over our first essay assignment in English 101, he told the class: "You must use gender neutral

188

language." Gender neutral? He proceeded to explain that in our essays we must either use *she*, alternate *he* and *she*, or add a line at the bottom of our essay stating that we had intentionally used the word *he* throughout. He gave us the song and dance about how the word *he* implied that women were excluded. I don't remember exactly what he said. I was too pissed off.

I couldn't quit thinking about what he'd said. I'd grown up in the world of *he* and never once thought myself not capable of doing something because the writer had used *he*. And here women were fighting for equality and looking like idiots because unless it said *she*, then a *she* wouldn't know she was capable of doing it. There was only one way to protest this new rule – I spent the entire semester using *he* in every essay and adding the disclaimer at the bottom.

X

"Please join us for an ice cream social after the service," my sister-in-law said to the congregation after the eulogy was delivered.

Ice: **1** freezing cold like I imagined my father's skin would have felt if I'd been brave enough to touch him; **2** numbing the pain I felt and causing my knees to buckle when I saw him lying in the casket; **3** providing relief from the sweltering heat; **4** melting into the tears streaming down my cheeks as I wondered who would answer the questions I would have in the future.

Cream: **1** rising to the top as my father had done both economically and professionally; **2** sweet like the stories friends and associates told, portraying a side of Daddy I'd never known; **3** a salve for the soul as I had begun to realize he'd made a difference in the lives of everyone he'd met; **4** mixing separate personalities together and making us a family.

Social: **1** a gathering of mourners on a hot July day; **2** shared stories of a man whose life had touched many other lives; **3** laughter as tales of long ago were told; **4** a gathering of family, friends and associates to celebrate a life well-lived.

Ice cream social: a gathering on July 18, 1995 of people from all walks of life and from all over the state, honoring Daddy's request that "the next time everybody's in town we need to get together and make some homemade ice cream."

> *When you get the choice to sit it out or dance,*
> *I hope you dance.*
> *(Time is a wheel in constant motion always.)*
> *I hope you dance*
> *(rolling us along).*
> (Quoted from "I Hope You Dance,"
> written by Mark D. Sanders & Tia Sillers)

--Diane Lang

Rhyme, Reason, and/or Rhythm

Haiku 145: Love

Men say Love may pass.
Fear of Wonder leaves Man cold.
For you I Burn bright.

--Steven Peano

reality

in harsh waves
belief stays afloat or sinks
down into the chasm of unbelief

within changing landscapes of
my imagination
God is; God is not

yesterday was pleasant
ending with a deep red sunset
i am certain painted by God

today is painful
as evil rises and children fall
i am confused; there is no God

i am certain; i am confused
i am a particle of life riding
a blue-green jewel through the galaxy—
        on the breath of the Logos
        which never stops speaking
even when i am unaware

--Terri DeFoor

Letting Go

I see the twinkle of sadness floating in the water of your eyes.
I see the tomorrow you have dreamed that won't come and the today that just won't give.
I heed the warnings in your voice that are a subtle hint that life is going to change.
I sit alone in the creaking of silence, turning every page of pain and laughter to allow a peace to reside next to me.
I exhale to the patience that I don't have and recline to the stillness of hope that came as a gift.
As the rains flood my soul and a glimpse of another day is passing, pieces of me realize the difficulty of letting go.

Sylvia Lane Edwards

Variations on a (Hackneyed) Theme

Nature gets me once a month.
Husband gets me when he wants.
But Thursday mornings,
I belong to Marcus.
Dreadful roar and hullabaloo!
Husband crackling, bristling, snorting:
Every manner of insult retorting,
Classifying my intentions
To ignore society's conventions
Among those same which, only latterly,
Motivated Lady Chatterly.
I stoke the fires of his indignation with the stalwart affirmation,
"I shall not be late on Thursday mornings."
Two hours once a week I ask:
Let me not be brought to task!
All the housework, laundry, shopping,
Toenail-clipping and hiney-mopping
Leave my spirit sodden, sour, sopping.

194

I stand in an infinity of raisin-ridden rugs
Equipped with chewing gum-stuck shrugs.
Laundry room muck up to my elbows
Prompts my desolated bellows,
"Never shall I miss that Thursday morning!"
Undaunted, fearless, away I drive.
Not permitting harsh invective
To becloud my soul's directive
I pursue my heart's desire
(Leaving my husband behind to perspire).
Steering slowly, by miniscule degrees
Toward my goal of expertise,
Faithfully I've practiced upon those piano keys.
Musically erudite? Well some Friday I might be
From playing there with Marcus Thursday mornings.

--Karen Lacey

Begetting Beginning

The year the syntax shifted,
Breeze inhaled the meadow
To breathe out cricket chirps grains
Of dirt rivulets banks of violets,
Hayricks of yesteryear.
Earth's systole murmured diastole-
Pumping rhythms, its Ur-Text
Belying syncopated bellows.
Shore sucked sea's breast, shells trilled.
Fired forms long resisting human ken
Emerge visible, possible now in
Palimpsestic overlay.
Sky realized new horizons—
Life, the swell of hope
Unknown unknowing.

--Karen Lacey

That Which Is Not Seen

Does the swell
I feel in my chest,
when I touch
titillating thoughts
only come from
within--
Self generated?
Or is it,
as it seems,
the spark
that flows
from that
sphere
once touched?
Does the soul
have the reach
to touch
that
which is not
seen?
To know
that of
which the
other senses
are unaware?

--Thompson Biggers

Strain and Twist

Strain and twist--
try to make of this life
what it "should" be.
Always wanting more--

196

never satisfied.
Hunger unquenchable;
thirst unabated.
The far pinnacle surmounted,
only to present the further.
Never enough.
No vision of enough.
So nothing could ever be.
Goals external.
Reality out there.
Inner peace never the goal.
Accompanies accomplishment?
Or never considered?

--Thompson Biggers

Light

The light peaks through the clouds,
Announcing a new day;
The light nurtures the flower,
Coloring the gray.

The light shines down the pole,
Securing the way;
The light signals security,
Keeping children's night fears at bay.

The light warms the human soul,
Encouraging all along life's way;
The light proclaims "Peace on earth,"
Imploring all to obey.
The light represents love,
Inviting us home to stay.

--Cliff Brown

Life's Last Quarter

When you get there—and I have,
You see years of venturing much, gaining a little,
And losing a lot of life's best hopes.
You gather around the table of last options,
Wondering what there is left to do.
You can rap on the table and call for more cards,
Or clutch tightly to the cards you've already been dealt,
Peeking out from behind your curtains
Watching the ones who ventured another hand.

--Rosemary McKelvey

Ink Blots Be Damned

Swiss psychiatrist Rohrschach designed his famous test,
Exploring personalities as patients gazed and guessed
The meanings of random ink blots.
He should have examined the secrets revealed
While cutting grass.

My true personality clearly came to the fore
When cutting the grass became my assigned chore.

I pushed the mower with wild abandon,
Creating circles, cutting pie wedges, linking
Them all together with rectangles below.

Not for me the dull monotony
Of up and down, up and down–no flight of fancy,
Seams overlapping until all lines meet.

I prefer to go off in all directions, at the end
Tying all the parts together in a neat green quilt.

--Rosemary McKelvey

Sonnet on Foucault

When I consider how we subdivide the world
In classes, races, gender, age, and health--
Identity proscribed by DNA,
Determining intelligence, our outer form--,
I ask what choices do we really make:
Can we escape the scepter's fateful swing
Assigning to us some space circumscribed
According to a list of duple traits
To realize a nightmare of the dream
Of order gerrymandered "objectively"
Upon the lonely landscapes of our lives?
The answer to my question nature yields:
Chance glances on our walkways show
Plants blooming where no plants should grow.

--Margaret Eskew

You and I

You and I--we go way back.
You saw me crawl, walk, then run.
I've seen your best,
I've seen your worst,
And I'm proud to be your son.

You and I--we survived a drowning.
Yes, "we," not "I," is true.
Because anything that torments me,
Torments my mother too.

You and I--we've been through trials,
Too many for me to tell.
And I know when my knees buckled,
Your knees did as well.

You loved me when I tried you.
You looked me in the eye,
And told me that you loved me--
Even if I'd made you cry.

You know me; I know you:
Our lives are intertwined.
You're a part of who I am today,
Body, soul, and mind.

You are gone; I can't see you.
I ask God to tell you things.
And I want you to know
That in my heart your voice still rings.

You told me that you loved me.
You've loved me from day one.
You care for me like no one else,
And I'm proud to be your son.

[Writer's Note: *This is a poem I wrote for my mother, Deborah Lynn Wells, on Mother's Day in 2005. My mother passed away on May 3, 2007, making these words even more meaningful to me. She was the most wonderful woman I have ever known. She was my strong supporter through every trial. She pushed me to conquer obstacles that I would have never thought possible. I added the last two verses after her death.*]

--Zach Wells

Raw

Three women
Unpatched or mended. Life left them whole:
Different materials, precious, unbroken.
Riotous, Raw and Rebellious,
Together they laugh at the world.
Together they roar with laughter like lions.

Robust, boisterous, half a word, world of meaning–

Men stand by unsure, waiting to re-claim.
Camaraderie, this laughter—who is she?
What about me? The cork is off for joie de vivre,
Not to be shared with mortal souls

Dangerous, Riotous, Raw, and Rebellious,
Obnoxious, annoying hosts and friends alike.
Eyebrows raise, jealousy paws, awareness making taller.
Sensing power and unencumbered, they feed off each other:
Society, religion, gender, all is gone.
Mount Olympus has been cleared; the view is splendid
For a moment.
A hand that pulls, a phone that rings, unknowing:
Back in the box, the power contained,
It's current now channeled, divided.
Polished they move among us, unbeknownst
Until we meet again, my friends.

--Yvonne Gabriel

The Stranger

How can I be a Stranger in a land I helped to mold—
Plantation homes, cotton gins and stories still untold?
I can be seen through old, tattered, and rusty screen doors:
Homes once filled with sounds of life and laughter
Are now filled with mold and spores.
Communities have been silenced:
No rhythm, no music, no band—
A people in disarray,
Desperately seeking a helping hand.
Families have been destroyed,
Moved from place to place,
Drifting like wanderers
Looking for space.
I shed a tear today for you.
I'll shed a tear tomorrow—

Can't bear to watch the news
Or see in your eyes the sorrow.

--Pamela Clark

Daydreams

Happiness rises when they arrive,
Emerging as I gaze the sky:
…removal from reality
…elixir for asperity
…possibility of chance, reign--
Downheartedness I exchange
I'm where and who I want to be:
Happy … fruitful … complete.
Yet they're caged, defended, disguised,
Despite their ability to hope-revive.
Despite my potential to actualize,
They're dormant; I'm paralyzed:
Genie in a bottle, sealed with cork;
Questions trigger mental torque.
How do I get from here to win?
What do I do to begin?
I pray for change; I sit and yearn.
I pray my flame bursts to burn

With grounded eyes I soon realize
Triumph begins with sloth's demise;
Thirsts are quenched through work and faith.
With God one can only do great--
Not great as in wealth, but great as in Will,
Using life for His purpose, my call to fulfill.

--Tiffany Tolbert

202

Borrowed Love

Please return, my love;
Come back.
Give me what you promised me,
For I lack companion.
I am not what most thought of me--and I am glad
Because I wrote you a song--versed a poem
In three words; I borrowed love.
I painted a cat--
Though I am not one for that.
I prefer dogs.
You know me better than that.
You can't go wrong when you borrow love.
I solved a puzzle,
But that was once--
I should have known
It had your name.
You've hidden stones beneath a rock.
But that was when
You borrowed love.
I washed my car while reading a book.
I thought I wrote this one for you.
You know me better than anyone does.
I mean so much--
Let me borrow your love.

--Dania Roker

Journey from Past to Present

From the moment I saw them I knew it.
It was bound to be a class reunion.
We'd met once before,
But when I offered them tea, we would meet again.
And, so, we did.

The day of our journey
I chattered away. I talked up a storm.
I was no longer cross word puzzled--
At least not while I searched for the map on the coffee table.
But, meanwhile, the bar was cold; we felt the chill of snow down
our spines.
By then, we knew we were getting old,
For only old age could tell us: go on your own.
Make room for a toast.
And the bartender would say to the barrister, "This goes on every
year; they meet, then they disappear."
After the bartender served us wine, we would have the barrister
make us coffee.
Then she'd say:
"Soup for supper is in the den,
The swan is cooked, the chicken laid."
The cup on the coffee table left a ring.

And he'd get on one knee and propose to her.

--Dania Roker

Atalanta

Graceful Atalanta, true as the wind and free as the Furies, bows
to no man.
Rather would she feel the warmth of the sun caressing her back,
her face and neck, than the possessive touch of a lover.
She is a light bird, who rides upon torrents of air like a Siren's
song, taunting men to curious damnation.
She is Torment; she is Divine.

Hippomenes must own her.
He cannot remove from his mind her hair, flowing behind her as
a maiden's garland, caught by Aeolus' sigh, her breasts heaving
high and proud, nor her thighs in mercury motion, charging over
men's lives.

204

And by the fruits of the Hesperades shall he win her, cage her
soul with his ripe desire and teach her the sun is no equal to his
own heat;

Yet Beauty must by Beauty be deceived, and the glimmering
apples are enough to quicken her beat, slow her so that he plucks
victory from her gleaming eyes.

In sunset dusk he takes her. She lies in wait, frozen in caged suffering, heart beating swiftly. The wind has stopped; outside their
window the blackening sky creeps in, like dark honey spilling
over.

Hypnos overtakes her,
      and she dreams of wilderness in the dawn,
      of gliding through tall and reaching boughs,
      of birds mysterious drifting out to meet the sun.
And somewhere behind, the roar of the beast still in the dark,
awaiting her return.

(In the original myth, Aphrodite blessed — or cursed — their union with mutual
love, but in their joy they forgot to give sacrifice to her, and she turned them
both into lions for ingratitude. The Greeks believed that lions could not mate.
I felt that by forcing love on one who was already in love — with freedom
and nature — Aphrodite committed an act of emotional rape, and sanctified
Hippomenes' obsession. At the end of the poem, the dream represents her
emotional state, and remains in line with the myth. She is a victim: forced
into love, then punished by the goddess.)

--Steven Peano

I Am Eros

I would freeze eternity for the sake of your eyes. You leave me
      breathless, the sun that beats upon my back, the oasis that
      slakes restless thirst, which goads to insanity. For you
      would I feel my fears, and dare to face them all, stay the
      gaze of these Gorgons and slay with the mirrored shield
      that is your strength.

Your touch is a gift of the Muses, and no beauty holds Apollo
or Aphrodite as your own golden soul, precious as the
golden apples to Hippomenes. Were I Orpheus, would I
have lost you much sooner: there in the very anteroom of
Hades, as you came to greet and follow? Such a hand
some Spirit I could never deny my eyes.

And when tears stream from your eyes--eyes the color of Jutur
na's own pool, eyes the color of crisp and autumn leaves
dancing in the wind of the dust-filled dusk—will I collect
them in the cup of my palm and cast them into the ne
penthian river, swim with you the waters of sweet for
getfulness, cleanse your pain.

I am Eros; you my Psyche. You will keep my commandments,
and I will give you my heart.

--Steven Peano

Essays

Haiku 37: Writer's Block

Expectant paper
blank as the moon's gaze,
Lingering in doubt.

--Steven Peano

The Birth of an Essay

Dear to my heart, this babe,
Born with defects
And a face that only a mother could love.

Oh—but the pain from whence she came!
The hours of wrenching labor!

"How much time she takes, dressing and redressing that child!"
My friends and relatives complain.
"When will she ever be done?"
"When will she admit blemishes, and stop adding trinkets and frills?"

> She is mine.
> She came from me.
> She is part of me.
> I am her Mother.
> I am her Creator.
> She is created in my image–
> Her imperfections are mine.

When does a god stop and say, "This is the best I could do?"

So, dear Doctor, inspect her with excruciating detail, if you must.

> But whatever Apgar score you assign,
> She will be forever mine–
> For better or for worse.

--Terri DeFoor

Living in Welfare

Like the women Alice Walker of Eatonton, Georgia, the eighth child of a Georgia sharecropper, described in "In Our Mothers' Gardens," my mother waited, never knowing who she really was or what artistic gifts she might have. My mother waited for "the first" to get her monthly welfare payment so she could buy groceries and maybe a long overdue pair of shoes for one of the children in addition to repaying the neighbors, relatives, and friends she had borrowed from to make it to the end of the month. She never could make it—our pantry was bare long before the end was in sight. Money for school supplies and field trips was nonexistent or delayed until the last moment, creating in the children anxiety about school and social events.

A child herself, my mother started having children at the age of fourteen. By the time she was seventeen, she had borne three children and decided to marry my father. Marriage didn't supply the necessary economic support, so she applied for government assistance. Like many men who cannot seem to find a productive place in the community, my father abused my mother physically and mentally. After repeated beatings, my mother finally got the courage and strength to leave my father. We became the quintessential one-parent family: a single mother with no education or job skills and five children, who knew only the despair, degradation, and daily hopelessness of living off the dole. Our mother and other mothers like her were the only role models we had.

Like my mother, my father had grown up in "the system," not ever having been exposed to men who went to work everyday and supported their families. His models were angry men who had been so devalued that they did not value themselves or anyone else. These men, usually living off the women, called the day the women received their monthly welfare check "Mother's Day." In the early days of welfare, men not only did not receive the check, the women couldn't receive welfare funds if the men lived in the same house with them. The caseworker would make her rounds at various times to try to catch the men at home. Creative warning systems developed in these communities to relay messages to the women so that the men could escape before the arrival of the caseworker, who could discontinue benefits. The dissolution of the black family effected under slavery was thus extended via the welfare system. The strengthening of families is not a national priority even today. Politicians pay lip service to family values, but rarely do they initiate programs to foster more stable relationships.

Changes in the welfare system eventually made it in some ways friendlier to families. Simultaneously, a new family-devaluing system developed especially in the South where the population of blacks and poverty levels are greater than in the rest of the nation: incarceration rates substantially increased for young black men. Like the mothers who waited on the monthly checks, young fathers now languished in jails across the nation. Freedom, if it ever came, often meant fewer job choices with a resulting lower wage-earning capacity. Like Robbie in John Wideman's "Our Time," young men turned to selling drugs for the greater possible earning potential. A young man might bring home more money in one sale than he could earn in a week. Unfortunately, many also became drug users, waiting for their next fix and selling drugs mainly to get it. The black family progressed to a new level of dissolution along with many especially poor white families across the nation—caught up in a cycle of poverty, drugs, and lack of education or job skills.

Within the cycle, it is almost impossible to find the way out. Einstein maintained that a problem cannot be solved on the level at which it is created. In a sense, the families involved did not create the problems with which they are now required to function as well as they can. Black people did not invent Jim Crow. White people did not invent the dust bowls, the Katrinas, the illnesses, and even the system of laws that favor the wealthy. Poor Southerners of all colors usually have to battle the standard English requirement to progress in school. They speak one way at home and in their communities and another way in institutions of education. The standard form of English is established on the basis of prestige, something in short supply in poor neighborhoods. Thus the poor often have to learn a "new language" to access the system of education successfully. They have to wait for someone to teach them—to tell them what is right and wrong. They have no idea of where they have to go and no idea how to get there—not even how to recognize when they have arrived.

The television pictures of New Orleanians at the Superdome after Katrina, waiting in vain for help to arrive, are forever seared in the national consciousness. Less visible are the faces of the more than 48 million Americans who must wait and wait for health care because they do not have health care insurance. In "Our Time," John Wideman introduces us to Garth, his brother's best friend, who suffers from an illness but is inadequately treated by uncaring and unconcerned doctors in the emergency room, leading to the deterioration of Garth's health and his eventual demise in his twenties. Garth was waiting for the doctors and the medicine they gave him to help him.

Like my mother, the Katrina survivors in New Orleans, the welfare fathers who couldn't come home, the young men in the criminal justice system, and Garth, I waited. Not having an available role model I could follow, I instinctively knew that the kind of life the welfare system afforded my family was really no life at all. This lifestyle affected my social and educational skills. It limited my ability to communicate with others. I always felt that someone was out to get me. Trusting in myself as well as in other individuals was a hard thing for me to do. There were

212

times when my heart was unbearably heavy, but I didn't have the courage to talk about the things that were hurting me inside. My education was limited by the poverty-stricken neighborhoods I was raised in. The schools in those neighborhoods had very poor academic standards, severely limiting effective learning opportunities. Sometimes students would be promoted to the next grade even though they had minimal or no reading skills.

I developed low esteem when I interacted with children from middle class neighborhoods. These children routinely made fun of my mother being on welfare, the neighborhood I lived in, the school I attended, and the clothes I wore, calling my mother "lazy," claiming she didn't want to work, and referring to her as "just a baby factory." I was embarrassed and deeply hurt. Remembering these acts of cruelty on the part of other children brings the hurt and trauma once again to the surface.

I recognized that my mother also suffered from low self-esteem. Like the women Alice Walker described, she had stopped believing in herself—stopped dreaming of a better life for herself and her children. I watched the interminable wait each month for the welfare check to arrive. Even though my mother knew $435.00 wasn't enough money to take care of eight children, not knowing what else to do, she chose to wait. She never had enough money to purchase clothes, shoes, and school supplies for her children. We were always in need of something. At the end of each month my mother had to borrow food from neighbors to feed us. She would promise to pay them back on the first of the month—when the check came. Poor people looked forward to "the first," "Mother's Day," or "Check Day." Many, like my mother, couldn't wait for the postman to bring the checks to their apartments. They would watch for the postman's truck and walk blocks to get their checks early.

It was a happy day for many, but a sad day for me. I was so fed up with waiting on the first of the month. Many times my siblings and I would have a field trip at school that required a small fee. Most of the time my mother had to borrow the money in order for us to go on the trips. It was impossible for her to

213

get out of the hole, because she always owed somebody some money. She had to pay the neighbors back the money she had borrowed for groceries. She had to pay the neighborhood store back when she "credited" food, formula and pampers for my baby sister. I became so frustrated with the way we were living that I began to beg my mother to look for a job–to which she replied, "One day."

I confessed to my mother that I was tired of lying to my friends that she worked at S&S Cafeteria. She didn't understand the negative effect the welfare system was having on me and my self-image. Like my mother, I began to doubt myself, asking myself big questions: Who am I? What is my purpose? Was I born on this earth just to suffer? Does anybody love me? How can I get out of this hellhole? I felt like I had nothing to be proud of: no identity, no dreams, no goals, and no happiness. In "The State," Edward Said wrote that the Palestinians, who were driven from their homeland to create the State of Israel, no longer knew who they were, where they came from, and what they were. I identify with Said's description of the Palestinians. Earlier in my life I didn't feel that I had an identity or voice either. Day in and day out these questions occupied my mind, eventually leading to thoughts of suicide. I couldn't get the picture straight.

At the age of sixteen I took a handful of my grandmother's sleeping pills. Fortunately for me, one of my younger brothers walked in on me as I swallowed the pills. He ran and got my mother, and I was rushed to the hospital. The doctor gave me some medicine that caused me to throw up the pills and admitted me to the hospital for evaluation. Some of the sleeping pills had dissolved into my system, causing me to sleep for hours. When I woke up, my mother was sitting in a chair near my bed, watching the heart monitor. She looked worried and sad. I couldn't explain to my mother why I no longer wanted to live. When the doctors entered my room, they asked why I had tried to kill myself. Angry and bitter, I refused to answer the question, keeping all my emotions bottled up inside.

214

The doctor referred me to a psychiatrist for treatment. After several sessions, I convinced my mother that I no longer needed to see the psychiatrist. Even though I stopped seeing my psychiatrist, I still suffered with depression. There wasn't a day that went by that I didn't find myself crying. My mother and I began to argue a lot. It seemed to me that she loved her boyfriend more than she loved her children. The close relationship we once had had begun to die. My best friend was no longer interested in the well-being of her children. The only friend I had, she no longer wanted to be bothered with me.

One night my mother and I got into an argument over my brother. She didn't seem to care how her boyfriend and his family treated him. When I began to confront her about these issues, she attacked me violently and threatened to have me locked up. In a moment of rage I jumped out of a two-storey window with no regard for my safety and life. God was so merciful to me, because I didn't suffer any major injuries. From that point on, our relationship was practically destroyed. I buried my feelings even deeper. I was convinced that people couldn't be trusted, causing me to have difficulties in relationships with others.

I then became entrapped in the very system that I hated: I became a pregnant teenager dependent upon low income housing and a check every month. The same system that had destroyed my mother's dream was now my only means of survival. It had become a repeated cycle of welfare, despair, and hopelessness. This system was the only way of life I knew. Now I was waiting for "the first."

When my son was four years old, I had the opportunity to participate in a "Welfare to Work" program. For the first time in my life, I had a job. I could support my son and myself. Even though he was only four, he was so happy for his mother that his eyes were shining. He must have sensed the tremendous difference that that intervention had made in my life. That achievement encouraged me to continue to develop myself. I am now working toward a degree in Human Services in Mercer University's College of Continuing and Professional Studies. I hope to develop the skills to help other families find their way out of a dead-end lifestyle.

While it is critical that families have a lifeboat for emergency situations over which they have no control, the welfare system as it is today prohibits individuals from reaching their full potential, resulting in their becoming complacent and unmotivated. The social environment promotes poverty, the use of alcohol and drugs, crime, broken families, and high dropout rates from schools and society. The welfare system teaches people to rely on the system, thus relieving them of accountability. Children tend to grow up thinking that this is a way of life that is passed down from generation to generation. In reality, this lifestyle hinders the personal growth of the individuals in the system. Long-term welfare recipients lose hope for the future, paring their dreams down to a Section 8 apartment and a monthly check.

--Mildred Smith

Giving Peace a Voice

After-Dinner Remarks
St George's House/Windsor Castle
England
January 28, 2009

I am truly honored to be here and to share this brief time with such a devoted and talented group of educators. Never before have I had the privilege of participating in such a gathering, and I want you to know how grateful I am to all those who have worked so long and so hard to make possible such an important event as this.

It's been a long day already for all of us. We are all tired, and the last thing any of us needs at this hour is a laborious, esoteric lecture about what to do in the classroom. In one way or another, we are all educators who know already some important things about learning, and I make no claim to knowing more

216

And by the fruits of the Hesperades shall he win her, cage her soul with his ripe desire and teach her the sun is no equal to his own heat;

Yet Beauty must by Beauty be deceived, and the glimmering apples are enough to quicken her beat, slow her so that he plucks victory from her gleaming eyes.

In sunset dusk he takes her. She lies in wait, frozen in caged suffering, heart beating swiftly. The wind has stopped; outside their window the blackening sky creeps in, like dark honey spilling over.

Hypnos overtakes her,
       and she dreams of wilderness in the dawn,
       of gliding through tall and reaching boughs,
       of birds mysterious drifting out to meet the sun.
And somewhere behind, the roar of the beast still in the dark, awaiting her return.

(In the original myth, Aphrodite blessed — or cursed — their union with mutual love, but in their joy they forgot to give sacrifice to her, and she turned them both into lions for ingratitude. The Greeks believed that lions could not mate. I felt that by forcing love on one who was already in love — with freedom and nature — Aphrodite committed an act of emotional rape, and sanctified Hippomenes' obsession. At the end of the poem, the dream represents her emotional state, and remains in line with the myth. She is a victim: forced into love, then punished by the goddess.)

--Steven Peano

I Am Eros

I would freeze eternity for the sake of your eyes. You leave me
      breathless, the sun that beats upon my back, the oasis that
      slakes restless thirst, which goads to insanity. For you
      would I feel my fears, and dare to face them all, stay the
      gaze of these Gorgons and slay with the mirrored shield
      that is your strength.

Your touch is a gift of the Muses, and no beauty holds Apollo
    or Aphrodite as your own golden soul, precious as the
    golden apples to Hippomenes. Were I Orpheus, would I
    have lost you much sooner: there in the very anteroom of
    Hades, as you came to greet and follow? Such a hand
    some Spirit I could never deny my eyes.

And when tears stream from your eyes--eyes the color of Jutur
    na's own pool, eyes the color of crisp and autumn leaves
    dancing in the wind of the dust-filled dusk—will I collect
    them in the cup of my palm and cast them into the ne
    penthian river, swim with you the waters of sweet for
    getfulness, cleanse your pain.

I am Eros; you my Psyche. You will keep my commandments,
    and I will give you my heart.

--Steven Peano

206

about education than anyone else in this room. What I WOULD like for us to do for the next few minutes is to think together about why we are here and about what we can hope to accomplish in the weeks and months and years that lie ahead.

Perhaps I can say best what I would like to say to you by telling you a story, a story about education that will probably be familiar to many, if not to most, of you. It's a story found in Plato's famous work *The Republic*, perhaps, some would say, the most important piece of literature to come from classical Greece. But before I tell the story, I want to explain the context. Plato's *Republic* is his attempt to describe what he believes would be the ideal society. As a literary form, it is what we would call a utopia, a vision or plan for a perfect, and therefore unattainable, world. What would such a world be like? In short, it would be a place where temperance, courage, wisdom, and justice govern the lives of individuals and of the society as a whole. Plato believed that no society can achieve its full potential if it cannot control its appetites, cannot endure in the face of adversity, and cannot make decisions in the present that will promote the long-term good of the society as a whole. Intemperance, cowardice, and foolishness will cripple, if not destroy, not only a person, but a society as well. If virtue, in other words, is overruled by vice, neither person nor society can expect to prosper indefinitely or to live for very long in harmonious relationship with others. The all-important question, of course, is this: Is a society ruled by virtue rather than vice really possible, and if so, what would be required in order to make it happen? Plato's answer to that question comes in the form of what we now call the thesis of *The Republic*. Plato writes: "Until philosophers are kings, or until the kings and princes of this world have the spirit of philosophy, that is to say, until power and wisdom come together in one, cities and states will never rest from their troubles."

What does this mean? What IS a philosopher? WHO is a philosopher? The Greek word *philosophia* combines two other Greek words, *philein*, a verb, which means "to love," and *sophia*, a noun, which means "wisdom." *Philosophia*, then, "phi-

losophy," means "the love of wisdom," and a philosopher is anyone who loves, seeks, and is guided by wisdom. Plato is saying
in the thesis of his *Republic* that not until our rulers, our leaders,
love, seek, and follow wisdom will we ever have the chance to
live in a prosperous and just and peaceful society. Power alone,
Plato believed, is never enough. Power must always be exercised with wisdom, and if our leaders are not wise, the exercise
of power will be ineffective, and, most likely, only destructive.
Many a nation, to its own shame, has failed to learn that lesson
until it is much too late, and there are others that need to learn
and take seriously the truth that power alone is not sufficient for
building a world we would all want to inhabit. There are even
now, as we know well, frightful displays of power all over the
world, but there is little evidence, I am afraid, that those garish
military outbursts are guided by wisdom. We cannot really expect, I think, to rid the world of hatred and resentment and anger
and fear and injustice with rockets and bombs. Power alone will
not bring us prosperity and justice and peace.

Now I would like to tell you the story I promised you a
few moments ago. It is found in Book VII of *The Republic*, and
Plato introduces it as a parable, an allegory, about education.
We customarily refer to it as the "Allegory of the Cave," and
the person telling the story is none other than Socrates himself,
Plato's teacher and the namesake of the Socratic Methodology.
Imagine, Socrates suggests, a cave in which there are prisoners
chained to the floor, unable to stand or move their heads about
to see behind them and able only to look at the wall in front of
which they sit. Behind them is the mouth of the cave, opening
to a world beyond, where there is light and a reality unknown
to the prisoners. The cave itself is dark, except for the dim light
filtering in from the world outside, and all that the prisoners see
are the shadows on the wall of the cave cast by the animals and
people and objects outside. These shadows the prisoners believe
to be real, and understandably so, because the shadows are all
they have ever seen. As Socrates is telling the story, one of his
students remarks, "What a strange image you have shown us,

218

Socrates, and what strange prisoners!" And Socrates responds, "Just like ourselves."

It's an allegory, you see, and WE, like the prisoners on the floor of the cave, are prisoners in our OWN caves, believing that only what WE have seen and experienced is the truth about reality. What do you think would happen, Socrates then asks, if one of the prisoners were released and were taken out of the cave into the world outside, a different world filled with light and strange objects? Initially, because of the bright light of this new world, the prisoner's eyes would be blinded and the prisoner would want to return to the cave, where the eyes were accustomed to the dim light of that underground abode. Eventually, of course, the eyes of the prisoner, initially blinded by the light, would adjust to the bright light of this new world, and the prisoner would finally begin to understand that what had originally been seen in the cave and believed to be real were actually only shadows cast by the objects in the world outside the cave. Astonishingly, what was thought to be true before is now seen to be but a pale image of what is really true! How terribly important it is to escape the cave, to begin to see beyond what one had originally believed to be all there is to be known! Enlightenment! Release from darkness into light! Education!

Our word **education** comes from the Latin *educare*, "to raise or bring up," and *educere*, "to lead out." "To have been educated" means "to have been brought up," "to have been led out." But "to educate" suggests more than "having BEEN brought up," "having BEEN led out." It means that we, the educators, are DOING the raising up, the leading out. And that is precisely the point that Plato makes in his allegory. Just as power alone is not enough for a person to be an effective leader, so having BEEN led out, having BEEN educated, is not all there is to BEING an educator. As important as it is to escape the darkness of the cave and to move into the light of a new world and of new understanding, it is equally important, Socrates argues, that those who would be effective leaders and educators must be willing to descend again into the cave and continue to work with those who remain chained in their own respective darkness.

Leaving the cave is never easy and always painful. Education—learning—is difficult, and relatively few dare to risk the journey, and it is often, if not always, the case that those who leave are LED. I do not know, I CANNOT know, where I would have been today if it had not been for Ralph Lynn, Wally Christian, Glenn Hinson, Bill Mallard, Manfred Hoffman, and Jean Hendricks—the teachers in my own life who took the time and invested the energy to meet me where I was, in my own darkness, and lead me into new paths and into ever greater understanding. Now it's payback time. Because those teachers did it for me, I can only, in good conscience, resolve to do it for those who come after me and who struggle still. After telling the allegory, after talking about turning the prisoner's body around toward the light, Socrates asks the sobering question, "How do you turn a SOUL around?" We know how to turn a BODY around, but how do you turn a SOUL, a LIFE, around? How do you lead a person from darkness and fear into light and confidence?

That, I think, is the question at the heart of every thoughtful and deliberate society and of every wise and compassionate teacher, and it is doubtful that a society can turn itself around until its citizens themselves begin to see the light. Do we not all know well what greed and arrogance and ignorance and dishonesty can do to a nation? Perhaps, in that light, it is not too much of an exaggeration to suggest that my own nation, America itself, is desperately in need of life-support. The critical question for me just now is, how do we turn America around? And perhaps from time to time you, too, ask a similar question about your own beloved native land.

Not so terribly long ago—it was in 1885—the famous Scottish poet and novelist Robert Louis Stevenson published his little book of poems called *A Child's Garden of Verses*. In that little volume is a short poem called "The Lamplighter." The story goes that, as a child, Stevenson, suffering from what may have been something like tuberculosis, lived with his parents in a little house on a hillside overlooking a village in his native

Scotland. Young Robert had become fascinated early on with the lamplighter (whom he called Leerie in his little poem) who nightly, with ladder and lantern, made his way through the village streets lighting the lamps so that all could make their way safely to and fro. One evening, as the young boy stood staring into the village below, his father asked him, "Robert, what are you looking at?" In boyish excitement, the young poet-to-be exclaimed, "Father, do you see that man down there? Do you know what he's doing? He's punching holes in the darkness!" Some 25 years or so later, Stevenson published his poem "The Lamplighter," in which he expressed the following inclination as to what he had imagined as a child that he would do with his life:

Now Tom would be a driver and Maria go to sea,
And my papa's a banker and rich as he can be;
But I, when I am stronger and can choose what I'm to do,
O Leerie, I'll go round at night
        and light the lamps with you!

Why are we here? Why do we do what we do? Why have we chosen the careers we have chosen? Is it for the money? Do we do what we do because we can make more money doing what we do than doing something else? Is it for the recognition we get from what we do? Are we here so that we can put on our resumes that we spent a couple of nights in Windsor Castle? No, of course not. None of that. Why, then, ARE we here?

The answer to that question has been given to us already. It's on the very first page of this little book.* The words read simply, "For the children." That's the answer. We are here for the children. We are here for our students. We are here for all those who live in darkness. But we are not BORN teachers. We CHOOSE to be teachers. I was born into a Christian family, but I didn't ask to be. I had wonderful parents, but I didn't choose them. I have light skin and blue eyes, but I didn't request them. I'm a native Texan and American, but I had nothing to do with where I was born. You didn't ask to be born Muslim or Jewish or Hindu or Buddhist, and you can't help it if you have black hair or red hair, brown eyes or green eyes, dark skin or light skin. You didn't choose any of that. There are some things we simply cannot control, but there are SOME things we CAN control. You—we—have CHOSEN to be teachers, and if we're serious about that choice, we must also take seriously the need to continue to work daily with those who, still in chains, have not yet seen the light.

The question was, and is, Why are we here? We might also consider briefly, of course, why we are NOT here. We are NOT here to preach at one another; we are here to dialogue. We are not here to monopolize the conversation; we are here to listen. We are not here primarily to defend some parochial point of view; we are here to consider possibilities that we may have dismissed before as incompatible with what we prefer to believe. As we consider for the next few hours the implications of our being here for the children, we are encouraged to be bold and to take some risks.

A few days ago I was reading through the St George's House website, and I came across a most interesting statement which, in reflecting on the mission of St George's House, issues both a challenge and an invitation. "We want people," it says, "to think the unthinkable." What does that mean, to think the unthinkable? And I wondered, "Is it not unthinkable to think that what we do in our classrooms might actually change things?" That's a tall order, changing things! And to think that it might happen as a result of how we teach!

But that's precisely what Colin Hannaford has challenged us all to do. I am so glad and privileged and proud to be here with all of you, but NONE of us would be here if it were not for Colin. We are here, Colin, because of you. We are NOT here, however, FOR you. We are here, as you have said, for the children, because in them, in the children, lies perhaps our only lasting hope.

A little over thirty years ago—it was in 1977—a movie came out entitled *Oh, God!* John Denver played Jerry Landers, a young grocery store manager, and George Burns played God.

At one point in the movie, Jerry, not quite yet convinced that the character played by Burns really is God, asks probingly, "How can you permit all the suffering that goes on in the world?" To which, God responds, "I don't permit the suffering. You do. Free will. All the choices are yours." Or again, from our own time, "If you're God, why don't you do something about the AIDS epidemic, or about the destruction and paranoia and fear and anger and resentment and injustice in the Middle East?!" The answer, of course, is, "Why don't you?!"

Rather than challenge God and ask, "Why don't you do something about the sorry plight of education in our world?" Colin Hannaford has decided to do something about it himself, and he has asked us all to join him in that task. Thank you, Colin, for all you have done and continue to do to help us understand that education is more than INformational; that it is, at its best, TRANSformational, because education at its very best can change a person's life. Perhaps, too, it might even change a nation—and dare we hope, in addition, that it might also change the world? "Father, do you see that man . . . over there? Do you know what he's doing? He's punching holes in the darkness!" So can we all. So let it be.

*The title of the book is Colin Hannaford's army number from his years with the military in England--473959, available online from Trafford Publishing Co., Oxford, England, at trafford.com.

--Duane Davis, Professor Emeritus of Liberal Studies, CCPS

Mathematics and Citizenship

In 2006, I was invited to Doha, Qatar (a small country bordering Saudi Arabia on the east) to give a presentation at an international conference about the social implications of teaching and learning mathematics through dialogue and contextual analysis of mathematical problems. During my presentation, I affirmed that the rate of change ought to be far more significant to leadership(s) of a given society than change itself. Change is a direction, exactly like democracy. Rates of change, on the other hand, take into account variables such as time, reflection, absorption of new ideas by individuals and groups, the impact of science and technology on culture, religious beliefs, and challenging the past with all of its trends and burdens.

During my presentation, I acknowledged that there must be time for reflection and response in society and by society as a whole in order for change to be meaningful and constructive. So, what is a rate of change? Is it not true that we discuss rates of change in a mathematics course? Here is an even more challenging question: what is mathematics?

Now, if you think of mathematics as a means to balancing your checkbook or managing your small business, or even as a gateway to a world of numbers, then I am afraid that you have a limited understanding of what mathematics is all about. Let's acknowledge, however, that mathematics has been defined by some as a science of patterns and by others as a universal language. Undoubtedly, these are good definitions. My choice, however, is to view mathematics and teach it as a series of arguments.

A proof, for example, consists of an argument or a series of linked arguments. Similarly, a debate can be seen as a series of arguments. Combined with an effective use of language and communication skills, arguments can become very powerful tools that cannot only help us connect with mathematics, but also with others.

Through debates we can establish dialogues with others and build society together; and as an outcome of debates we can build habits of mind that have the potential for transforming the mind itself and all of society through the diversity of thought processes. As Humboldt, a philosopher and linguist, once remarked, "If freedom is to exist, there must be diversity."

According to my colleague Colin Hannaford from Oxford, England, "The original purpose of mathematics teaching . . . is unknown to all but a handful of classical historians. They know that the style of argument on which mathematics depends was always intended to give more political freedom to ordinary people, to increase their confidence in democracy. Its purpose is to persuade people to accept logical truths freely and voluntarily, not to be bullied or oppressed by dogma or dogmatists to accept their ideas as absolute truths."

Did you ever solve a mathematics problem and witness freedom, justice, peace, harmony and even honesty, all of which are ingredients of fine citizenship? Aside from joy and fulfillment, solving a mathematical problem, simple or complex, is one of the most rewarding journeys one can embark upon.

We must not be afraid to change our perspectives about life as a whole or about mathematics as a subject. Change can be very healthy when it comes from within. Change is also necessary for survival in a world that is heavily shaped by all sorts of advancements in the sciences. Mathematics, therefore, can be seen as a philosophy of liberation. Yes, mathematics can transform our lives in meaningful ways and through meaningful debates.

My teaching philosophy, a part of my own professional journey, has been greatly inspired by mathematics. As a person who was exposed to a long history of religious, ideological, and cultural beliefs, I maintain that much of our knowledge–including our beliefs and attitudes toward mathematics–is strongly related to our history and distinct ways of living. I also believe that differences among people, including the ability to do mathematics, ought to be celebrated, negotiated and appreciated, not belittled.

I have lived most of my life in a wheelchair and spent the last 20 years in the classroom growing with students of various mathematics backgrounds and diverse cultural legacies. Fifteen years out of those 20 years were spent at Mercer University teaching adult students at the Regional Academic Centers.

I believe that with the appropriate methods of teaching, the appropriate utilization of technology in the classroom, and the deep understanding of how students develop their perspectives about mathematics as a subject and about themselves as learners and doers of mathematics, much of students' hindering beliefs, misconceptions, and negative attitudes toward mathematics and toward themselves as learners and doers of mathematics can indeed fade away. I do believe that all students can do mathematics, but this belief does not stand alone.

Students come to the mathematics classroom bringing with them a spectrum of abilities, ideas, experiences, stories, and sometimes very difficult conditions involving their very personal existence. Many of them feel that they were deprived of the necessary education and ignored by educational institutions; many feel lonely in their search to achieve success or to continue achieving success. Sometimes they even lack the support of their closest friends and family members. I do believe that all students can do mathematics, and I believe that I can make a huge difference in their expectations, their lives, and their journeys in discovering the beauty of mathematics and the inner self, and therefore, in discovering the uniqueness of others.

By growing with my students I share with them my own stories in life, my own struggles, dreams, and my journey to this great nation. I tell them that being in a wheelchair is just one difference between myself and others, a difference that I celebrate and do not regret, a situation that I live and do not forget, a fact that I accept and build on every day of my life. I tell them about my love for mathematics, the rigors of mathematics, and the joy of doing mathematics. I tell them about my friends, my family, and my journey to the United States of America and toward achieving my dream of obtaining higher education. I tell them that my dream remains to be with them in the classroom and to help them achieve their goals of becoming excellent professionals in their own fields of study. I listen to students and I let them believe that combining effort and perseverance is the only way toward success in mathematics and throughout life. It is learning and adapting that will set us free in this global world. Do not be afraid to change.

Let us lead by example and help others discover themselves as unique people with unique perspectives. I believe in the power of respect, the power of mathematics and words, the power of mind and articulation, and the power of celebrating differences through genuine and credible debates.

Finally, let's deepen our understanding of citizenship and respect through insight and mathematical inquiry. Let's help each other develop mathematical literacy at higher and higher levels in order to strengthen our understanding of a truly democratic society and of a truly genuine citizenship.

Mathematics has indeed contributed to my freedom at both the professional and intellectual levels. I hope that it will contribute to your life in meaningful ways as well.

Hani Khoury, Chair,
Department of Mathematics, Science, and Information Systems

Sustainability and Education

One of the definitions of "regenerate" is to restore to a better, higher, or more worthy state (Webster's Seventh New Collegiate Dictionary, 1969); therefore, when an organization or society undergoes regeneration, it should become a better, higher, or more worthy state. This action of regeneration in an organization or in society would be called organization development (OD) or organization change. A change that I'm passionate about promoting is the teaching of others about the importance of regenerating our environment. This change starts with the individual and grows as others become knowledgeable and involved with some aspect of recycling, conservation practices, green practices, or sustainability practices related to our environment.

As we move forward in the development of products, farming, electricity generation, and other activities that are necessary for creature comforts, we have to begin to think of the impact of what we do on future generations. This process is known as sustainable development. One of the highest regarded definitions of this practice was penned by Brundtland: "Sustainable development is development that meets the needs of the present without compromising the ability of future generations to meet their own needs" (As cited in Barlett & Chase, 2004, p.6).

A clear example of this practice would be related to the effects of the quality of air as we engage in meeting our current needs as a society as our standard of living increases. Air pollution is not something new. It has been with us for more than two centuries and there is growing evidence that air pollution was around even in some primitive societies. There are some studies that suggest that the air in our homes may be more polluted than the outside air. However, most air pollutants have been much reduced in today's world over measurements taken in the early 20th century with the exception of ozone and carbon dioxide. Ozone is formed by the chemical reaction of other pollutants. Carbon monoxide is a poisonous gas produced from combustible fossil fuels used in automobiles, home heating, and many manufacturing processes (Brown, 2002).

Senge, *et al*. (2008) offers an excellent model for use by corporate America for initiating and building sustainable practices in organizations. The key ingredient is administrative support from the top of the organization to the bottom. This support is manifested by informing the corporation's employees of the corporate strategy of sustainable practices and putting training programs about green practices in place for those employees. Corporations are finding that in order to survive and grow, there has to be a strategic plan at the mega level that not only addresses the strategy of the corporation but also includes a strategy about environmental issues in the local communities in which it does its business. This model is adaptable to other types of institutions such as universities, religious groups, and nonprofits.

I strongly believe that one way to approach sustainable practices is through the process of education, both formal and informal. The petro-chemical companies would have you believe that recycling plastics is a sustainable practice but a closer examination discloses this not to be true. The paper companies would have you believe that paper is the correct choice and that choice is also not true. Both products require much water in the manufacturing process and the manufacturing process creates and expels many air particulates that add to the already overly-taxed air quality. Remember, we breathe this stuff. The absolute best practice is to use reusable tote bags. (See HYPERLINK "http://www.treehugger.com" and HYPERLINK "http://www.mnn.com" for further information.)

An example of how education works involves some organization leadership program students, all ladies. In a course titled Contemporary Issues: A Leadership Perspective, two of the ladies presented papers about how the use of paper and/or plastic bags was a serious issue in society today and that the correct sustainable action to take was the use of reusable tote bags. A third student responded that she was completely unaware of the impact that plastic and paper bags could have on the environment and she proclaimed to the class that she would not use them again because of the compelling evidence presented by the other two students. She was an instantaneous convert to the tote bag. Education works. My plea to all students, staff, and faculty members is to think critically about individual habits and change them to be more in tune with the needs of future generations.

Last year in a "Lunch and Learn" session, I observed that one of the best ways to conserve water is to conserve electricity. Water is withdrawn from a lake or river to cool the steam and water after it has been used to drive the power generating turbines. This water has to be cooled before it can be discharged back into the lake or river or else it will kill the fish and destroy the ecosystem of that lake or river. Several in the audience did not know this. We had a lively discussion about the topic; another teachable moment.

Last year when water conservation was the media darling, I was discussing a practice that my wife and I had already begun to practice to water plants. When we shower, we place open containers on the shower floor and catch the water. We then pour that water into a larger container in the garage and use it to water plants. One student responded that he had never thought of doing anything like that. The problem was not that he was ignorant about water conservation; he was in some respects, but he simply was not well informed. Again, these topics are worthy of classroom discussion as well as written assignments and maybe some of it will stick with our students, staff, and faculty members; after all, it's about education.

Understanding the environment and researching the truth about sustainability or green practices or environmental conservation are more important to our future generations than they are to us. Wouldn't it be great to wake up one morning and discover an active program at Mercer University to become a leader in sustainability practices, not only in the act of recycling on the various campuses, but incorporating some aspect of environmental awareness and green practices in the classroom. It would work in any course.

References

Barlett, P. F. & Chase, G. W. (Eds.). (2004). Sustainability on campus: stories and strategies for change. Ambridge, MA: The MIT Press.

Brown, R. H. (2002). The greening of Georgia: the improvement of the environment in the twentieth century. Macon, GA: Mercer University Press.

Senge, P., Smith, B., Kruschwitz, N., Laur, J., & Schley, S. (2008). The necessary revolution: how individuals and organizations are working together to create a sustainable world. New York: Doubleday.

-- Richard R. Bohannon, Ed.D.
Assistant Professor of Counseling and Human Science

Beecher versus Grimké:
Reasoned Arguments on Abolition and a Woman's Place

Outspoken intellectuals Angelina Grimké and Catharine Beecher debated the issue of slavery in 1836 and 1837 through a series of published letters. This exchange yields the opportunity to examine their opposing attitudes about a woman's proper role in nineteenth-century America, while also providing a snapshot of the public and private discussion of this issue. Beecher and Grimké used the sensitive question of slavery to highlight another volatile subject—the proper place for a woman—and they did it using the "masculine" trait of rational deductive reasoning. In one sense, the debate juxtaposed the conservative Beecher with the radical Grimké. But in another very real sense, they were *both* advocates of the expansion of women's roles in the antebellum period and beyond.

Grimké, the daughter of a wealthy slaveholding Charleston planter, wrote *An Appeal to the Christian Women of the South* that was published in pamphlet form by the American Anti-Slavery Society in 1836. It caught the attention of Beecher, a well-known advocate for female education, who published in 1837 a rebuttal entitled *An Essay on Slavery and Abolitionism, with Reference to the Duty of American Females.* Later that same year, Grimké replied in a series of stinging *Letters to Catharine Beecher,* published in *The Liberator* and *The Emancipator.*

There was a countless array of various reform movements in the nineteenth century, as the new nation moved into a turbulent adolescence. Evangelical revivals swept the country and gave birth to numerous benevolent societies, answering the call of sundry problems associated with the industrial boom. The vision and direction of the republic was being hammered out, and cheap available print was the soapbox around which citizens gathered. One of the most controversial movements was that of the Garrisonian abolitionists, which began in earnest with the first publication of *The Liberator* in January 1831; it rejected gradualism and colonization, and called for the immediate abolition of slavery.[1] That summer, Nat Turner led his slave insurrection in Southampton County, Virginia; many laid the blame squarely on William Lloyd

---

[1] Christopher Stokes, "Colonization, Abolitionism, and Race" (lecture, Mercer University, Macon, Ga., September 13, 2006).

Garrison's fringe element. Passions and fears rose, especially in the southern slave states, and defenses mounted against the meddling northern abolitionists.[2]

In the midst of the slavery controversy, an unlikely future cohort of the abolitionist cause relocated from Charleston to Philadelphia. Angelina Grimké followed her older sister Sarah there in 1829 (who would later follow Angelina into the abolitionist movement), and adopted her newfound Quaker beliefs.[3] The sisters were daughters of a wealthy slaveholding planter who served on the South Carolina Supreme Court. Most of the family's slaves worked on their Union County plantation, some two-hundred miles away, but the Grimké sisters grew up among the Charleston elite, surrounded by house slaves; all eleven siblings were each given a companion slave close to their own age. Mrs. Grimké was a stern administrator over her slaves and her children, with a keen awareness of their "standing" in society. She was dogmatically devoted to her Episcopalian faith and an active member of Charleston's Ladies Benevolent Society, through which she "visit[ed] the needy, the destitute sick, [and] the sinful woman prisoner."[4] The Grimké matron was all that society expected her to be within her appropriate "sphere." She would later have a strained relationship with Angelina and Sarah, who stepped out of the "natural" bounds appropriate for females, and into swirling controversy over abolition, another subject on which mother and daughters would stand at polar opposites.

During a visit to Philadelphia, Catharine Beecher had met Angelina Grimké briefly, and had invited her to visit her Hartford Female Seminary. Beecher had been impressed enough with Grimké's superior intellect that she offered to instruct her for six months, and thereafter employ her as a teacher at the school. Grimké's July 1831 visit to the seminary was a positive

2 Charles Sellers, *The Market Revolution* (New York: Oxford University Press, 1991), 387.
3 Katharine Du Pre Lumpkin, *The Emancipation of Angelina Grimké* (Chapel Hill: University of North Carolina, 1974), 58–59.
4 *Ibid.*, 6.

experience, opening her mind to new possibilities. She was quite impressed with Beecher and her school, and when she and a traveling companion left at the end of the month, Beecher accompanied them as far as New York. Grimké recalled fondly times of laughter and friendship as they traveled.[5] It was likely the last time that she felt amicable toward Beecher, though they would address each other in later public letters as "friend."

Upon returning to Philadelphia, Grimké learned that her newly adopted Quaker Society would not give her permission to attend Beecher's seminary, warning her that it would be dangerous to mix so closely with "Presbyterians."[6] The Grimké sisters settled somewhat bumpily into their Society of Friends, disagreeing with some of the unyielding authoritarianism, but drawn by the calm simplicity, which was in so many ways opposite from their tense, busy upbringing.

The American Anti-Slavery Society was formed in Philadelphia in December 1833, and three days later a group of abolitionist women organized the Philadelphia Female Anti-Slavery Society.[7] Yet the two women who would in a few short years be leading the charge were not among the founders. Angelina and Sarah had for some time been reading American and English publications on the question of slavery and emancipation, and shortly after the abolition societies were formed, they began taking Garrison's *Liberator*. Angelina was particularly interested in the possibility of taking up the cause, and against the advice of her sister and her Quaker overseers, she attended a lecture by British abolitionist George Thompson in March 1835.[8] Two months later, she joined the Philadelphia Female Anti-Slavery Society, and four months thereafter wrote her infamous letter to William Lloyd Garrison, who promptly published it without her permission in the September 19, 1835 issue of *The Liberator*. In it she proclaimed her willingness to

5 *Ibid.*, 62–65.
6 *Ibid.*, 66.
7 Bruce Dorsey, *Reforming Men and Women* (New York: Cornell University Press, 2002), 166.
8 Pamela Durso, *The Power of Woman* (Macon, Ga.: Mercer University Press, 2003), 70.

be persecuted for the cause of immediate abolition, expressing her "deep, solemn, deliberate conviction that *this is a cause worth dying for.*"[9]

Less than a year later, Angelina wrote her *Appeal to the Christian Women of the South*, published by the American Anti-Slavery society in the summer of 1836. It wasn't long before Sarah became convinced of God's call on both of their lives, and followed her younger sister into the fray. After a stern rebuke from their Society of Friends, the sisters left the Quaker group, and would later speak of the restrictive oppression they had endured. They continued, however, in their "plain" attire, and in the basic tenets of Quakerism.[10]

In November, the sisters were the only females invited to attend the Agents' Convention of the American Anti-Slavery Society.[11] Beginning in 1837, and for the next few years, Sarah and Angelina Grimké traveled New England, drawing larger and larger crowds. Thunderous and constant were the opposing voices. Not only were these women speaking and writing about the sins of the South *and* the North, but they were daring to step outside their "sphere" as women and address "promiscuous," or gender-mixed, audiences. Conservative clergy began to speak out against them and warn their congregations to stay away. This seemed to have the reverse effect, as the sisters became somewhat of a spectacle.[12]

During Angelina Grimké's explosion onto the public scene, Catharine Beecher was in Cincinnati, where in 1832 she had followed her father, well-known Congregational minister Lyman Beecher. He was serving as president of the newly formed Lane Theological Seminary, after leaving a ministry position in Boston. Catharine left the Hartford Female Seminary that she had founded in 1823 with the hopes of beginning another facility to train young women to teach school. A vast

[9] *Ibid.*, 86–87, author's italics.
[10] *Ibid.*, 72–74.
[11] *Ibid.*, 92.
[12] *Ibid.*, 94–102.

need was developing as more Americans pulled up stakes and headed west, and educating children was an appropriate—indeed, an exalted—feminine endeavor. Catharine Beecher was beginning to see herself as a pioneer of women's education.[13]

The Beecher children had grown up in a vastly different environment from the Grimké clan. A meager minister's salary always assured shortcomings, and Catharine remembered her mother, who birthed nine children in thirteen years, adding more to an already impossibly hectic schedule by running a small boarding school. If a burgeoning household was not enough, Lyman Beecher was absent for long periods, and whenever he was at home, he was prone to "dyspepsia." The described episodes were more depression than indigestion, and would show up later in other family members. Catharine would grow up close to her stern but loving father, but somewhat distant from her mother.[14]

As the eldest, Catharine was a domineering sister; the tendency to involve herself in the business of others would later earn her the reputation of a meddler.[15] This caused inconsistency much of the time between her ideals about the proper place of a woman and the role she allowed for herself. As one historian observed, she "did not hesitate to join in the most controversial theological, economic, or political debates of the era."[16] Beecher family biographer Milton Rugoff related a time when Catharine Beecher created a local scandal while "helping" a former student vindicate her bruised honor. Though she was forbidden by local clergy and her brothers, she published a book about the entire incident, which prompted a New York literary critic to christen her "busybody general."[17]

When Lane Seminary theology student Theodore Dwight

13 Marli Weiner, "Rural Women." *A Companion to American Women's History* (Oxford: Blackwell Publishing), 162.
14 Milton Rugoff, *The Beechers* (New York: Harper and Row, 1981), 13, 20.
15 *Ibid.*, 190–192.
16 Robert Nelson, "The Forgetfulness of Sex: Devotion and Desire in the Courtship Letters of Angelina Grimké and Theodore Dwight Weld." *Journal of Social History* (2004), 487.
17 Rugoff, 191–192.

Weld requested permission to organize a debate to determine the merits of abolition versus colonization, Lyman Beecher naively allowed it, smugly convinced that common sense—and the colonization position—would prove triumphant.[18] The result of the eighteen-day event would prove disastrous for the school when Weld convinced students of the merits of abolitionism and the prejudice underlying the colonization movement. When the students put feet to their convictions and began to mingle publicly with blacks, Cincinnati was in an uproar, and Lane's board of trustees insisted that Beecher put a stop to the "rebellion." An overwhelming number of students transferred to evangelist Charles Finney's Oberlin College, and the financial backing of the New York Tappan brothers went there as well.[19] According to the observations of Rugoff, "[n]othing could have seemed more perverse [to president Beecher] than that a band of theological students should suddenly have staged such a devastating revolt."[20] Catharine Beecher must have been incensed at the treatment of her father by these abolitionist radicals, and while her own female institution was suffering from a lack of students (albeit for very different reasons), her father's student body would dwindle to barely a handful.[21]

Beecher, then, was thoroughly familiar with abolitionist positions well before Angelina Grimké wrote her *Appeal* in 1836. To be sure, she was abreast of all the Lane debates and the actions of the students. She perceived, as did most of America, that the entire lot of abolitionists were menacing radicals bent on pushing their dangerous agenda, without considering social order and decorum. Worse still were those few outspoken females who had joined their ranks, and when Grimké's pamphlet reached her, Beecher's dutiful response was inevitable.

In her *Appeal to the Christian Women of the South*, Grimké used systematic reasoning and passionate rhetoric

---

[18] *Ibid.*, 144–146.
[19] Sellers, 235, 403.
[20] Rugoff, 151.
[21] Sellers, 403.

designed to reach both head and heart of her female audience. After claiming the Bible as her "ultimate appeal in all matters of faith and practice,"[22] Grimké listed seven arguments against slavery. Five appealed directly to scripture, one to the Declaration of Independence, and one to the human rights of natural law. She then laid out four things that women in the South could do to "overthrow slavery."[23] They should inform themselves by reading on the subject, they should pray, they should speak—using "the tongue, the pen, and the press"—and they should act.[24] This call to action required setting free any slaves that they owned; but if their slaves chose to remain, they should be paid wages and taught to read.[25]

The *Appeal* then uses examples of heroic women throughout history, beginning with the Old Testament through the Middle Ages down through colonial time. Grimké ended this march through time with the recent heroines of the Ladies' Anti-Slavery Society in Boston, whose "lives were jeoparded [sic] by an infuriated crowd."[26] The remainder of this pamphlet is devoted to defending the measures of the abolitionists as non-insurrectionary.

Beecher opened her address, *An Essay on Slavery and Abolitionism, with Reference to the Duty of American Females* with a lengthy justification for publishing her response to Grimké's *Appeal*. Her first argument against Grimké's abolitionist assertions begins by differentiating the "principles" from the "measures" of abolitionists. She argued that the principles of those who are striving for gradual emancipation and those insisting on immediate abolition are virtually identical, but that their actions differ profoundly.[27] In answer to this, Grimké asserted in her *Letters to Catharine Beecher* that proponents

---

[22] Angelina Grimké, *An Appeal to the Christian Women of the South* (New York: American Anti-Slavery society, 1836), 3.
[23] *Ibid.*, 16.
[24] *Ibid.*, 16–17.
[25] *Ibid.*
[26] *Ibid.*, 21–23.
[27] Catharine Beecher, *An Essay on Slavery and Abolition with Reference to the Duty of Females* (Philadelphia: Henry Perkins, 1837), 6–7.

of gradual emancipation did not at all agree in principle with Abolitionists, as their very first tenet is that "man cannot rightfully hold his fellow man as property," and that "therefore... *every slaveholder is a man-stealer.*"[28]

To illustrate her call for the gradual end of slavery, Beecher then used the examples of Thomas Clarkson and William Wilberforce, men who had worked tirelessly for several years to end the slave trade and then outlaw slavery in the British Empire. They accomplished this using "a modest and lowly spirit," and "benignity, gentleness, and kindheartedness."[29] These are among the very attributes that Beecher used to characterize women who are operating within their proper "sphere." She then compared the behavior of these men to the abrasive conduct of William Garrison, who used coercion and incendiary language.[30] But later, when discussing gendered spheres of societal operation, she considered that:

> A man may act on society by the collision of intellect, in public debate; he may urge his measures by a sense of shame, by fear, and by personal interest; he may coerce by the combination of public sentiment; he may drive by physical force, and he does not outstep the boundaries of his sphere.[31]

By this we may conclude that Beecher considered Garrisonian abolitionist men as having overused or abused the natural inclinations of masculinity, while she applauded the "feminine" qualities of Clarkson and Wilberforce.

Gender bifurcation of the nineteenth century left male converts to evangelicalism in a quandary, for to adopt the meekness and gentleness called for by Christianity meant entering into a distinctly feminine arena.[32] For Beecher, the natural inclinations of women allowed them moral superiority,

---

28 Angelina Grimké, *Letters to Catharine Beecher* (Boston: Isaac Knapp, 1838), 4.
29 Beecher, 22.
30 *Ibid.*, 21–24.
31 *Ibid.*, 100.
32 David Kling, "For Males Only: The Image of the Infidel and the Construction of Gender in the Second Great Awakening in New England." *Journal of Men's Studies* (1995), 335–346.

though they must operate from inside a sphere subordinate to men.[33] They must use their influence to quietly manipulate change. According to this model, then, the male who adopts feminine characteristics would have the most influence for reform, since he has become superior in morals but without the societal constraints placed on women.

Grimké's *Letters to Catharine Beecher* was first published by the *Liberator* and the *Emancipator* in a series from June through October in 1837. In it, she maintained that the Bible does not teach this idea of separate spheres, but calls all to the same "rule of action."[34] She challenged Beecher's authority as a judge of societal roles and pointed to biblical examples of men with gentleness and women with leadership roles.[35]

Beecher's address to Grimké proclaims that those women who best administer their proper role of influence will instigate the changes they seek with ease. "Woman is to win every thing [sic] by peace and love," she asserted, "by making herself so much respected, esteemed and loved, that to yield to her opinions and to gratify her wishes, will be the freewill offering of the heart."[36] Grimké's challenge to this lofty ideal is decisively potent: "This principle may do as the rule of action to the fashionable belle, whose idol is *herself*, whose every attitude and smile are designed to win the admiration of others to *herself*, and who enjoys, with exquisite delight, the double-refined incense of flattery which is offered to *her* vanity, by yielding to *her* opinions, and gratifying *her* wishes, because they are *hers*.[37]

Grimké proclaimed that truth and the "higher motive" of following Christ are to be esteemed, rather than the desires of an irresistible female. Grimké counseled that women should not be dependent on men, but that both should be equally dependent on God.[38] Presumably, for Beecher this decree was rather symbolic;

---

33 Beecher, 128–129.
34 Grimké, *Letters to Catharine Beecher*, 103.
35 *Ibid.*, 105–106.
36 Beecher, 100–101.
37 Grimké, *Letters to Catharine Beecher*, 104 (author's italics)..
38 *Ibid.*, 104, 107.

practical societal hierarchy required women to be dependent upon men.

Grimké's views were radical for her time. Before she married Theodore Weld (the student who led a "rebellion" at Lyman Beecher's seminary) in May of 1838, they crafted—through a three-month prenuptial letter exchange—what the ideal Christian marriage should look like. Using creative language, at times comically gymnastic, they determined to have a marriage of equality as two disembodied spiritual beings, without reference to gender.[39] According to Beecher, a woman voluntarily put herself into a submissive role as wife. Once married, her influence should become private and meek.[40]

After lecturing Grimké in her *Essay* on all the reasons that women should not be involved in the public arena of party politics, Beecher pointed to a more effective and legitimate role–that of teacher. She reminded Grimké of the pressing need for educated teachers, especially in the new western frontier. Grimké expressed concern that a democratic nation could not function properly without an educated populace.[41] This idea of "republican motherhood" contended that women, in their private role, determined the rise or fall of the nation. They must teach their young children, or employ someone who can. The energy that Beecher saw the intelligent Grimké display for the misguided cause of abolition would be better applied to the more constructive role of teacher. Education was the key to changing the hearts of the nation on the issue of slavery.[42]

Grimké responded by questioning why educating children had to be the sole responsibility of women. She asked why it was considered a menial task beneath men, given the brevity of the charge to instill truth into the minds of the young. Launching into grandiosity, Grimké proclaimed abolitionism as a healthy part of a thorough education, concluding that

---

39 Nelson, 665.
40 Mark David Hall, "Beyond Self–Interest: The Political Theory and Practice of Evangelical Women in Antebellum America." *Journal of Church and State* (2002), 488.
41 Beecher, 105–107.
42 *Ibid.*

"Intellectual endowments are *good*, but a high standard of moral principle is *better*, is *essential*."[43]

Rampant reform movements attest to the overarching belief in the eventual perfection of the world, and as millennialists both Beecher and Grimké understood humankind's role in ushering in a new and better age. In her *Appeal*, Grimké named various reform movements that were "walking abroad through the earth scattering the seeds of truth" and keeping at bay the "black clouds of vengeance" that would cause in America the same "fate of the devoted cities of the plain."[44] Grimké saw the abolitionist movement as the ultimate reform movement, and one that must take place before the millennial reign could begin. For Beecher, ideals about social order and place, as well as the patience to wait for a gradual, bloodless solution for emancipation, would be the path toward a perfected world.

Grimké reflected the impatience of the Abolitionists in her *Essay* when she warned that "there are only two ways in which [immediate emancipation] can be effected, by moral power or physical force, and it is for you to choose which of these you prefer."[45] Beecher charged that because of Abolitionist rhetoric, the "minds of men [are] thrown into a ferment, and excited by those passions which blind the reason, and warp the moral sense."[46] She prophetically warned that one of the results of this uproar may be the severing of the Union. She called for common sense and compassion on both sides.[47]

Catharine Beecher was an advocate for the education of women in such a way as to empower them to reach their full potential without overstepping the appropriate boundaries. An important role within that sphere was the education of children by women as mothers and schoolteachers. She assigned moral superiority to females because of their "natural inclination" to virtue and goodness, but cautioned that the wise and educated

43 Grimké, *Letters to Catharine Beecher*, 124–125, author's italics.
44 Grimké, *An Appeal to the Christian Women of the South*, 27.
45 *Ibid.*, 24.
46 Beecher, 94.
47 *Ibid.*

woman should use those attributes in a softly manipulative fashion in order to sway opinion and action.

Grimké was a woman with the thoughtful rational abilities that Beecher sought so earnestly for all women. But her reasoning led her to evaluate the cause of radical abolitionism as worthy, and she employed all of her powers as an intelligent southern Christian woman to further that campaign. Her involvement in the issue of the rights of women was inevitable the moment her letter to Garrison was published, and it was heightened to a frenzied level when she later stood at the public podium, addressing audiences of men and women. The women's movement would mature at a snail's pace, but here it was born, the younger sibling of radical abolitionism.

Beecher idealistically envisioned educated women using their intellect inside the appropriate sphere of influence, but neither she nor Grimké would live up to that ideal. The bifurcated roles of gender would remain the status quo well into the twentieth century, in spite of the few outspoken females, mostly regarded as dangerous radicals.

BIBLIOGRAPHY

Primary Sources

Beecher, Catharine. *An Essay on Slavery and Abolition with Reference to the Duty of Females*. Philadelphia: Henry Perkins, 1837.

Grimké, Angelina. *An Appeal to the Christian Women of the South*. New York: American Anti-Slavery society, 1836.

Grimké, Angelina. *Letters to Catharine Beecher*. Boston: Isaac Knapp, 1838.

Secondary Sources

Dorsey, Bruce. *Reforming Men and Women*. New York: Cornell University Press, 2002.

Durso, Pamela. *The Power of Woman*. Macon, Ga.: Mercer University Press, 2003.

Hall, Mark David. "Beyond Self-Interest: The Political Theory and Practice of Evangelical Women in Antebellum America." *Journal of Church and State* (2002): 477 – 500.

King, David. "For Males Only: The Image of the Infidel and the Construction of Gender in the Second Great Awakening in New England." *Journal of Men's Studies* (1995): 335 – 346.

Lumpkin, Katharine Du Pre. *The Emancipation of Angelina Grimké*. Chapel Hill: University of North Carolina, 1974.

Nelson, Robert. "The Forgetfulness of Sex: Devotion and Desire in the Courtship Letters of Angela Grimké and Theodore Dwight Weld." *Journal of Social History* (2004): 663 – 680.

Rugoff, Milton. *The Beechers*. New York: Harper and Row, 1981.

Sellers, Charles. *The Market Revolution*. New York: Oxford University Press, 1991.

Stokes, Christopher. "Colonization, Abolitionism, and Race." Lecture, Mercer University, Macon, Ga., September 13, 2006.

--Terri DeFoor

The Capacity for Grace:
A Comparison of The Grandmother and the Misfit
In Flannery O'Connor's
"A Good Man is Hard to Find"

Flannery O'Connor's stories and their characters typically operate in two dimensions. While the physical action unfolds, a point of demanding spiritual application is usually ushered in violently. "A Good Man Is Hard to Find," written in 1955, is such a story. It chronicles a family's encounter with a violent criminal and the resulting tragedy, climaxing in a spiritual encounter between the two main characters. A careful comparison of the Grandmother and the Misfit reveals two distinctly different operations of philosophy or worldview. The Grandmother is a believer whose beliefs have hardly transformed her daily life. The Misfit is an unlikely spiritual seeker of sorts who realizes the true implications of belief as well as unbelief.

The grandmother's obstinate self-centeredness quickly becomes apparent as she tries to manipulate her son into taking the family to Tennessee to "visit some of her connections," instead of to their intended vacation site in Florida. She has seen an article in the paper about an escaped convict known as the Misfit who is purportedly heading for Florida; she pounces shamelessly on her son Bailey in an effort to change his plans—"'I wouldn't take my children in any direction with a criminal like that aloose in it'" (658). When that doesn't work, she self-righteously counsels her daughter-in-law about the need for the children to "'see different parts of the world and be broad'" (658). The next morning she sneaks her cat Pitty Sing into the car and is ready to go. Instead of pouting about not getting her way, she dresses up like the proper lady she believes herself to be, pronounces it to be a good day for driving, and, assuming the role of the ideal grandmother, begins to point out interesting landmarks to John Wesley and June Star, who sit on each side of her in the back seat. She bounces the baby on her knee, makes jokes, and tells stories from her childhood, priding herself on her "naturally sunny disposition" (661).

After a stop for lunch and a few short catnaps, the Grandmother begins reminiscing about a nearby plantation that she had once visited as a young lady. Overcome by memories, she wants to see the place again, but knows Bailey is not willing to make a stop. So she lies about a "secret panel" in the house, suggesting that the family who lived there during the Civil War may have hidden their gold behind it when Sherman marched through on the way to Savannah. This has the desired effect of getting the children excited enough to cajole their father into turning off the highway down a twisting dirt road in search of the old plantation house. The crafty grandmother is not above using these modern, demanding children for her own plans.

In a somewhat comic scene, the Grandmother is startled when she remembers the house is in Tennessee and not Georgia, upsetting the basket that holds the cat. Pitty Sing jumps onto Bailey's shoulders, causing him to lose control of the car. After the accident, the Grandmother lies about an "injured organ," hoping that will keep Bailey from being too angry with her. She decides it is wise to keep the reason for her jolt a secret. The shaken family gathers to access their situation. They are ten feet below the old dirt road in a clay ditch surrounded by dusty trees. The children's mother, who has suffered a broken shoulder, suggests that perhaps a car will come by. In just a few minutes one appears above them on the road, carrying three gun-toting occupants.

When the Misfit and the Grandmother first meet, he is soft-spoken and polite. The grandmother exaggerates the accident by saying the car flipped twice, and he corrects her, saying that he and his companions saw it happen, and it flipped only once. He asks them to all sit down. The Grandmother shouts her realization that he is the Misfit, dooming the entire family. Bailey reacts harshly, saying "something to his mother that shocked even the children" (665). When she begins to cry, the Misfit tries to comfort her: "'Don't you get upset.... I don't reckon he meant to talk to you thataway'" (665). She dabs her eyes, and in a selfish disregard for the rest of the family, she asks him, "'You wouldn't shoot a lady, would you?'" (665).

The Grandmother has caught a glimpse of what O'Connor called the Misfit's "capacity for grace" (111), so she begins to appeal to him in desperation: "'I know you're a good man.... I know you must come from nice people!'" (665). He reminisces about his family, and then looks at the family huddled together in front of him, making polite small talk about the weather. The grandmother tries once again to appeal to the Misfit as a "good man at heart" (665). As Bailey and John Wesley are escorted into the woods by the Misfit's companions, she continues to try to convince herself and the Misfit that he really is a good man and "not a bit common" (666). He counters that he is not a good man, but he "ain't the worst in the world neither" (666). The Misfit claims that his father called him a "different breed of dog" from his siblings, saying "'it's some that can live their whole life out without asking about it and it's others has to know why it is, and this boy is one of the latters'" (666). Conscious of expected social etiquette, he apologizes for not having a shirt on in front of the ladies. Desperate to save her own skin, the grandmother tries again to persuade the Misfit to change his ways, advising him that he should pray. Hearing gunshots from the woods, she calls out sadly, "Bailey Boy!" (667). The Misfit continues to talk to her about being in prison, confessing he was accused of killing his father, but claiming he didn't do it. After yet another appeal from the Grandmother concerning prayer, he tells her he doesn't pray because he doesn't need any help.

When the Misfit's two companions return, the rest of the family is taken into the woods, leaving the Grandmother alone with the Misfit. He softly converses about his punishments not equaling his crimes, explaining that he named himself the Misfit because he could not reconcile the consequences he paid with the bad things he had done. The Grandmother's desperation peaks when she hears more gunshots. She is now the sole survivor of the family; she knows she will be next.

As the Grandmother urgently seeks the divine spark in the Misfit in order to change the inevitable outcome of their chance meeting, he quietly and politely answers her questions and explains his philosophical quandary. He theorizes that Jesus threw everything off balance when He raised the dead. "If He did what He said, then it's nothing for you to do but thow [sic] away everything and follow Him," he says, "and if He didn't, then it's nothing for you to do but enjoy the few minutes you got left the best you can—by killing somebody or burning his house or doing some other meanness to him" (668).

The Misfit's voice cracks slightly when he says that if he had had physical proof of Jesus' resurrection, he would have lived his life totally differently. The Grandmother looks at him and at once sees clearly the picture before her. The believer sees the skeptic with spiritual eyes as "one of [her] own children" (669). With her own safety momentarily forgotten, she reaches out and touches him on the shoulder. The gesture so startles the Misfit that he immediately shoots and kills her. When his companions return from the woods, one of them comments on the talkativeness of the Grandmother, and he replies, "[S]he would have been a good woman if it had been someone there to shoot her every minute of her life" (669). The Misfit had recognized the Grandmother's inconsistencies soon after they had met: she had lived in a pragmatic denial of the faith she confessed. Her spiritual nature, though, had finally surfaced, and it had caught him off-guard. Following his violent reaction, he admits to his companion that her urgency had, in the end, uncovered her true nature.

The Grandmother had lived her life as a relatively decent Christian woman, not doing any great harm to anyone. But her beliefs did not sink too deeply. She had a good heart even though she was selfish and not above manipulation or dishonesty to get her way. She sometimes equated "good" with social standing, in stark contrast to the teachings of the Jesus she claimed as her Savior. But in the final instant of her life, she acts out her faith like the selfless Christian she was meant to be: she reaches out to the Misfit after a moment of spiritual clarity exposes her human connection to him, across all boundaries. In comparison, if the Misfit had been a believer, his would not ever have been a casual belief. He understands that radical belief in Jesus should be life-changing and permeate every part of one's existence. Conversely, the ambiguity and confusion of his unbelief are powerful enough to keep him off-balance. He may be polite and soft-spoken, and even empathetic toward others, but he is also a murderer.

Perhaps the reason for the Misfit's immediate and violent reaction toward the Grandmother's spiritual gesture was the recognition that only true selfless faith based on the power of a historically resurrected Christ could have caused such a moment. He was much more comfortable when the Grandmother was squirming in desperate self-preservation. It is interesting that this breakthrough moment between them was immediately preceded by the Misfit's expressed desire for proof of the resurrection power of Jesus. When the proof was offered and placed squarely in front of him, he shot it right through the heart.

REFERENCES

O'Connor, Flannery. "A Good Man Is Hard to Find." *The Story and Its Writer*. Ed. Ann Charters. New York: Bedford/St. Martin's, 2003.

O'Connor, Flannery. "A Reasonable Use of the Unreasonable." *Mystery and Manners*. Eds. Sally and Robert Fitzgerald. New York: Farrar, Straus, and Giroux, 1969.

--Terri DeFoor

The Road to Tolstoy

A Russian writer who created *Anna Karenina* and *War and Peace* is the extent to what most of us know about Tolstoy. What could possibly be the connection between him and the steady stream of literature we read at Mercer that mainly addresses the development of the individual and civil rights issues? The discovery of these connections was an interesting journey in the curriculum of the courses I have been taking in the College of Continuing and Professional Studies at Mercer.

In the book *Ways of Reading* used in the Liberal Studies 175-180 classes, I came face to face with my own pre-conceived ideas about American society. I was born in the Netherlands, a country that profited from slavery by capturing and buying the slaves from Africa and transporting them to America. However, in The Netherlands we never had slaves in that sense of the word or even an ethnic minority with that heritage in our nation. We pride ourselves on being one of the most tolerant nations in the world: the Netherlands is a safe haven for all refugees. To us, black people are totally cool and confident. They are better athletes and performers, always in high demand.

Coming to the States and working in Grady Memorial Hospital, I was shocked to discover the undercurrent of hostility between blacks and whites that took just a small flame to ignite into a furious battle. I was shocked to see the results of drugs, poverty, poor healthcare, and poor education. I thought all black people lived a "cool" life--which is of course a stereotype in itself, but one of admiration rather than pathos. I had seen "Roots" and "The North and South" with Patrick Swayze and I had

248

learned in school about the horrible suffering of the black people in Africa, but I felt that that was history, long ago, and over.

Why do black people look at me with distrust? Why do they keep to themselves? Why don't they just "get over it and move on"? They're physically stronger and just as smart. So what's holding them back? Some of the essays in *Ways of Reading* answered many of those questions.

Paulo Freire explains in his essay "The Banking Concept of Education" that if the teacher does not develop a dialogue with students and allow those students to solve problems--including their own reality, which for African Americans is vastly different from that of whites--, the students will not fulfill their true potential. From Richard Rodriguez's essay, "The Achievement of Desire," I learned that in order for students with different cultural backgrounds to succeed in the current educational system, they pretty much have to divorce themselves from their personal identity and conform to the established norms in matters of language and accents. In addition, they have to be able and willing to isolate themselves in a manner quite unnatural to some cultures, often creating a rift between family members.

John Wideman describes this alienation among family members in his essay "Our Time." An educated black man and acclaimed writer, Wideman writes about his brother, who chose to stay in the ghetto and take the consequences, refusing to be "square." As soon as you get ready to judge him, Susan Griffin in "Our Secret" reminds us that the monster lies within all of us. It just takes a certain set of circumstances to bring it out as in Heinrich Himmler's role in WW II.

For me, however, James Baldwin is the one writer who shed the most light on the issue. Disadvantaged, he somehow managed to educate himself to a level that enabled him to enter the literary world where he was heard. In other words, he got through that glass ceiling. His ability to describe what being black means in America has made me understand what it means to be cut off from your cultural heritage: to live in a country and to love certain elements of a culture that "your" people cannot claim. I never fully realized that I myself carry a certain amount of pride in the European culture and what that means for my identity. Baldwin's essay, "Stranger in the Village," is brilliant in its ability to describe so objectively the different way white people respond to him in Switzerland than in America--in the absence of the struggle of various ethnicities trying to come together and create one common history and staking an equal claim to all that this country has to offer, since it does not belong to the white people anymore. Instead of bitterness and the desire to evoke pity, Baldwin recognized the many problems, yet expressed a love for America and a recognition that Americans need to work together to create a common culture.

James Baldwin was a personal friend of Martin Luther King, the great leader of the Civil Rights movement in the sixties. Interviewing Joan Godsey, the wife of the Chancellor of Mercer, Dr. Kirby Godsey, about Civil Rights issues made me realize how recent the struggle was for equal rights. After all, Joan Godsey was at the forefront of white people in the South willing to teach black children. The sixties? That was when I was born. It's really not that long ago—hard to imagine.

Fast forward to 2009. I am reading a commentary by Tolstoy on Chekov's story "The Darling." In this story, a seemingly dependent woman only has a sense of identity when she is coupled with a man. His life, work, and ideas become the single focus of her efforts and thoughts. Without a significant other, she is utterly lost. In our emancipated times it is easy to crucify this character, but I was interested in reading what Tolstoy had to say about it—his being regarded as one of the most important authors of all times. Having read his two most famous works, I was delighted to discover something written in his own voice rather than in the novel form. What could this great man have had to say about this little story? What I read blew me out of the water and made me fall in love with the man instantly. I have to quote him since nothing else will do justice.

First, Tolstoy quotes the Bible, which surprised me. Tolstoy? Russian? Christianity? Yes, this was before communism!

250

Check your history. But what a discovery nevertheless:

> But a woman's work is from her very vocation different from man's and so the ideal of feminine perfection cannot be the same as the ideal of masculine perfection. Let us admit that we do not know what that ideal is; it is quite certain in any case that it is not the idea of masculine perfection. Men cannot do that highest, best work which brings man nearest to God—the work of love.

Those sentiments just made me speechless--what a profound truth, what a wonderful thinker. I became feverish in my pursuit. I googled Tolstoy and learned that he came from an aristocratic background. Sent home from school because he was impossible to teach and unwilling to learn, he became a gambler and traveled a lot. Tolstoy's Christian beliefs were based on the Sermon on the Mount, particularly on the phrase, "turn the other cheek," which he saw as a justification for pacifism, nonviolence, and nonresistance. Tolstoy relied most on the passages of the Bible that comprised the actual words of Jesus. He believed that being a Christian made him a pacifist and, due to the military force used by his government, being a pacifist made him an anarchist.

What else did I discover on our beloved Wikipedia page? Tolstoy was an inspiration to Martin Luther King! More credible searches verified Wiki. It was true: Jesus, Tolstoy, Martin Luther King, civil rights, America, Africa, Europe--what connections, what discoveries! Who would have thought a couple of English classes would lead to this?

I am not the same. I have learned so much about myself and about this country that I now live in. I don't think it is possible to explain to people that going to a building in little Macon, Georgia, after a hard day's work, you can find a new universe. While the time spent is the same as if I were sitting in front of a television set, I am now changing. I look at the people around me in a new way. So what if I'll be fifty before I get a degree-- that is just a piece of paper. It is what I am learning and how it is changing me that really makes a difference. It is what you use from it in your daily life that matters. Dare I quote Miley Cyrus in the same paper as Tolstoy? She's got a new song: "Ain't about how fast I get there, Ain't about what's on the other side. It's the climb . . . ."

--Yvonne Gabriel

Student Athletes in Untenable Situation

"Beware of how you take hope away from any human being." -- Oliver Wendell Holmes

"An athletic scholarship is renewed every year. The only reason it would be taken away is because of academics or off-court issues." These are the words an assistant coach at the University of Texas Pan America used in his efforts to recruit me during my senior year of high school. My mother and father and my seven siblings sat around the family dining table along with two other coaches, all bearing witness to the promises of the spokesperson. It was one of the best days of my life.

Almost exactly two years later I was at my girlfriend's apartment, tears streaming down my face, the words that coach had said that day at my dinner table screaming in my brain. Silence would fill the room for several seconds, then deep, gasping breaths--moans of sorrow. Convulsions would take my body, causing me to cry out--I suppose to set free some of the grief. It was the type of grief one experiences when dreams are shattered. Everything I had worked for, including my personal identity, was being stripped away--through no fault of my own. "What am I going to do now? What am I going to do?" This question kept repeating itself aloud.

Those were the emotions I experienced immediately after being informed that my athletic scholarship would be revoked for the coming year. The end of my basketball career was not the main cause of my anguish: how was I going to pay for school? What would happen to my girlfriend? What are all

252

of my friends back home going to think? How could I be such a failure? How can I ever trust anyone again?

I had moved nearly a thousand miles away from my hometown of Oklahoma City to Edinburg, Texas for one reason: to play NCAA Division 1 college basketball. I had put in countless hours of practice from the time I was twelve years old toward my goal of playing college basketball. I had made very good grades in high school, insuring that if I were offered a scholarship, I would qualify and be able to play. Suddenly, and without warning, my scholarship was gone.

One of the assistants had called to tell me that the head coach wanted to meet with me. I thought it was simply going to be an end of the year meeting, in which we might talk about what I needed to work on for the following year, or maybe go over my academic progress. When I walked into his office, he told me to have a seat. The assistant who had called me in was sitting to the right of the head coach's desk. Coach Davenport was sitting behind his desk. I immediately noticed the stern look on his face. *He always has a stern look on his face,* I thought to myself. He asked me how I was doing, and I responded: "I'm fine, Coach."

He looked at me for a second, and then he began: "I called you in here today to let you know that I won't be renewing your scholarship for next year." I am sure that my face lost all color. My brain went numb. "We don't feel that you will ever reach your full potential as a basketball player, because of the injuries you have experienced," he continued, "and we need to use your scholarship for someone else." He looked at me, maybe waiting for a response, but I couldn't move my mouth. "This has nothing to do with your commitment to the team or your academics. You have done a great job in those areas. We just need someone who can be more effective on the basketball court. I will try to help you find somewhere else to play. Do you have any questions?"

I did have questions, but I was in shock and couldn't formulate the words. I said nothing. I just shook my head. "I'm sorry I had to do this. Clean out your locker as soon as you can." Tears were welling up as I stood and walked out the door in silence.

I saw one of my best friends. She looked at me and said "Hi!" And when I did not answer, she asked: "What happened? What's wrong?" I could not speak. I walked past her in a daze. All of this transpired the week before I was to take the final examinations of my freshman year, leaving me little or no time to find a place to play the following year. I was crushed.

College athletes are being taken advantage of all over the United States of America. College coaches and administrators have the power to destroy the dreams of college students on a whim. There are no checks or balances. A college coach can take away a scholarship for any reason and experience no repercussions. Experiences that I am personally familiar with include injuries, medical conditions, personality conflicts, and the inability of the athlete to meet the coach's expectations on the athletic playing field.

I lost my scholarship because of injuries. I was told that I had done everything expected of me academically and that I had fulfilled my responsibilities to the team. There are hundreds of women who have lost scholarships due to pregnancy or medical conditions. Emily Sherrill lost her scholarship at Gardner Webb because of a disagreement with her coach. Gil Verner lost his scholarship at Nicholls State going into his senior season. The coach suddenly decided that Gil was not good enough to play on his team. When Steve Spurrier was named the head football coach at the University of South Carolina in 2004, he revoked seven football scholarships from recruits made by the previous coach. He had not even seen them perform on the court. Eight athletic scholarships at Portland State in 2008 were terminated for reasons that were suspect. The list of infractions goes on and on.

If you are a student athlete, or you have a child who plays sports, then this subject should be of great concern to you. Otherwise, you might ask: "What does this have to do with me?

254

My child doesn't play sports so this does not affect me."

If that is your outlook on the situation, then you would be wrong for several reasons. First, you should be concerned that the system is not fair to the student athlete. In theory at least, the university exists for students. If athletes opt to transfer to another school, they are penalized by being forced to sit out an entire year of athletic competition before they can play for their new team. If a coach, however, wants to take away a scholarship, he can do so as long as it is before June 1, and he can do so for any reason while experiencing no consequences. If student athletes want to avoid sitting out a year after transferring, then they have to make an appeal to the NCAA and give a valid reason for transferring. A college coach, on the other hand, has to do no such thing when revoking the scholarship of a student athlete.

If your child is in college or planning to go to college, then it should be understood that at most universities, athletics pay huge dividends for the academic community. This is especially true at large state schools, the choice of the majority of students in America. The University of South Carolina football program, where the seven players lost their scholarships, made a profit of over 28 million dollars last year and over 4 million of that went directly to the university. The Notre Dame football program profited more than 45 million and donated 21 million to the university. The University of Texas football program made a profit of more than 45 million and over 7 million of that went to the University. The reality is that student athletes are being used to make huge sums of money for universities, and as soon as they are deemed incapable for any reason, they are dumped and never heard from again. The bottom line is that every student is benefiting from the success of college athletics. Therefore, everyone should be concerned when student athletes are mistreated. The library where you (or your child) study or the computer you are using might have been paid for by university athletics.

Finally, you should be concerned because student athletes are young and impressionable. Having a scholarship revoked can have a wide range of effects on the individual; some will have a loving family to fall back on; some will find a scholarship at another school; however, many will never recover, never get a college degree, and never fulfill their dreams. When these young people are recruited to play division 1 athletics, they are promised everything imaginable. I was promised that my scholarship would not be taken away as long as I fulfilled the academic and personal conduct standards of the university; most athletes get promised much more, as coaches who are desperate to keep their jobs do everything within their power to get the player they want. If that player does not turn out to be as great as the coach thought, then he will do everything in his power to get rid of him or her, maybe even a year later.

The mere mention of the words "college athlete" inspires negative thoughts in the minds of some. All college athletes are egotistical, lazy in the classroom, and basically over-privileged, right? This can be a valid description of a very limited number of college athletes. Unfortunately, this stereotype has made it easy for the general public to overlook the travesty afflicting the large majority of college athletes. There are 126,000 scholarshiped NCAA Division 1 and 2 student athletes in the United States of America. Of those 126,000, only a small percentage fit into the conventional image that most people have. People react to what they see--and they see football and basketball at major division 1 programs. Those are the sports that tend to have major issues in the classroom and off the court. Those are the sports that are deemed most exciting, which means the programs receive much more media scrutiny. When something bad happens, everyone hears about it. Most college athletes are great kids who work hard, make good grades, and do not get in trouble; most of them do things the right way. But those are not the ones we hear about. We hear about the the quarterback who is getting paid under the table or the basketball player who gets in a fight at the local bar. Those are the images that stick in the minds of people who are not directly involved with sports, and that must be a part of the explanation for the apathetic attitude taken toward student athletes.

The apathy I describe has been underscored by research. It was very difficult to find articles on the subject. When I did find something written about a scholarship taken away unjustly, it was because it concerned a special individual. Ken Burger, of the *Charleston Post and Courier*, wrote an article about Ray Ray McElrathbey, who had his football scholarship revoked by Clemson University. McElrathbey's scholarship loss caused a public outcry because of his personal situation. Here are some excerpts from Ken Burger's article: " When it comes to the Ray Ray McElrathbey story, Clemson's ham-handed football factory fumbled this story from start to finish. It all started back in 2006 when the Atlanta native took in his younger brother, Fahmarr, because their mother was addicted to drugs and couldn't provide a decent place for the child to live."

As the media scrutiny intensified, they finally came up with a solution that allowed donations to flow into a trust fund for Fahmarr. Meanwhile, the school relished all the feel-good stories that followed. Through it all, Ray Ray represented his university favorably from coast to coast. He even appeared on the Oprah Winfrey Show. But what happened next is part of the ugly underbelly of college football most fans never see--or want to see. Every year, coaches call marginal or injured players into their offices and tell them it's over. Their scholarships are not being renewed. Hit the road.

Most kids on the bubble are simply run off by assistant coaches who know how to make their lives a living hell. Usually, they are nobodies who quit, transfer or disappear without anybody taking notice. Somebody, however, forgot to tell Clemson coach Tommy Bowden that Ray Ray McElrathbey was not a nobody whose fate could be traded for a better player to be named later. When word of Ray Ray's dismissal got out, it was front-page news and the backlash seemingly caught the Clemson football staff by surprise. The real loser is Clemson. How could they have not seen this coming? Why didn't somebody step up and say, "You know, this might not look so good"? That's because it looks like what it is: college football programs use players until they are of no use to them anymore. Then, when nobody's looking, they kick them to the curb. The only difference is that this time everybody's looking.

The hypocrisy of this situation is thick; hundreds of student athletes are "kicked to the curb" each year, but the only time the general public takes notice is when that athlete is somewhat of a public figure. What if Ray Ray had not been a public figure? What if he had not had the support of his community? He would have been left with a drug addicted mother, the responsibility of raising his little brother, no scholarship to complete his education, and few prospects outside of football. He would have fallen through the cracks, taken a bad job, and struggled through the rest of his life. How many students have experienced this scenario? I can not be sure, because the NCAA does not keep track of student athletes whose scholarships have been revoked. I can not be sure because the NCAA has no stipulations as to the reasons a coach can take a scholarship away. I can not be sure, because as Ken Burger said, no one is paying attention to this "ugly underbelly" of college athletics. Something must be done. Coaches must be held accountable for their actions.

I understand that college coaches have a difficult job. I want to be a college basketball coach, and I am fully aware that most coaches do not last more than 3-4 years at a particular university. There is a lot of pressure in the coaching profession, although not every coach takes advantage of the lax rules of the NCAA in this area. There are coaches of high integrity who refuse to allow the business of college athletics to get in the way of their moral values. The hours of coaches are long and hard. It is also true that NCAA Division 1 coaches are paid very lucrative sums of money to do their job. Of the 58 teams that made it to the NCAA tournament last year, the average salary of the head coach was $800,000; the average salary of a Division 1 football coach (119 schools) is $950,000 a year. It is inexcusable that someone paid that much money can lie to a 17-year-old and get away with it. It is inexcusable that the student athlete, who is the reason that the coach is paid so well, is viewed as an expendable object. It is inexcusable that an organization as powerful as the NCAA has turned a blind eye and allowed so many student athletes to be mistreated. It is inexcusable that university officials stand by and allow such a travesty to happen repeatedly.

Zach Wells

Biographical Sketches
of the Regeneration Writers

Brown, Cliff

Alert, responsible, and always prepared, Maconite Cliff Brown, a skills trade worker at Mercer for eight years, takes his studies and his work as the "key man" in the maintenance department at Mercer seriously. He is tenacious in seeking ways to add value to his job performance, constantly observant of the state of the facilities. A light out in the parking lot communicates a safety concern to Cliff, who moves quickly to address the problem, even though it is not part of his job description.

Cliff's devotion to his family is a large part of his motivation to continue his studies. Being a good role model for his two sons, Darren and Trent, informs his decisions. The surprise 40th-birthday celebration for Cliff planned by his wife Becky attests to the respect and affection Cliff enjoys among a wide circle of family and friends.

Cliff likes the process of solving problems, which is probably why he has chosen to major in organizational leadership. He serves as a disaster relief volunteer for the Georgia Baptist Convention. During Hurricane Katrina he provided communication support for cleanup recovery teams.

Cliff's writings range from the comical to the reflective and philsophical and include both narrative and poetry. He confesses that he enjoys experimenting with different genres, a characteristic congruent with his longtime hobby as an amateur ham radio operator.

Crocker, Janet Horne

"I am only one, but still I am one. I cannot do everything, but still I can do something; and because I cannot do everything I will not refuse to do the something that I can do." –Helen Keller

Janet Crocker's favorite quotation from Helen Keller

reflects her optimism. The myriad tasks she accomplishes each day and sometimes against great odds remind us of the power of one. Whether she is arranging photography for a Mercer publication, responding to her beautiful daughter on Facebook, or making contacts to place a homeless kitten, the Coordinator of Marketing Communications at Mercer University brings a tremendous intensity, vitality, and creativity to the completion of her tasks. Modestly, she confides: "I do consider myself to be a very resourceful person." She credits Liberal Studies courses in the CCPS with helping her find her writing voice once again, claiming that "my love for writing was long lost until I enrolled in the Issues of Justice Class on capital punishment." Reflecting back on sometimes exuberant classroom discussions, she wheedles, "If everyone would just follow the Golden Rule, life would be so much easier."

In her ninth year at Mercer, Janet openly expresses her love for her job. She happily reports that she gets to do all of the things she likes most: working with photography and interacting with people. She credits Dr. Priscilla Danheiser, Dean of the CCPS, for encouraging her to further her education. For seven years, Janet worked at Wesleyan College as administrative assistant to Dean Danheiser, who helped her refine her listening skills and taught her that sometimes silence is the best response. Janet describes Dr. Danheiser's grace under pressure as legendary.

Photo editor for the Georgia College newspaper three decades ago, Janet served as photography editor for this first volume of *Regeneration*. Her stories fall firmly under the rubric of Southern literature, delivering an acute sense of place, tradition, and time—and identify for us one more Steel Magnolia who weathers the storms of life with beauty and a contradictory fragility. Janet graduated from Mercer with a degree in Human Services in May 2009.

DeFoor, Terri

Like many students in the College of Continuing and Professional Studies, a personal calamity motivated Terri

DeFoor's return to school. As she explains, all she had ever wanted was to be a wife and a mother—and now that was being wrenched from her. Faced with having to support herself, she opted to come to Mercer to get the educational background necessary for a job that would pay more than minimum wage.

One of the few students in the college who began Mercer with no prior college experience, Terri poured herself into her classes, earning top grades in every class. She arrived with a love for history and writing. In a class on the short story, she created a digital story, testifying to the aliveness she had experienced in her Mercer journey. She wrote perceptive essays in her history and literature classes, dealing with topics ranging from the leadership roles of women in education to grace in the short stories of Flannery O'Connor. She crafted powerful short stories and applied her creative genius to the composition of poetry. She has demonstrated repeatedly a willingness to tackle new things and an open mind toward assessing and acquiring new knowledge—and revisioning events and positions through new lenses.

Terri served as editor-in-chief for *Regeneration!* The journal elicited over 100 entries of poems, narratives, art works, and essays from students, staff, faculty, and alumni, requiring hours of organizational work and communication with the contributing writers. A practitioner of lifelong learning, Terri embodies the values that the College of Continuing and Professional Studies seeks to develop in all students: integrity, critical thinking, reading, writing, an informed and regenerative worldview, and world citizenship. Terri received the top award for scholarship from Liberal Studies and from the College of Continuing and Professional Studies at her graduation from Mercer in May 2009.

Eskew, Harry

An avid hymnologist, Harry Eskew is the author of two books and several hundred articles. His book, *Sing with Understanding*, written together with fellow hymnologist Dr. Hugh

McElrath, is used in seminaries and colleges around the world. He served eight years as editor of the journal of the Hymn Society of America. A shape-note singer and researcher of this Early American tradition, Harry lent his expertise to the class of emerging writers. Most recently he has organized lecture demonstrations and church hymn sings centered around the contributions of William Walker, the hymn tune compiler and composer who first published the traditional tune and the words of John Newton's "Amazing Grace" together.

Harry is married to Margaret Eskew, the teacher of the writing classes and his favorite editor.

Fluellen, Elnora

A person of many talents, Elnora worked for almost two decades for the United States Postal Service. She has also been employed in various capacities at a medical center, an insurance company, and a tax preparation service. She has recently achieved the rank of independent sales director with Mary Kay. While in the military, she earned an associate degree in general studies with a concentration in business from Troy State Universtiy.

Elnora has a radius of positive energy around her that infects all who are near. She carries life with a large dose of humor, revealing a talented comedian. The sun always shines around Elnora which is why it is hard to recognize her in some of her writings. Underneath all her fun and games lies a sensitive, caring heart able to feel the pain of a friend.

Elnora is majoring in organizational leadership at Mercer. She has a vision of working with young people to prepare them academically for success in college courses. She is currently working as a church secretary, where she thrives on the diversity and complexity of her work.

Gabriel, Yvonne

A native of the Netherlands, a resident of the U.S. for two

decades, a registered nurse with significant hospital experience, and a seasoned international flight attendant, Yvonne Gabriel epitomizes the new world citizen. She has openly embraced many of the cultures of the world and the people of those cultures have returned the embrace, indicative of the genuine respect and trust she has given and engendered.

An artist since childhood, Yvonne has expanded her flair for color, form, and energy to the written word, including the creation of essays, short stories, poetry, and children's books. She keeps a diary and has a fondness for short stories and "funny stuff." She has great respect for writers who can make readers laugh with just their written words. Among her aspirations is to write a *Bildungsroman*, a type of novel concerned with the education, development, and maturation of a young protagonist.

Yvonne has just completed her freshman year at Mercer, where she is working on a bachelor's degree in liberal studies with concentrations in writing and literature. She finds the students in the evening classes amazing. She describes them as "a special kind of people: strong, motivated, intelligent, and focused." Fellow Regeneration Writer Gloria Jordan spoke for all her classmates when she wrote: "Yvonne enters your life and leaves footprints of genius all over your heart."

Jordan, Gloria

An excellent narrative writer, Gloria Jordan comes alive in the midst of a group of children, weaving stories as she teaches them in her job as a paraprofessional the basics of learning and good citizenship. She creates for the children stories, songs, and rhymes and punctuates them with repeated movements and facial expressions worthy of a fine actor. A member of a dance team in her teen years, Gloria has retained an impeccable sense of timing, a dedication to team effort, and a formidable work ethic. If you want a job done right, give it to Gloria Jordan—or GloJo as she is affectionately known. Sometimes her preschoolers from many ethnic groups slip and call her "Mama."

It is perhaps the engaging aura Gloria gives off that draws others to her and provides the necessary trust and affirmation to broach difficult topics in group discussions. The smile in her eyes belies the great tragedies Gloria has suffered. She lost the father she never knew when he, a decorated veteran of the Korean War, in jail on a $40 check forgery charge since before her birth, broke out to be there on her first birthday. He was arrested for rape, convicted under Jim Crow laws, executed, and buried with military honors within three months—today DNA tests would probably prove the innocence of the "Gentle Giant." How does such an event affect a family? Gloria chronicles some of the aftermath in her stories. The mother of three, she dares to revisit family relationships and social history in an effort to piece together unknown parts of the past to find clues to the present.

Vice President of the Bibb Association of Educators, member of the Educational Support Personnel Committee of the Georgia Association of Educators, National Education Association Delegate, preschool Sunday School teacher at Church of Christ at Houston Avenue, and board member of Georgians for Alternatives to the Death Penalty, Gloria Jordan has a reverence for education and an unquenchable hunger for new knowledge. This hunger led her to join the Mercer on Mission team to spend three weeks in Guatemala working with children at an orphanage, where she endeared herself to all the children and brought them all home with her in her heart. When fellow classmate Barbara Sellers asked Gloria what topics she most enjoyed writing about, Gloria responded: "I love fact finding and expressing what I know in all forms of writing. Usually my mood determines what I write about at certain times. Since childhood, I have used writing as a way to escape dark periods of my life."

The recipient of a several scholarships and awards and a veteran of several writing conferences, Gloria will graduate in May 2010 with concentrations in writing and literary studies and a minor in education. Gloria describes her experiences at Mercer as "awesome." Classmates describe Gloria as an "awesome presence" in class.

Lang, Diane

A military wife and mother of two, Diane Lang had no choice but to assume responsibility for the entire family during her husband's deployments. Possessed of unusually sharp instincts and the uncanny ability to get to the heart of the matter, Diane knows how to take care of business. Although she is highly organized and typically runs a tight ship, she is nevetheless filled with compassion for those around her. A survivor and a fighter, she always stays the course, sometimes allowing her hilarious, edgy humor to carry her through--a treat when she shares it!

Diane takes writing seriously, carefully crafting each sentence. She listens intently to the responses of her readers, meticulously choosing vocabulary and images for maximum effectiveness. However, nothing is so sacred that it can escape the force of her humor. With the deftness of a skilled surgeon, she eviscerates the words that hold the power of taboo over us, stalking topics from which many of us take flight. She will definitely not sweep anything under the rug.

It was Diane who introduced the writing class to the round-table method of reviewing works. Bravely, she brought her own manuscript to the class for review on the first evening, coaching us on how to respond constructively. She set the tone for all of the classes that followed, demonstrating how to withhold any comments until all reviewers had concluded their remarks and then modeling how to accept and respond to suggestions or criticisms.

The quintessential writer, Diane has several books at various levels of completion. She plans to graduate in December 2010 with concentrations in writing and literary studies.

Legare, Andrew

Born in Massachusetts, Andrew Legare is married to veteran teacher Mary Palmer, the daughter of a Virginia physician. With a penchant for fine detail, Andrew is skilled in electronics and enjoys working with wood. An active member of the Glad River Congregation that meets on the Mercer campus on Sundays, Andrew is happiest when he is helping other people. A published poet, Andrew searches for meaning through his writings. His early inspiration for poetry came from a Walt Whitman poem he memorized and recites for his friends:

> I saw in Louisiana a live-oak growing,
> All alone stood it and the moss hung down from the branches,
> Without any companion it stood there uttering joyous leaves of dark green,
> And its look, rude, unbending, lusty, made me think of myself,
> But I wondered how it could utter joyous leaves standing alone there without its friend near, for I knew I could not,
> And I broke off a twig with a certain number of leaves upon it, and twined around it a little moss,
> And brought it away, and I have placed it in sight in my room,
> It is not needed to remind me as of my own dear friends,
> (For I believe lately I think of little else than of them,)
> Yet it remains to me a curious token, it makes me think of manly love;
> For all that, and though the live-oak glistens there in Louisiana solitary in a wide flat space,
> Uttering joyous leaves all its life without a friend or lover near,
> I know very well I could not.

Andrew's poetic essay included in this collection inspired artist Yvonne Gabriel to paint the cover picture of the flower breaking through the tough terrain of the concrete—evidence for Andrew and Yvonne of the resilience of life and the promise of redemption.

McKelvey, Rosemary

A mother of five adult children, Rosemary joined the Regeneration Writers after a successful career as Vice President for Development at Wesleyan College, where she completed her undergraduate degree as an adult student. A Southern writer, Rosemary communicates an acute sense of place and time in her writings. Originally from the Mississippi Delta, she recreates the outrage she felt as a child when exposed to blatant racism.

Her poignant piece on aging and the meaning of life leaves readers contemplating their own questions.

Reid, Kevin

Definitely understated, Kevin Reid is big on family and modest about his own accomplishments. Most of his peers do not know that he was a member of the Green Beret during his career in the military. However, they soon learn about his grandmother who was a tremendous force in his life. They learn about his parents, both of whom were educators and about his dreams for his daughter and son--his son is now a student at Mercer.

Unlike any of the other writers, Kevin started his college career at Mercer, leaving when a friendship failed to meet expectations. He was determined to complete what he had started two decades ago. A full-time employee at another college in Macon, Kevin was teased by coworkers when his picture was plastered on billboards advertising the evening program at Mercer.

Kevin has been tapped to work to increase the number of young African American men graduating from college. Focused, disciplined, creative, and determined, Kevin is a good role model for us all. His "Everything Can Kill You" is hopefully only the first of many writings about the military. He also leaves readers wanting to hear more "Miss Bay" adventures.

Sellers, Barbara

Mercer University's Acquisitions Supervisor in Tarver Library, Barbara Sellers, was hooked on books from the time she learned to read. Born in Hawkinsville and raised in Cochran, until recently she had never ventured far from middle Georgia—except in books. It was no wonder that when a position in the Cochran library came available that Barbara was asked to apply. She accepted the job and found the library was a perfect fit for her. She has since moved twice—both times to positions in libraries, coming to Mercer in August 2003.

Barbara combines her love of books with a love for writing. Before her employment in the Cochran library, she worked at the newspaper office there and was eventually asked to write articles in addition to her other duties. During that time, her older sister Emily wrote feature articles for the Cochran paper, inspiring Barbara to continue writing. Barbara's primary goal in learning to write was to preserve some of her family stories. The story of her grandparents is vintage rural Georgia, revealing in a few short pages the family dynamic in a way that begets instant recognition and spontaneous laughter.

It is not surprising that Barbara's all-time favorite book is *To Kill a Mocking Bird*, a book she first read in middle school. It is the story of a family and the struggles they go through as the father decides to represent a black man in Jim Crow Alabama. It was the children in the story, Scout and Jem, with whom Barbara immediately connected. Barbara confesses, "I always wanted to be like Scout."

The mother of two adult children and grandmother of two, Barbara works to maintain strong family ties. When her son was in Iraq, he wrote that he wanted to be able to give school supplies to the Iraqi children whose schooling had been interrupted by the American occupation. Tarver Library served as a collection site for those school supplies. Knowing the daily danger her son faced during his tour of duty, Barbara's efforts to collect the school supplies not only helped the time pass more quickly, but ultimately contributed to the safety of the soldiers.

On Barbara's first journey outside the United States, she chose to participate in Mercer on Mission with a group of students and faculty who worked with children in an orphanage in Huehuetenango, Guatemala. Barbara's kindness and caring bridged cultural and language gaps as evidenced by the spontaneous affection she received from the Guatemalan children, intensified in a little boy named José, who would hardly let Barbara out of his sight. A lifelong learner, Barbara testifies that this experience profoundly affected who she is, changing her worldview in dramatic ways. Research editor for *Regeneration*, Barbara will graduate from Mercer with a degree in Liberal Studies in May 2010.

Zach Wells

The son of a pastor and the youngest writer in the class, Zach brought a unique perspective to the class. Homeschooled in Oklahoma by his mother, he was left devastated by her premature death from cancer. His works reveal his efforts to keep her memory alive and to come to terms with his tremendous loss. One of eight children, Zach felt a responsibility to help his younger siblings work through their grief.

Zach is tall, blonde, and muscular. A former basketball player whose career and scholarship were cut short by an injury, Zach works with Coach Hoffman and the Mercer basketball team. His dream is to one day become a coach himself. The sense of unfairness Zach experienced due to his dismissal from the team fuels other writings, where Zach is trying to come to terms with who he is and what he is to do with his life.

A Mercer on Mission trip to Guatemala revealed Zach's gift for working effectively with children. Somewhat fluent in Spanish, Zach attracted the young children from the orphanage they were serving. Starved for a male presence, the children were delighted to have Zach among them..